T0022550

HISTORY COMICS

HIP-HOP
THE BEAT OF AMERICA

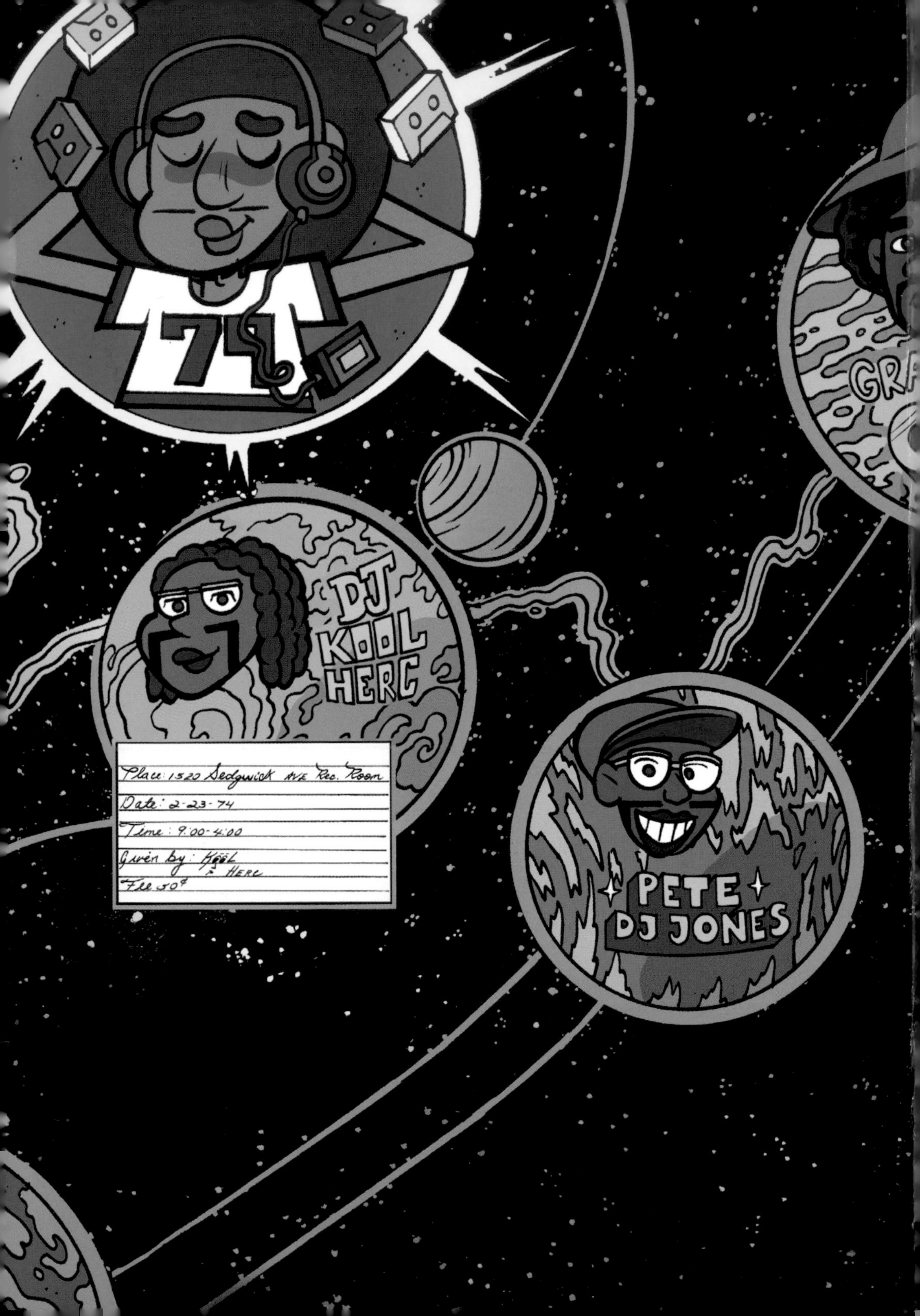

77
DJ KOOL HERC
Place: 1520 Sedgwick AVE Rec. Room
Date: 2-23-74
Time: 9:00-4:00
Given by: Kool Herc
Fee 50¢
PETE DJ JONES

HISTORY COMICS

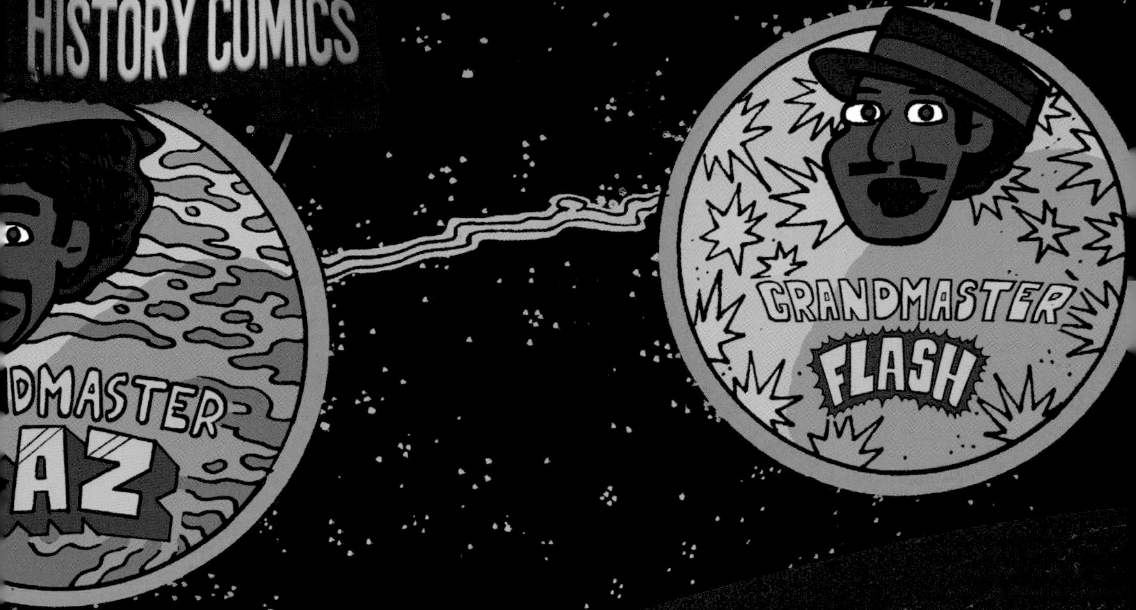
DMASTER
AZ
GRANDMASTER
FLASH

HIP-HOP
THE BEAT OF AMERICA

JARRETT WILLIAMS

color by
JOEY WEISER

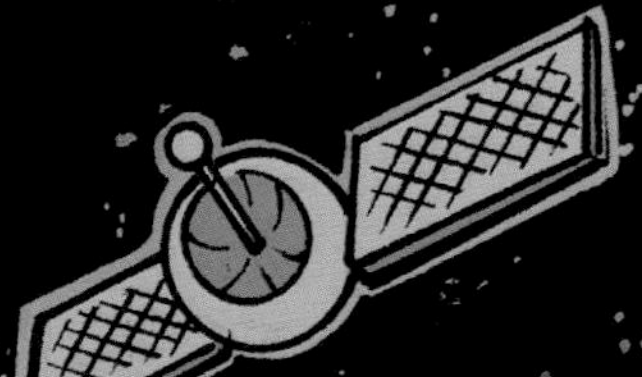

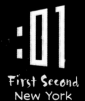

:01
First Second
New York

:01

First Second

Published by First Second
First Second is an imprint of Roaring Brook Press,
a division of Holtzbrinck Publishing Holdings Limited Partnership
120 Broadway, New York, NY 10271
firstsecondbooks.com
mackids.com

© 2024 by Jarrett Williams
Introduction © 2024 by Claude "Paradise" Gray
All rights reserved

Library of Congress Control Number: 2023937813

Our books may be purchased in bulk for promotional, educational, or business use.
Please contact your local bookseller or the Macmillan Corporate and Premium Sales Department
at (800) 221-7945 ext. 5442 or by email at MacmillanSpecialMarkets@macmillan.com.

First edition, 2024
Edited by Dave Roman
Cover design by Sunny Lee and Casper Manning
Interior book design by Casper Manning and Angela Boyle
Production editing by Avia Perez
Color by Joey Weiser
Lettering by Kevin Burkhalter
Historical consultant: Prime Minister Pete Nice
Special thanks to Ryan Douglass, Rose Van de Walle, Martha Diaz, the Hip Hop Education Center, and the
Universal Hip Hop Museum

Penciled with Prismacolor Col-Erase Blue Pencil on Smooth Bristol Paper. Inked with Sakura Pigma Micron and
Pentel Brush Pens. Colored digitally in Photoshop. Digitally lettered with the Soliloquous font from Comicraft.

Printed in China by Toppan Leefung Printing Ltd., Dongguan City, Guangdong Province

ISBN 978-1-250-79576-2 (paperback)
10 9 8 7 6 5 4 3 2 1

ISBN 978-1-250-79575-5 (hardcover)
10 9 8 7 6 5 4 3 2 1

Don't miss your next favorite book from First Second!
For the latest updates go to firstsecondnewsletter.com and sign up for our enewsletter.

For me, hip-hop always went hand in hand with comic books, which is why I identify with this story wholeheartedly! I grew up on the streets of the Bronx, always looking up to my big brother, Michael. For a while he was into collecting stamps and coins, which didn't really interest me much. Then he started collecting comic books and they  immediately had my full attention. Unfortunately, he was a comic book *collector* and I was a comic book *reader*, which can be like oil and water! Michael kept his comics all clean and pristine, packed away in tight plastic bags, and I just wanted to set them free and access the amazing stories within!

When I first saw hip-hop flyers they immediately reminded me of the art styles that appeared in comic books. Graphic designers like Phase 2 and Buddy Esquire made flyers (Bronx Deco) so incredible that they created a hip-hop universe that rivaled the Marvel and DC universes.

The names on the flyers all sounded like superheroes—Grandmaster Flowers, Pete DJ Jones, DJ Kool Herc, the Herculords, Grandmaster Flash, and Grand Wizzard Theodore. Many of the early flyers even had comic characters like Iron Man on them, and I started collecting them the same way my brother did with comic books! I had all the ghetto superstars in my collection. I just kept it moving from there, collecting magazines, ticket stubs, posters, and more. If it was hip-hop, I saved it.

When I was a kid, I first really learned about Martin Luther King Jr., Coretta Scott King, Rosa Parks, and all the other civil rights workers and activists because of a comic book called *Martin Luther King and the Montgomery Story* that was first printed in 1957.

The illustrated story of "we shall overcome" went all around the world and was translated in many different languages, helping to spread the word of what really happened during the Civil Rights Movement.

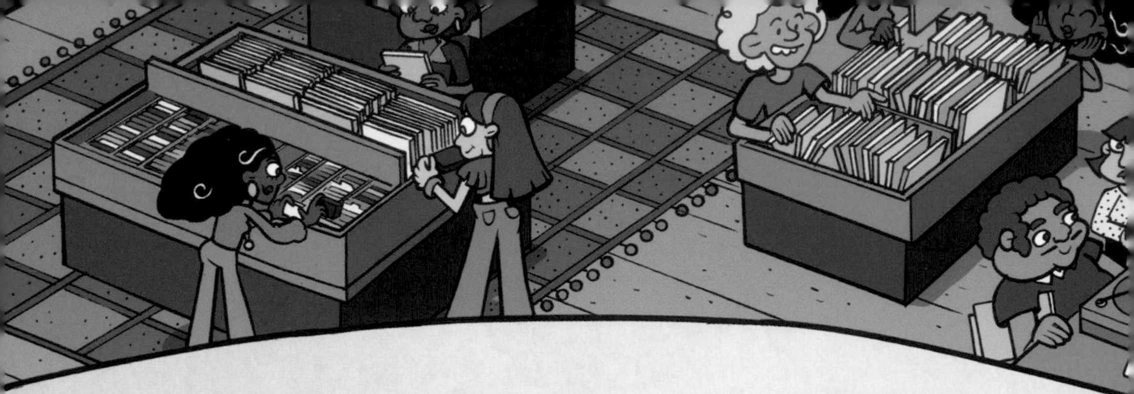

I think that comic books can be a very important teaching tool to break down a lot of barriers, and they instilled in me a lifelong love of reading. I would go to the library and stay there until it got dark. I was amazed when one day the librarian told me that I was actually allowed to take the books home—that I don't have to sit there until close every night. I was like, "What? I can take these home?" and she was like, "Yes." After that it just opened up a whole new world to me, and I literally read myself off the corners of the Bronx.

Between 1986 and 1988, I would go on to host the earliest hip-hop nights at the Latin Quarter in Times Square, a high-profile club that showcased groundbreaking acts like EPMD, Eric B. & Rakim, KRS-One, Queen Latifah, Public Enemy, Salt-N-Pepa, 3rd Bass, and A Tribe Called Quest. When I cofounded the politically conscious hip-hop group X-Clan, I was able to take my passion for civil rights and education and channel it through our music. Rap music is very powerful, and I've tried to use it to inspire people to get involved, fight back against oppression, and protect communities like the one I grew up in.

I wish I could have had a book like *History Comics: Hip-Hop: The Beat of America* when I was a kid growing up in the projects. Oh my god! It would have opened my universe even more. For this work of art to exist for young people to read is an incredibly great resource for them. I didn't know it at that time, but when some older brothers were showing their brothers the streets, my older brother was showing me the stars and universe.

—**Claude "Paradise" Gray,**
chief curator of the Universal Hip Hop Museum

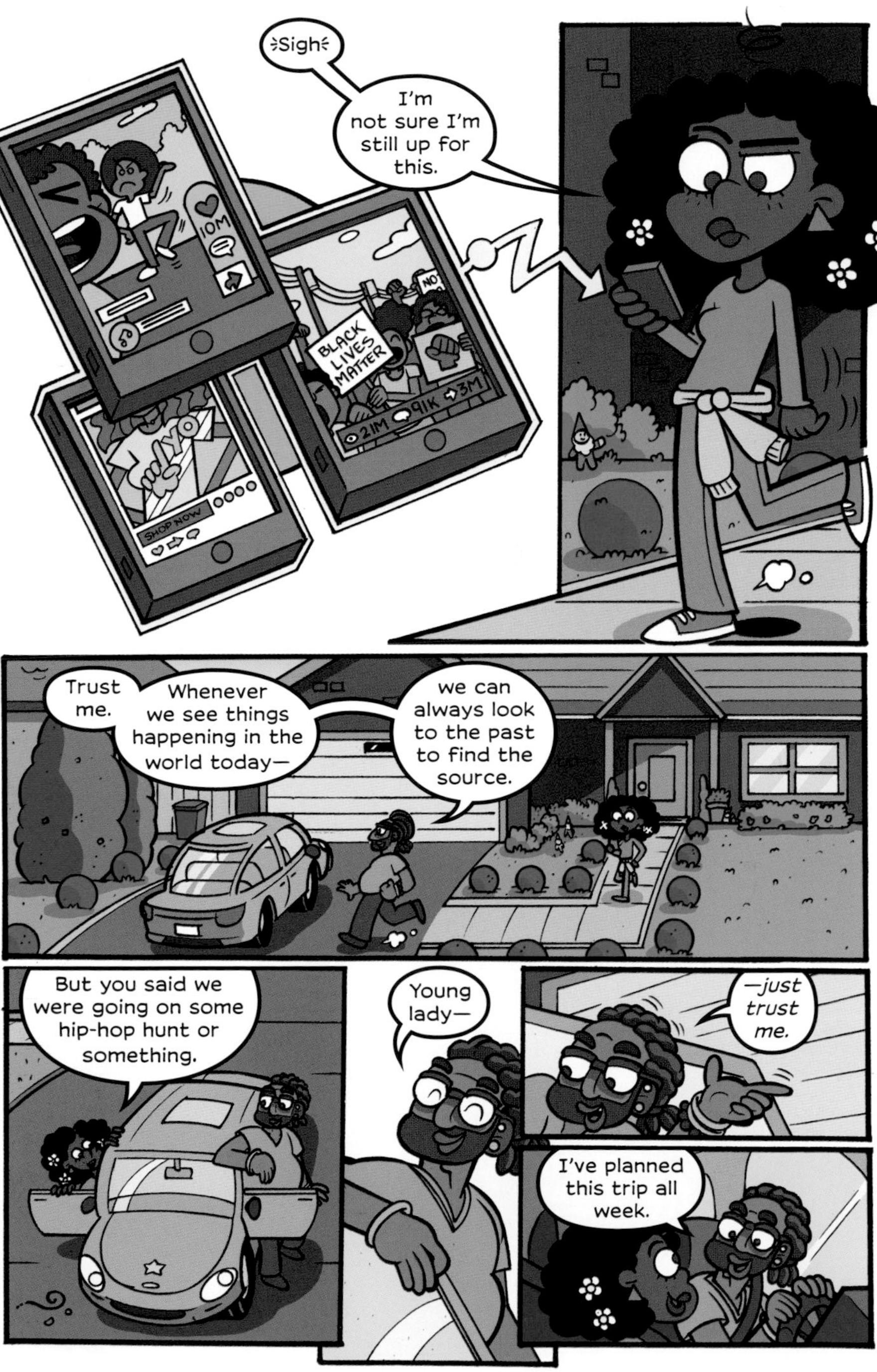

Sigh
I'm not sure I'm still up for this.
10M
NO
BLACK LIVES MATTER
21M 91K 3M
YO
SHOP NOW
Trust me.
Whenever we see things happening in the world today—
we can always look to the past to find the source.
But you said we were going on some hip-hop hunt or something.
Young lady—
—just trust me.
I've planned this trip all week.

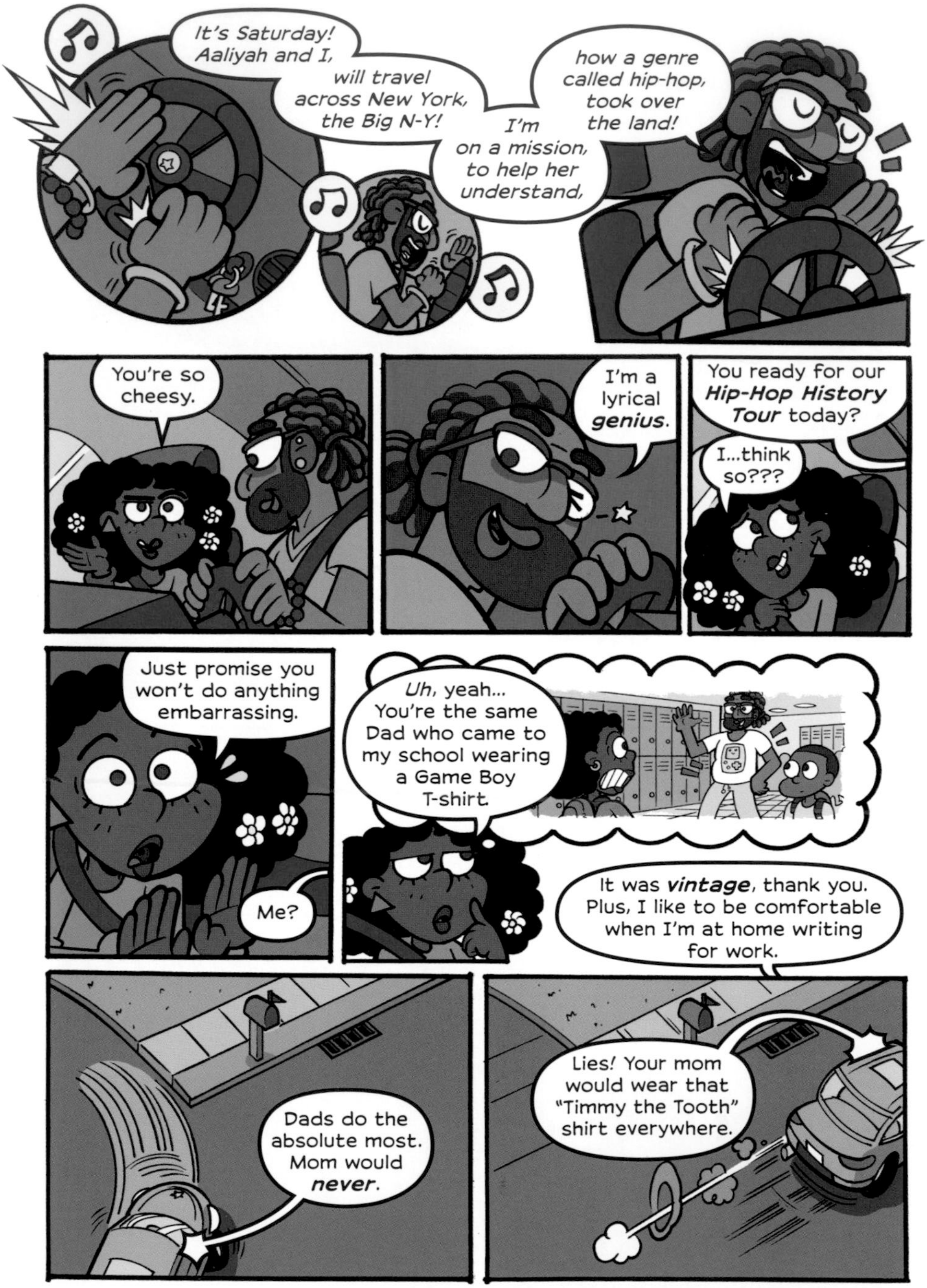
It's Saturday! Aaliyah and I,
will travel across New York, the Big N-Y!
I'm on a mission, to help her understand,
how a genre called hip-hop, took over the land!
You're so cheesy.
I'm a lyrical genius.
You ready for our Hip-Hop History Tour today?
I...think so???
Just promise you won't do anything embarrassing.
Me?
Uh, yeah... You're the same Dad who came to my school wearing a Game Boy T-shirt.
It was vintage, thank you. Plus, I like to be comfortable when I'm at home writing for work.
Dads do the absolute most. Mom would never.
Lies! Your mom would wear that "Timmy the Tooth" shirt everywhere.

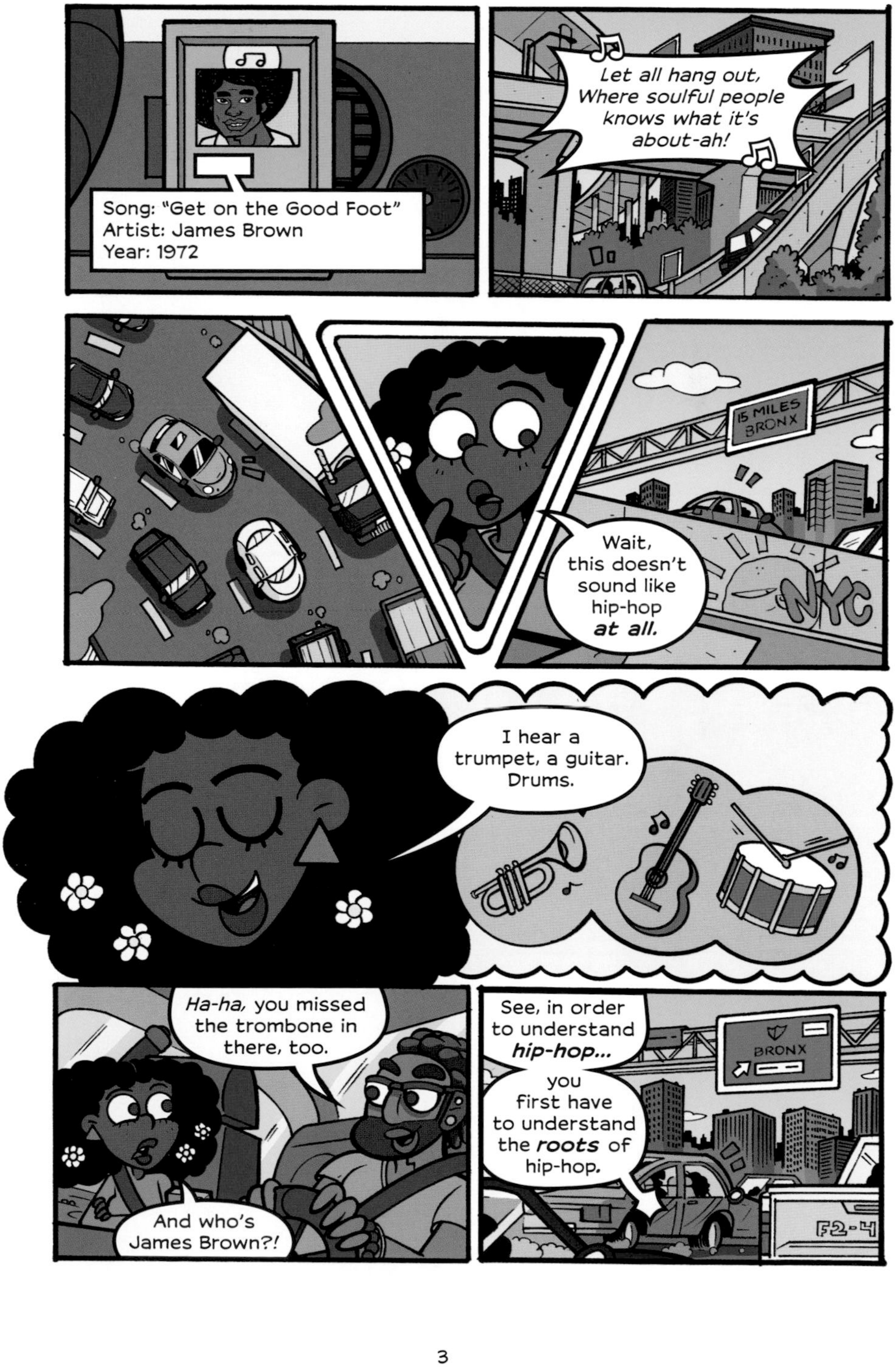
Song: "Get on the Good Foot"
Artist: James Brown
Year: 1972
Let all hang out, Where soulful people knows what it's about-ah!
15 MILES BRONX
NYC
Wait, this doesn't sound like hip-hop *at all.*
I hear a trumpet, a guitar. Drums.
Ha-ha, you missed the trombone in there, too.
And who's James Brown?!
See, in order to understand ***hip-hop...***
you first have to understand the ***roots*** of hip-hop.
BRONX
F2-4

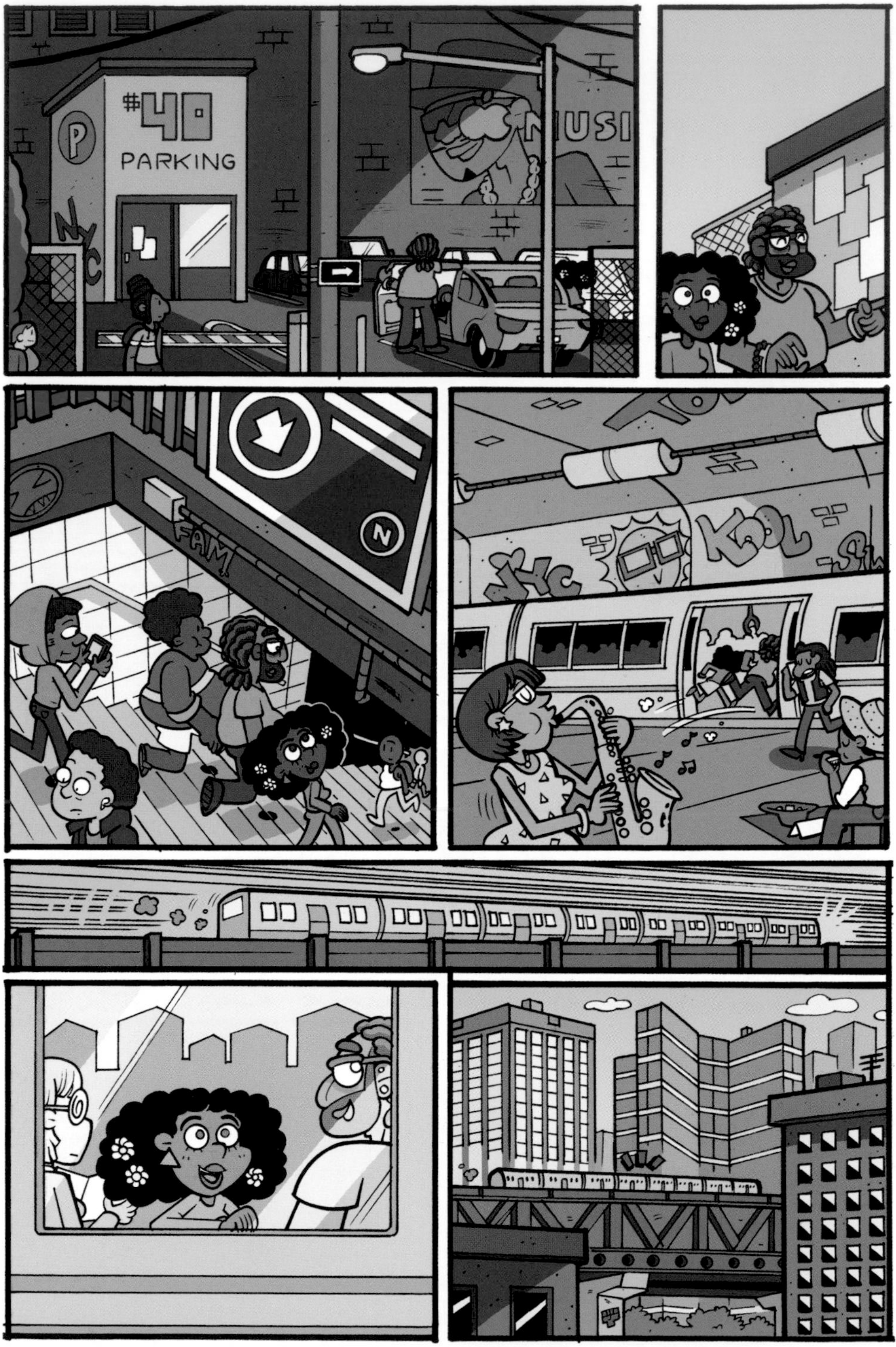
$40
PARKING
MUSI
FAM

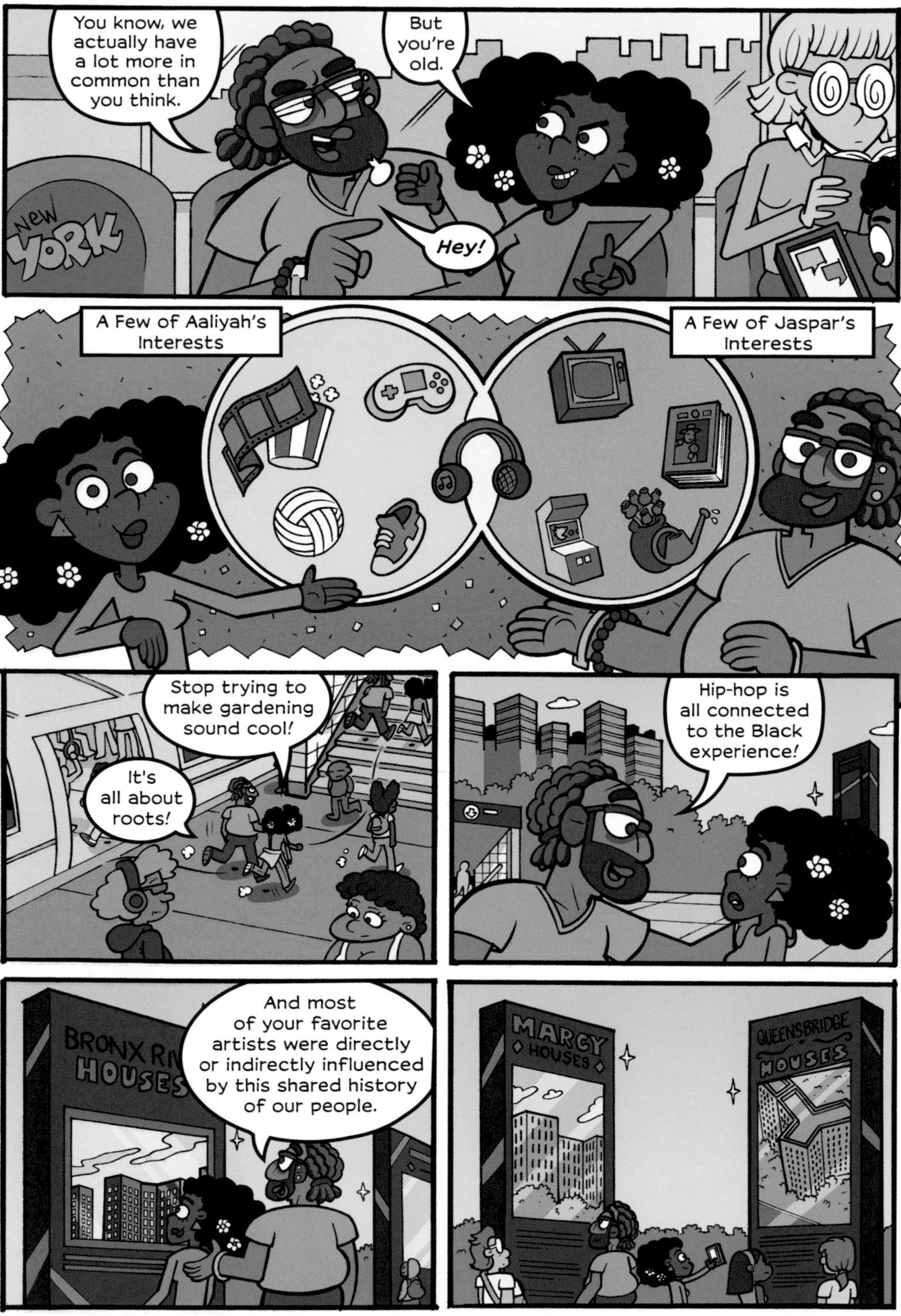
You know, we actually have a lot more in common than you think.
But you're old.
NEW YORK
Hey!
A Few of Aaliyah's Interests
A Few of Jaspar's Interests
Stop trying to make gardening sound cool!
It's all about roots!
Hip-hop is all connected to the Black experience!
And most of your favorite artists were directly or indirectly influenced by this shared history of our people.
MARGY HOUSES
QUEENSBRIDGE HOUSES

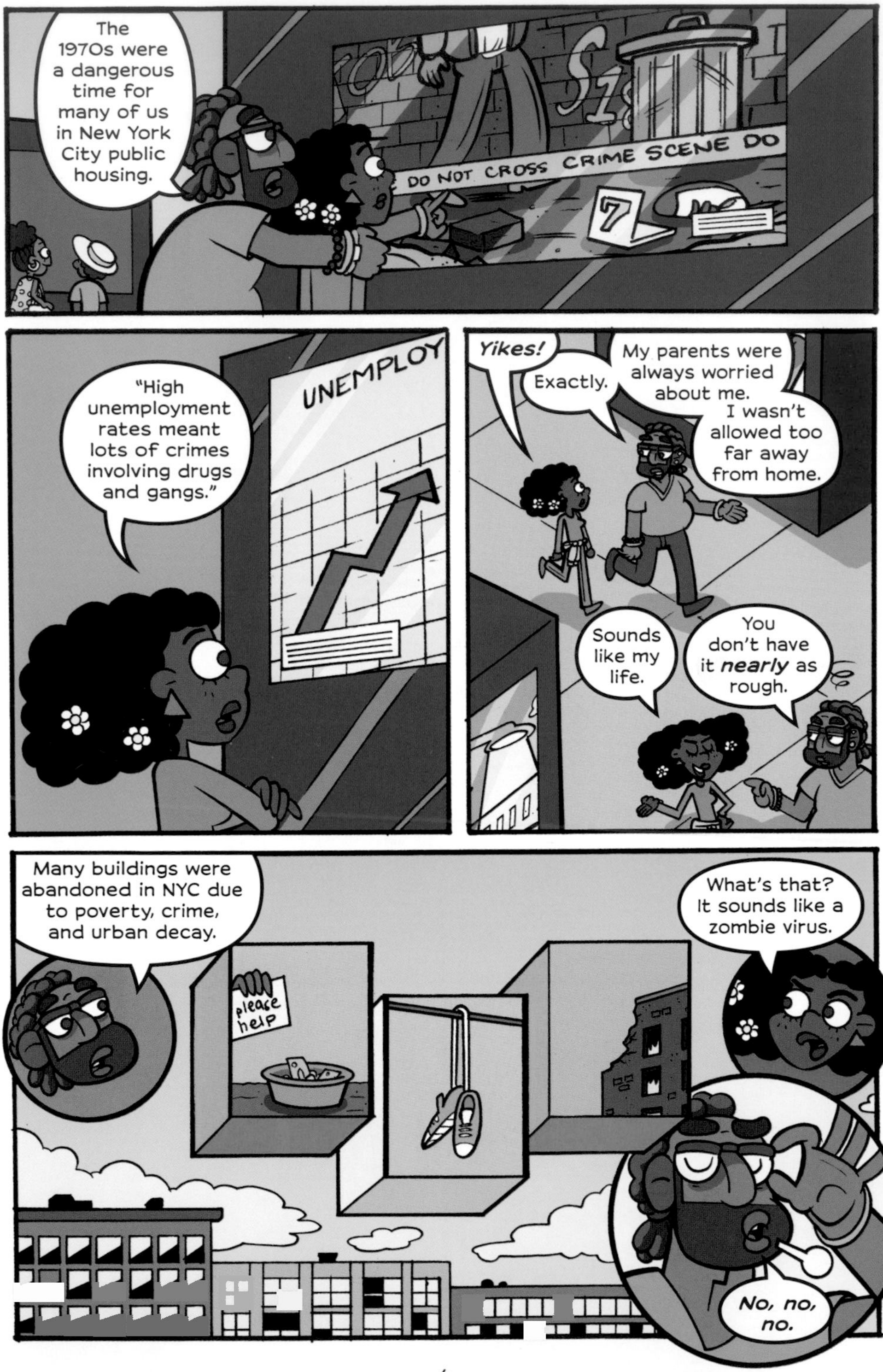
The 1970s were a dangerous time for many of us in New York City public housing.
DO NOT CROSS CRIME SCENE DO
7
"High unemployment rates meant lots of crimes involving drugs and gangs."
UNEMPLOY
Yikes!
Exactly.
My parents were always worried about me.
I wasn't allowed too far away from home.
Sounds like my life.
You don't have it *nearly* as rough.
Many buildings were abandoned in NYC due to poverty, crime, and urban decay.
please help
What's that? It sounds like a zombie virus.
No, no, no.

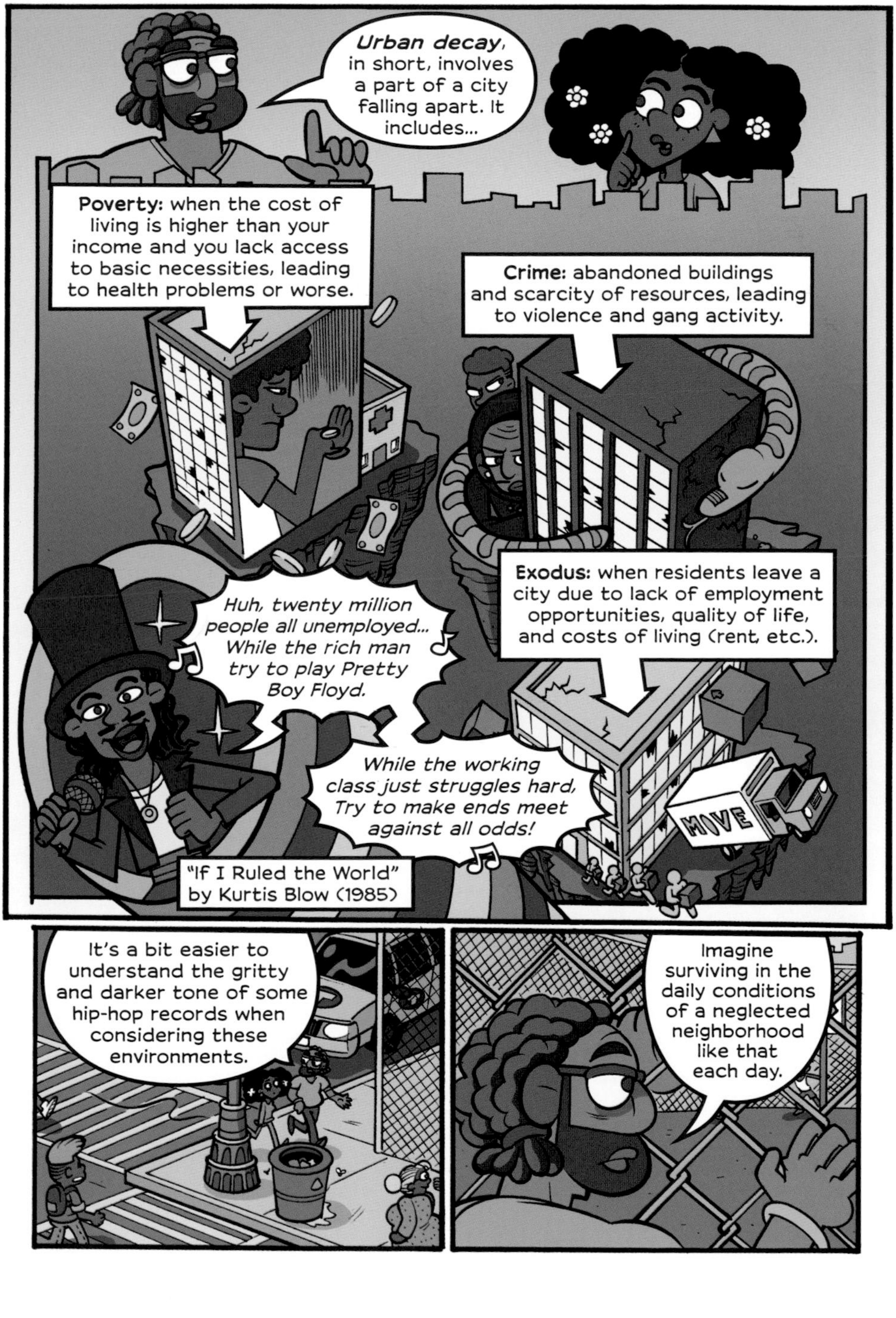
Urban decay, in short, involves a part of a city falling apart. It includes...
Poverty: when the cost of living is higher than your income and you lack access to basic necessities, leading to health problems or worse.
Crime: abandoned buildings and scarcity of resources, leading to violence and gang activity.
Exodus: when residents leave a city due to lack of employment opportunities, quality of life, and costs of living (rent, etc.).
Huh, twenty million people all unemployed... While the rich man try to play Pretty Boy Floyd.
While the working class just struggles hard, Try to make ends meet against all odds!
"If I Ruled the World" by Kurtis Blow (1985)
MOVE
It's a bit easier to understand the gritty and darker tone of some hip-hop records when considering these environments.
Imagine surviving in the daily conditions of a neglected neighborhood like that each day.

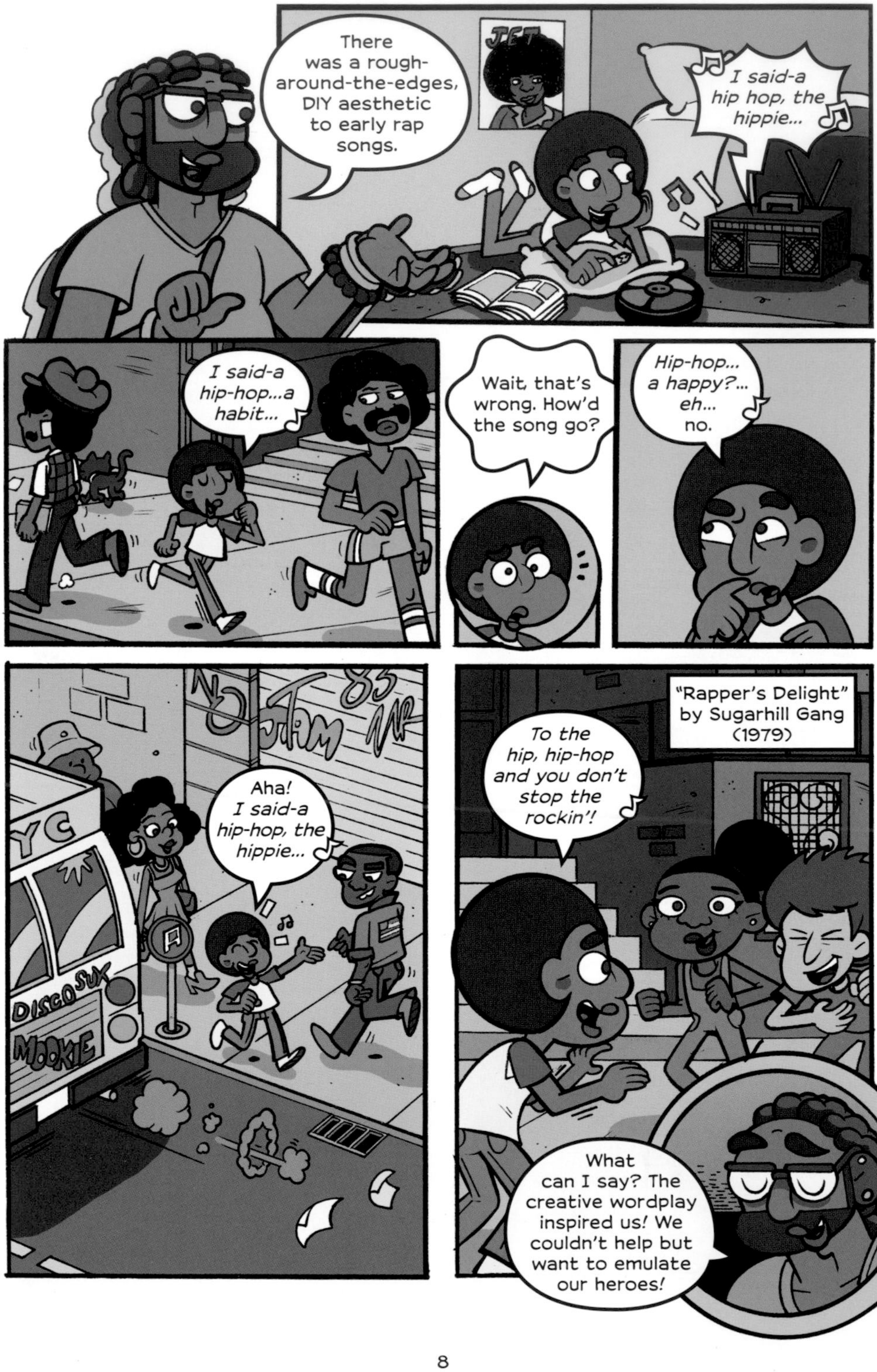
There was a rough-around-the-edges, DIY aesthetic to early rap songs.
JET
I said-a hip hop, the hippie...
I said-a hip-hop...a habit...
Wait, that's wrong. How'd the song go?
Hip-hop... a happy?... eh... no.
NO JAM
Aha! I said-a hip-hop, the hippie...
DISCO SUX
MOOKIE
"Rapper's Delight" by Sugarhill Gang (1979)
To the hip, hip-hop and you don't stop the rockin'!
What can I say? The creative wordplay inspired us! We couldn't help but want to emulate our heroes!

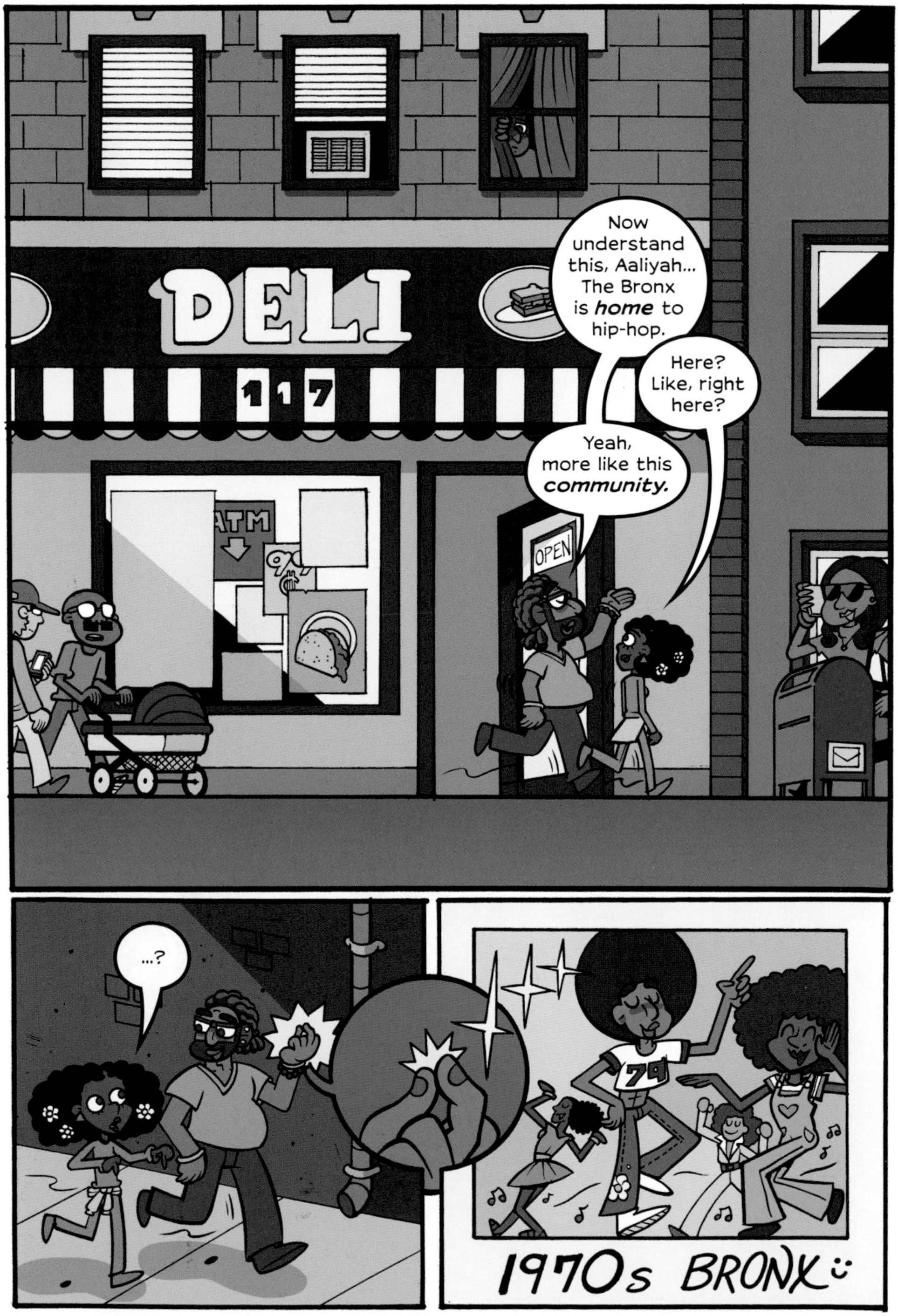
DELI
117
ATM
OPEN
Now understand this, Aaliyah... The Bronx is ***home*** to hip-hop.
Here? Like, right here?
Yeah, more like this ***community.***
...?
79
1970s BRONX

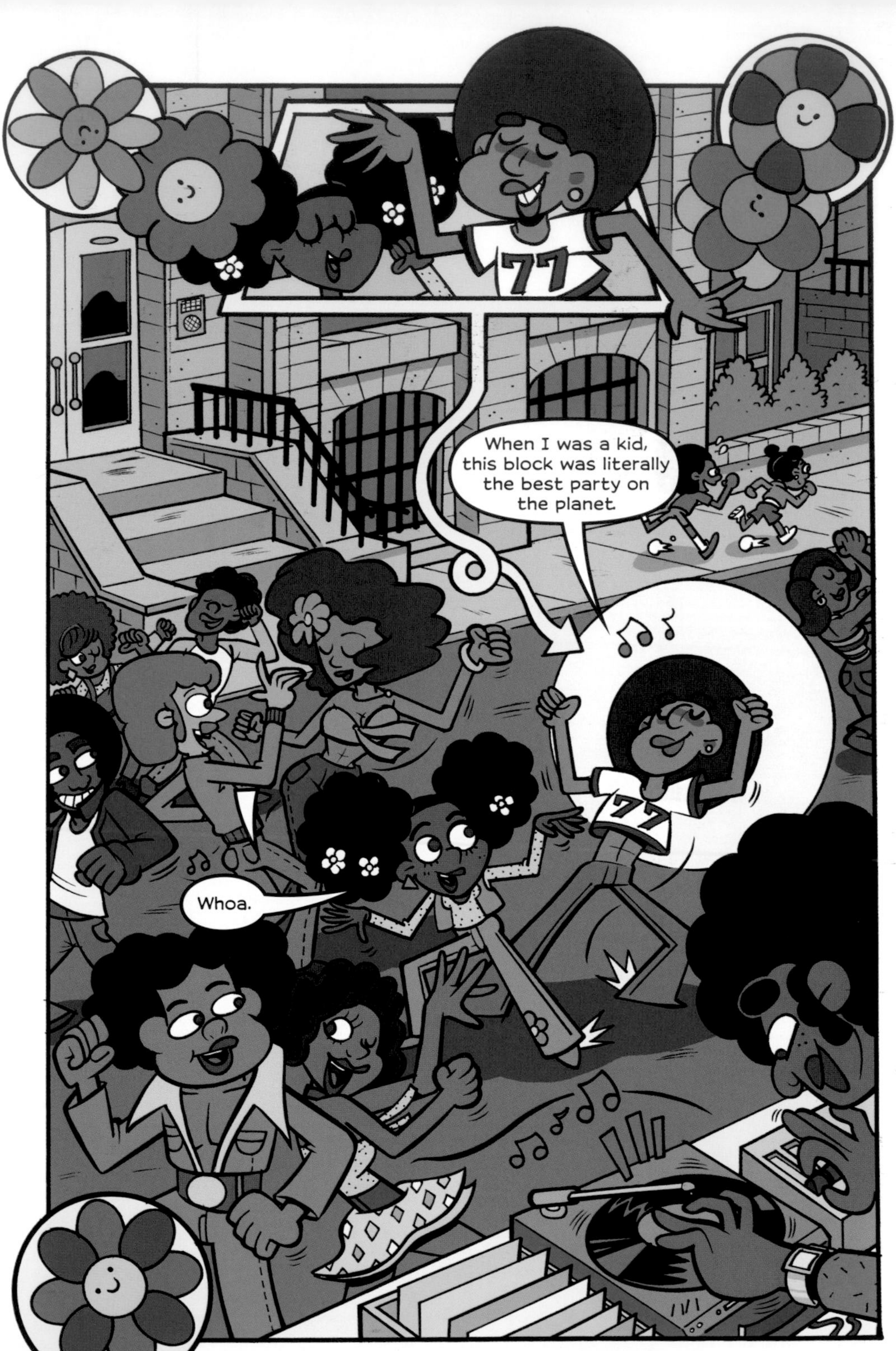

When I was a kid, this block was literally the best party on the planet.
Whoa.

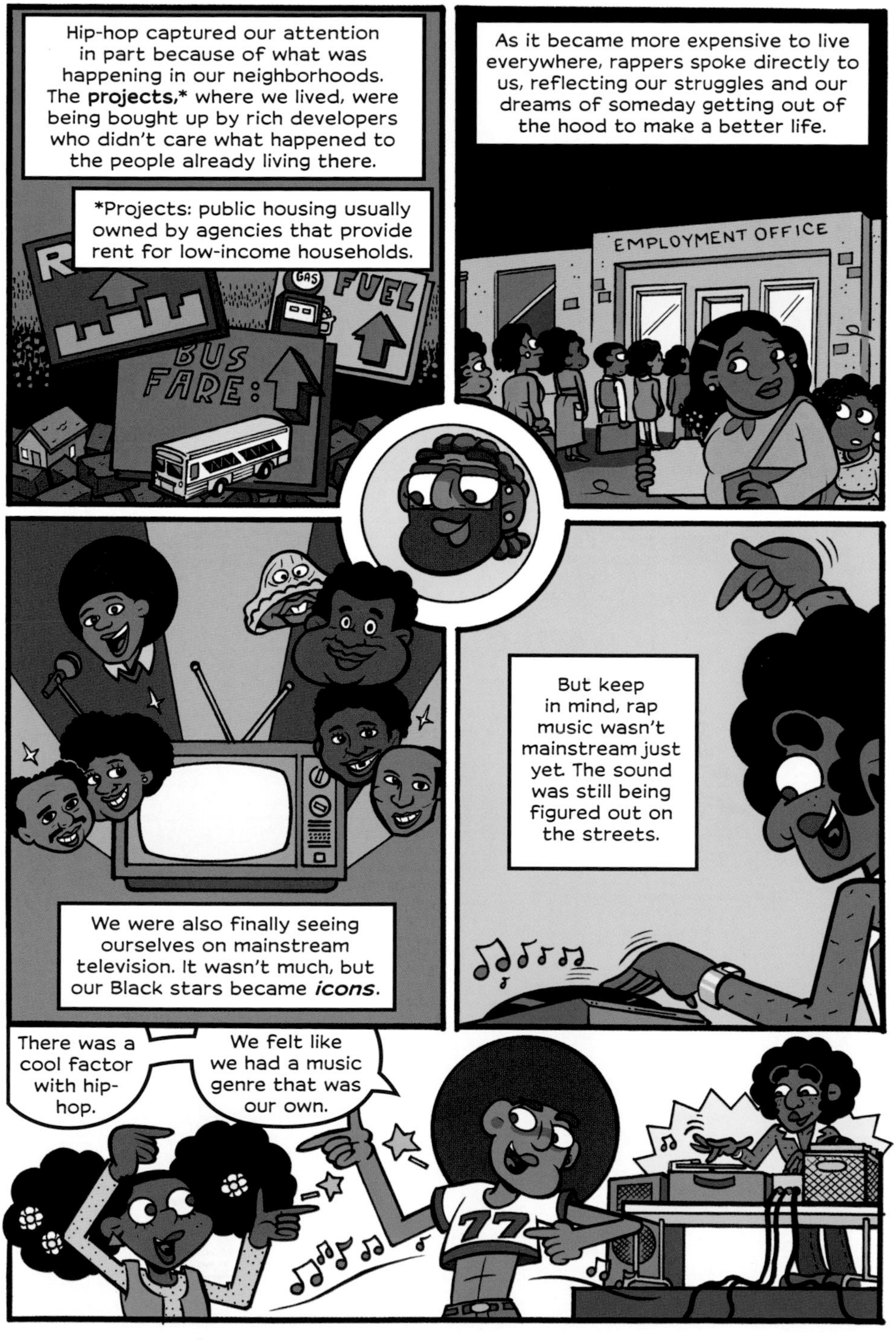
Hip-hop captured our attention in part because of what was happening in our neighborhoods. The **projects,*** where we lived, were being bought up by rich developers who didn't care what happened to the people already living there.
*Projects: public housing usually owned by agencies that provide rent for low-income households.
FUEL
GAS
BUS FARE:
As it became more expensive to live everywhere, rappers spoke directly to us, reflecting our struggles and our dreams of someday getting out of the hood to make a better life.
EMPLOYMENT OFFICE
We were also finally seeing ourselves on mainstream television. It wasn't much, but our Black stars became *icons*.
But keep in mind, rap music wasn't mainstream just yet. The sound was still being figured out on the streets.
There was a cool factor with hip-hop.
We felt like we had a music genre that was our own.
77

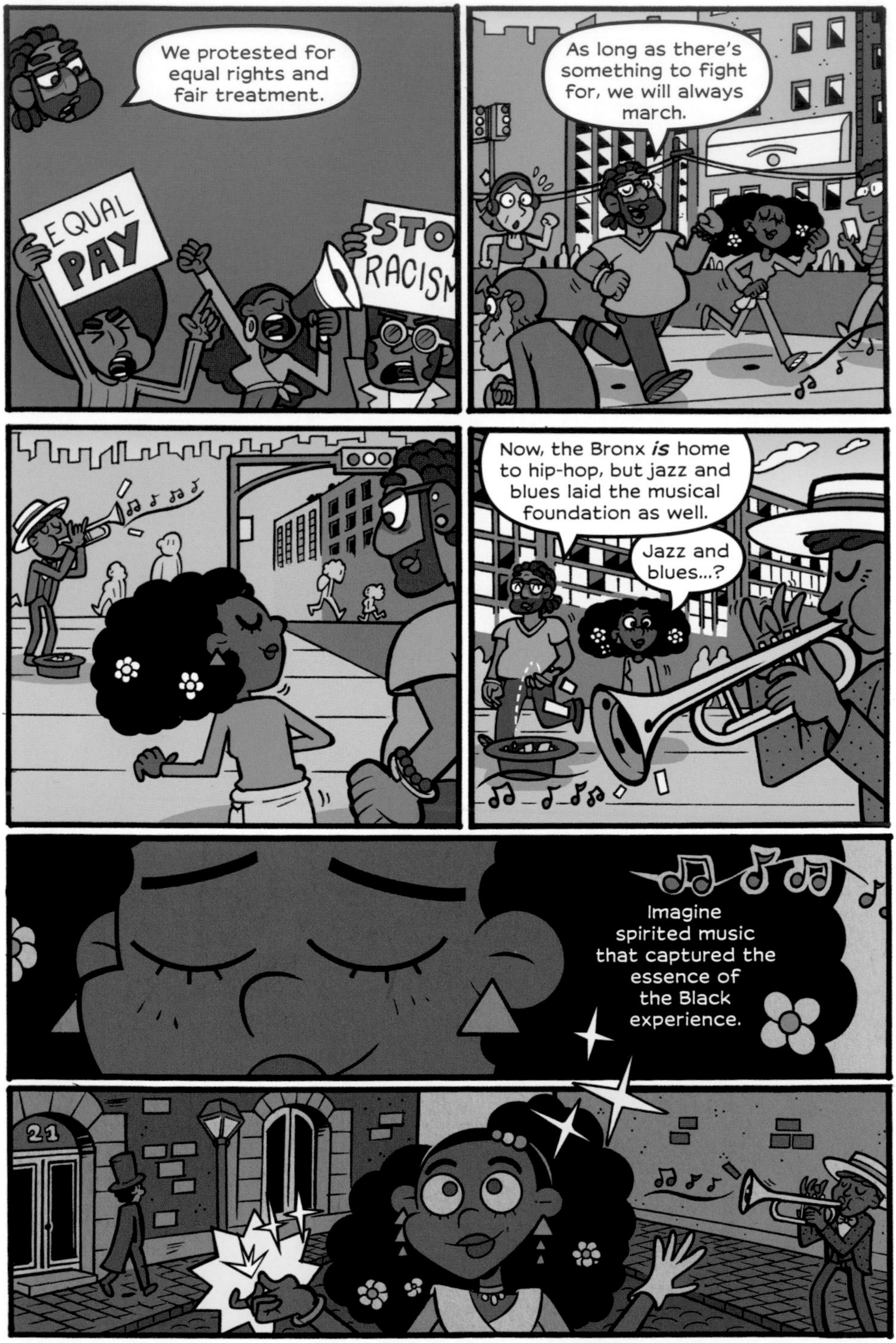
We protested for equal rights and fair treatment.
EQUAL PAY
STOP RACISM
As long as there's something to fight for, we will always march.
Now, the Bronx *is* home to hip-hop, but jazz and blues laid the musical foundation as well.
Jazz and blues...?
Imagine spirited music that captured the essence of the Black experience.
21

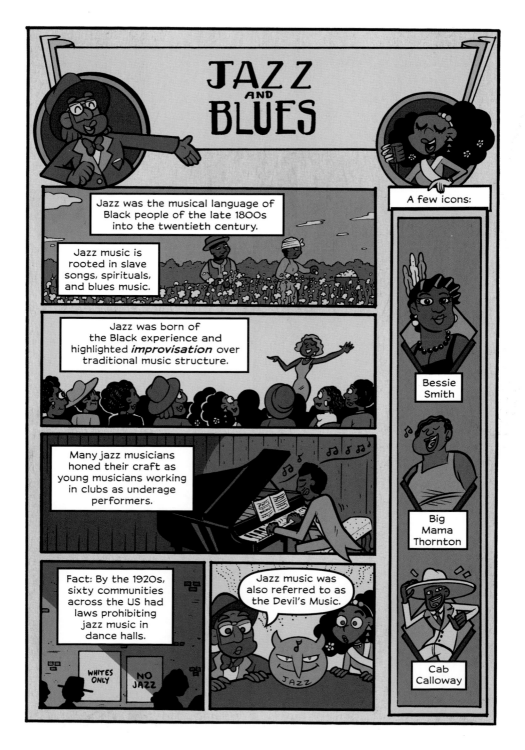

JAZZ AND BLUES

Jazz was the musical language of Black people of the late 1800s into the twentieth century.

Jazz music is rooted in slave songs, spirituals, and blues music.

Jazz was born of the Black experience and highlighted *improvisation* over traditional music structure.

Many jazz musicians honed their craft as young musicians working in clubs as underage performers.

Fact: By the 1920s, sixty communities across the US had laws prohibiting jazz music in dance halls.

WHITES ONLY

NO JAZZ

Jazz music was also referred to as the Devil's Music.

JAZZ

A few icons:

Bessie Smith

Big Mama Thornton

Cab Calloway

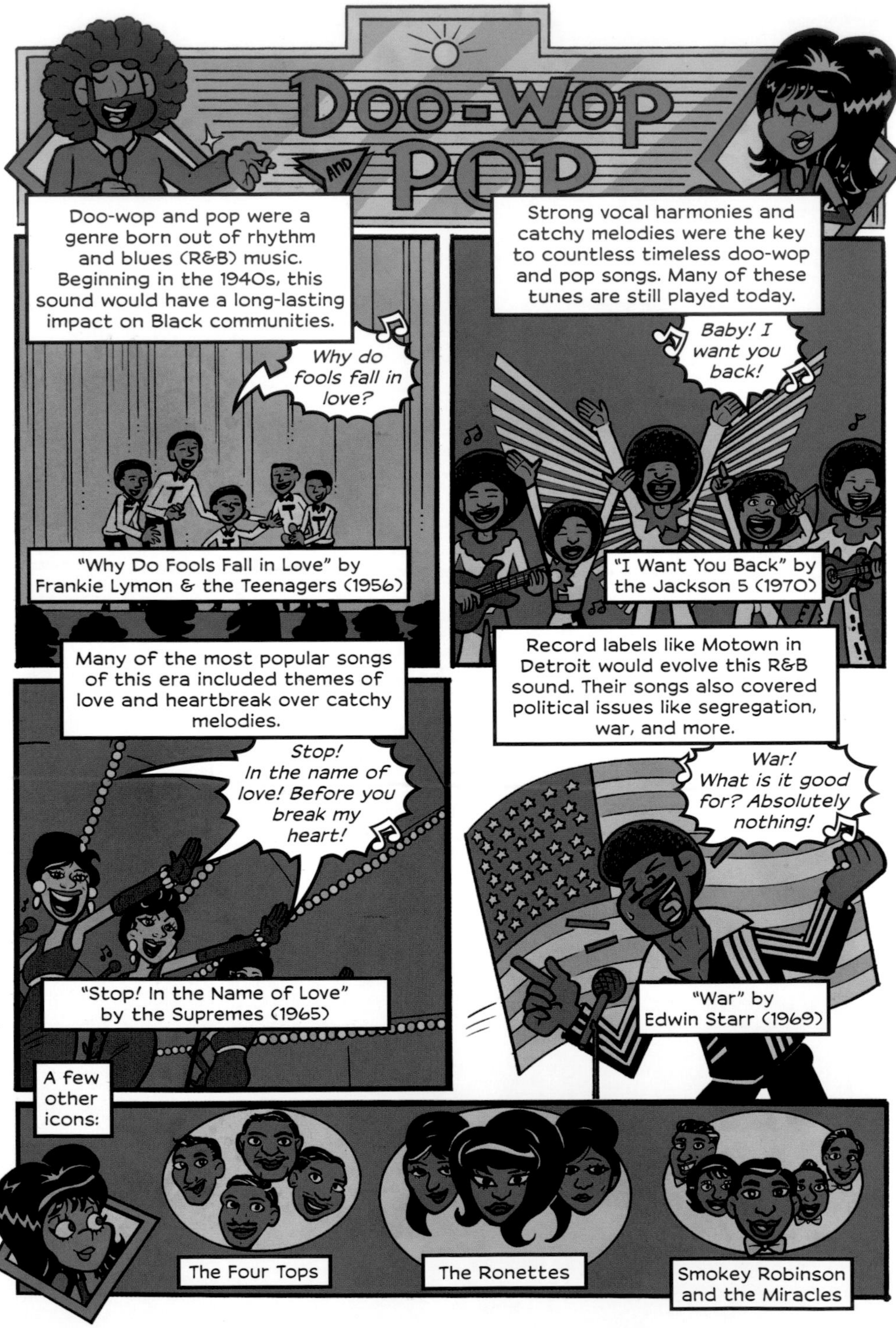

DOO-WOP AND POP
Doo-wop and pop were a genre born out of rhythm and blues (R&B) music. Beginning in the 1940s, this sound would have a long-lasting impact on Black communities.
Why do fools fall in love?
"Why Do Fools Fall in Love" by Frankie Lymon & the Teenagers (1956)
Strong vocal harmonies and catchy melodies were the key to countless timeless doo-wop and pop songs. Many of these tunes are still played today.
Baby! I want you back!
"I Want You Back" by the Jackson 5 (1970)
Many of the most popular songs of this era included themes of love and heartbreak over catchy melodies.
Stop! In the name of love! Before you break my heart!
"Stop! In the Name of Love" by the Supremes (1965)
Record labels like Motown in Detroit would evolve this R&B sound. Their songs also covered political issues like segregation, war, and more.
War! What is it good for? Absolutely nothing!
"War" by Edwin Starr (1969)
A few other icons:
The Four Tops
The Ronettes
Smokey Robinson and the Miracles

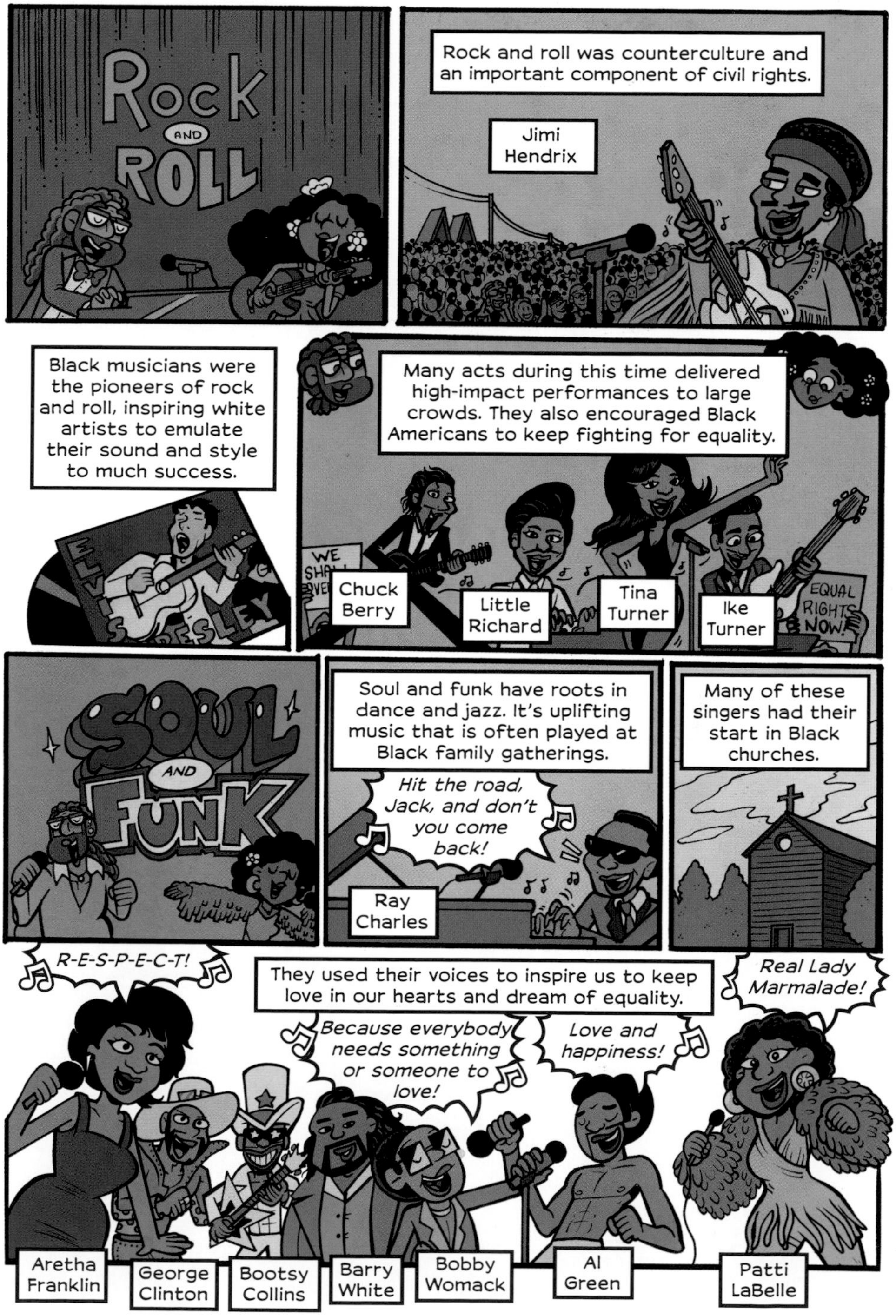

Rock AND ROLL
Rock and roll was counterculture and an important component of civil rights.
Jimi Hendrix
Black musicians were the pioneers of rock and roll, inspiring white artists to emulate their sound and style to much success.
ELVIS
Many acts during this time delivered high-impact performances to large crowds. They also encouraged Black Americans to keep fighting for equality.
Chuck Berry
Little Richard
Tina Turner
Ike Turner
EQUAL RIGHTS NOW!
SOUL AND FUNK
Soul and funk have roots in dance and jazz. It's uplifting music that is often played at Black family gatherings.
Hit the road, Jack, and don't you come back!
Ray Charles
Many of these singers had their start in Black churches.
R-E-S-P-E-C-T!
They used their voices to inspire us to keep love in our hearts and dream of equality.
Real Lady Marmalade!
Because everybody needs something or someone to love!
Love and happiness!
Aretha Franklin
George Clinton
Bootsy Collins
Barry White
Bobby Womack
Al Green
Patti LaBelle

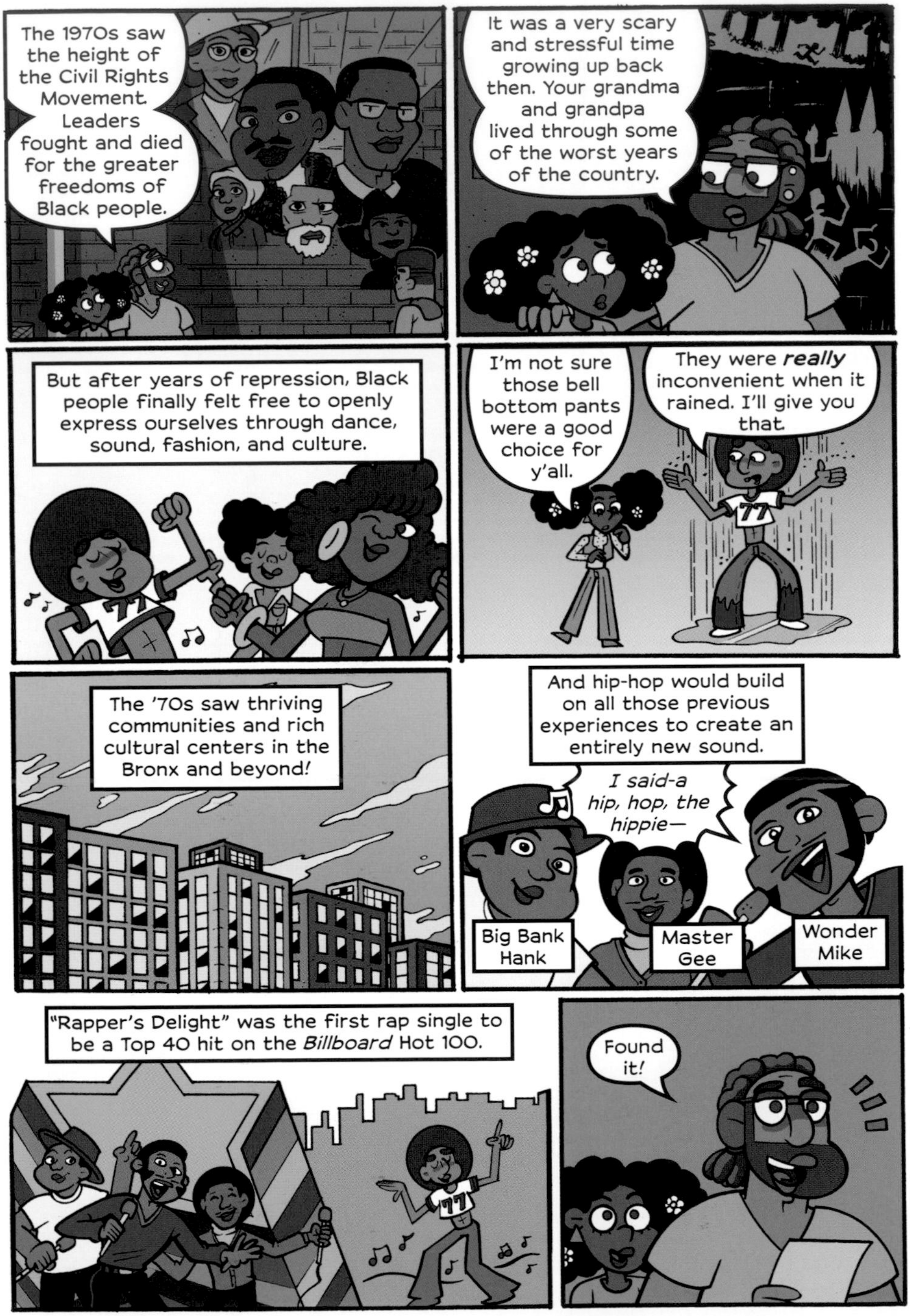
The 1970s saw the height of the Civil Rights Movement. Leaders fought and died for the greater freedoms of Black people.
It was a very scary and stressful time growing up back then. Your grandma and grandpa lived through some of the worst years of the country.
But after years of repression, Black people finally felt free to openly express ourselves through dance, sound, fashion, and culture.
I'm not sure those bell bottom pants were a good choice for y'all.
They were ***really*** inconvenient when it rained. I'll give you that.
The '70s saw thriving communities and rich cultural centers in the Bronx and beyond!
And hip-hop would build on all those previous experiences to create an entirely new sound.
I said-a hip, hop, the hippie—
Big Bank Hank
Master Gee
Wonder Mike
"Rapper's Delight" was the first rap single to be a Top 40 hit on the *Billboard* Hot 100.
Found it!

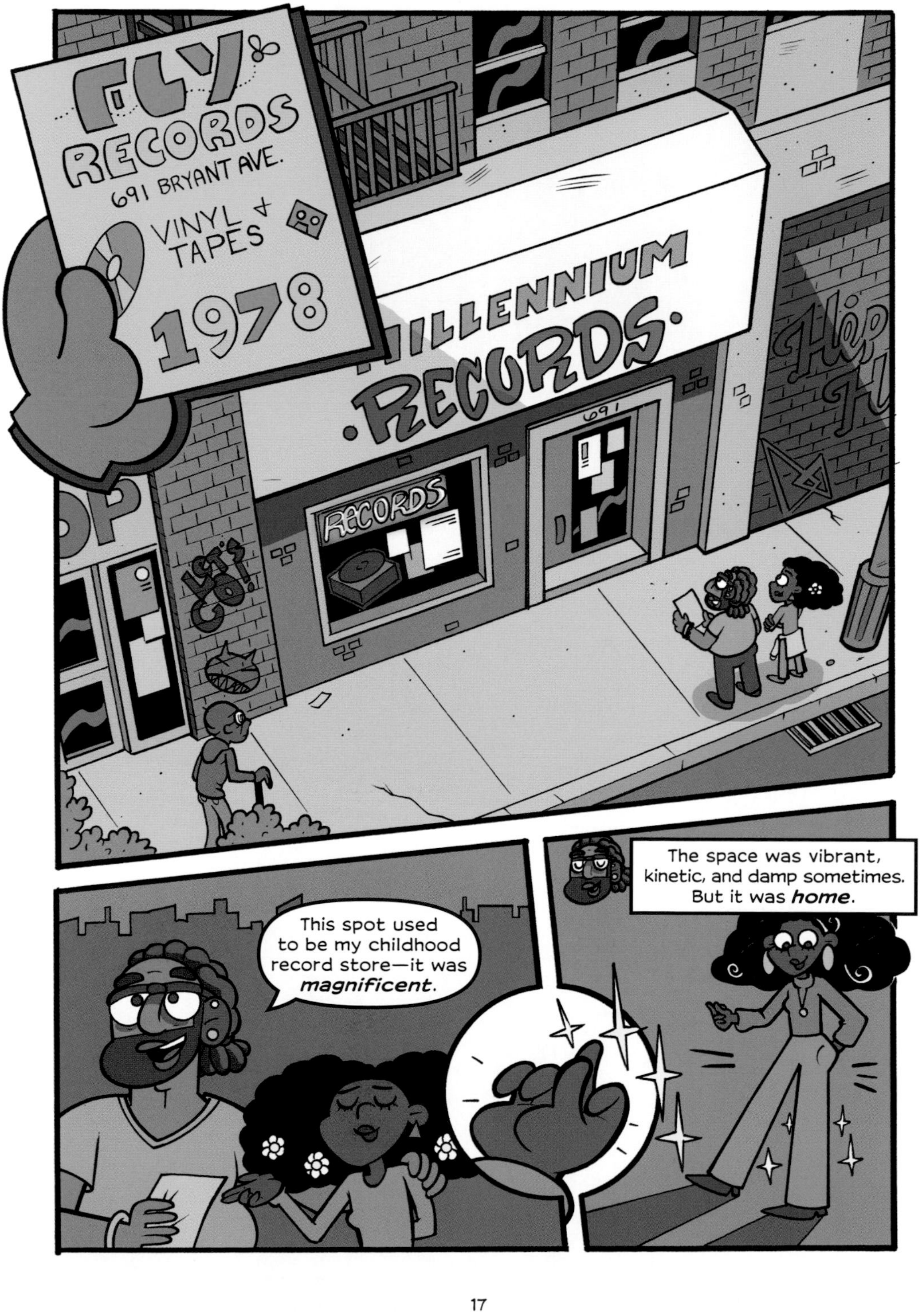
FLY RECORDS
691 BRYANT AVE.
VINYL & TAPES
1978
RECORDS
691
RECORDS
This spot used to be my childhood record store—it was ***magnificent***.
The space was vibrant, kinetic, and damp sometimes. But it was ***home***.

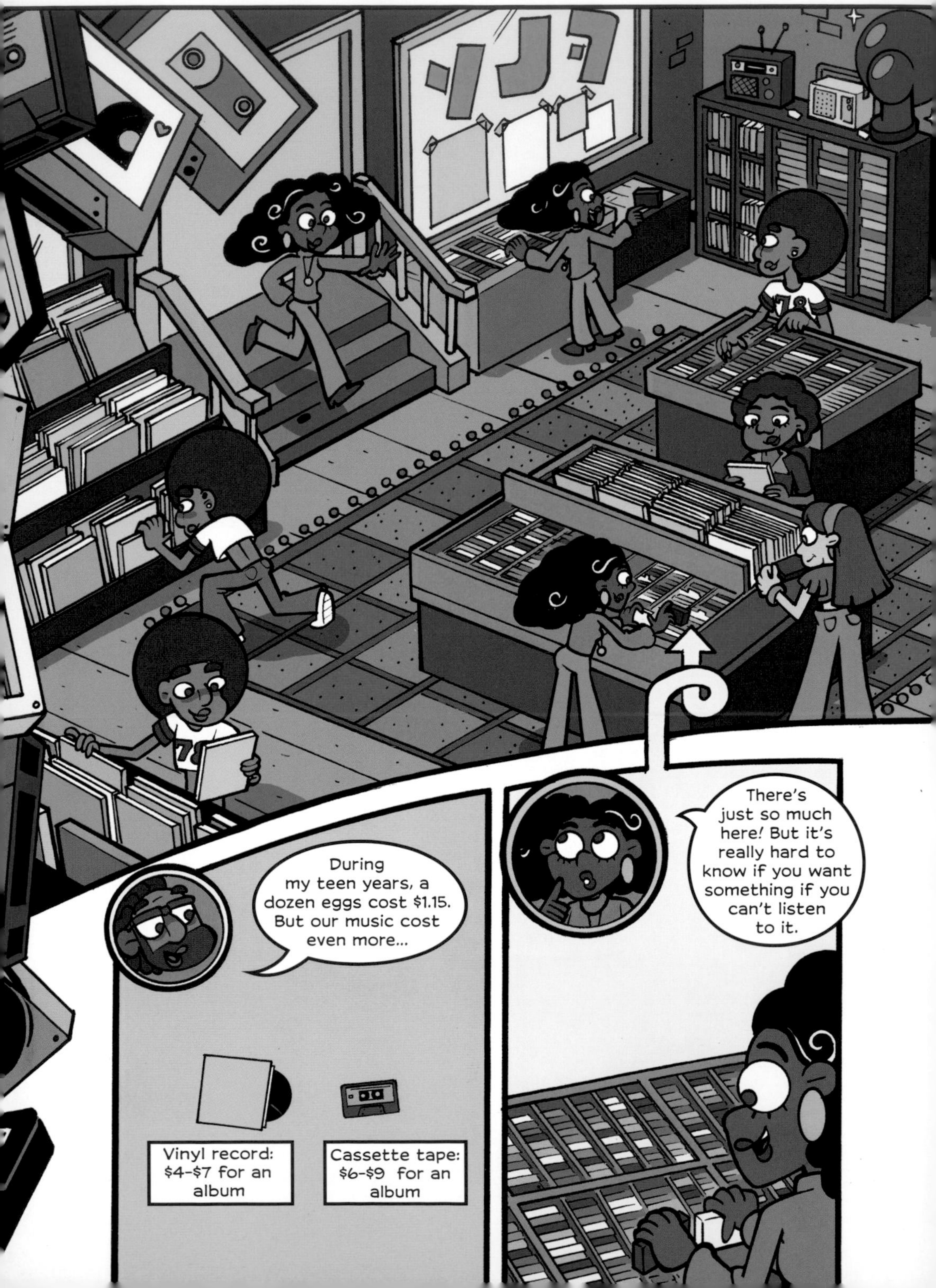
During my teen years, a dozen eggs cost $1.15. But our music cost even more...
Vinyl record: $4–$7 for an album
Cassette tape: $6–$9 for an album
There's just so much here! But it's really hard to know if you want something if you can't listen to it.

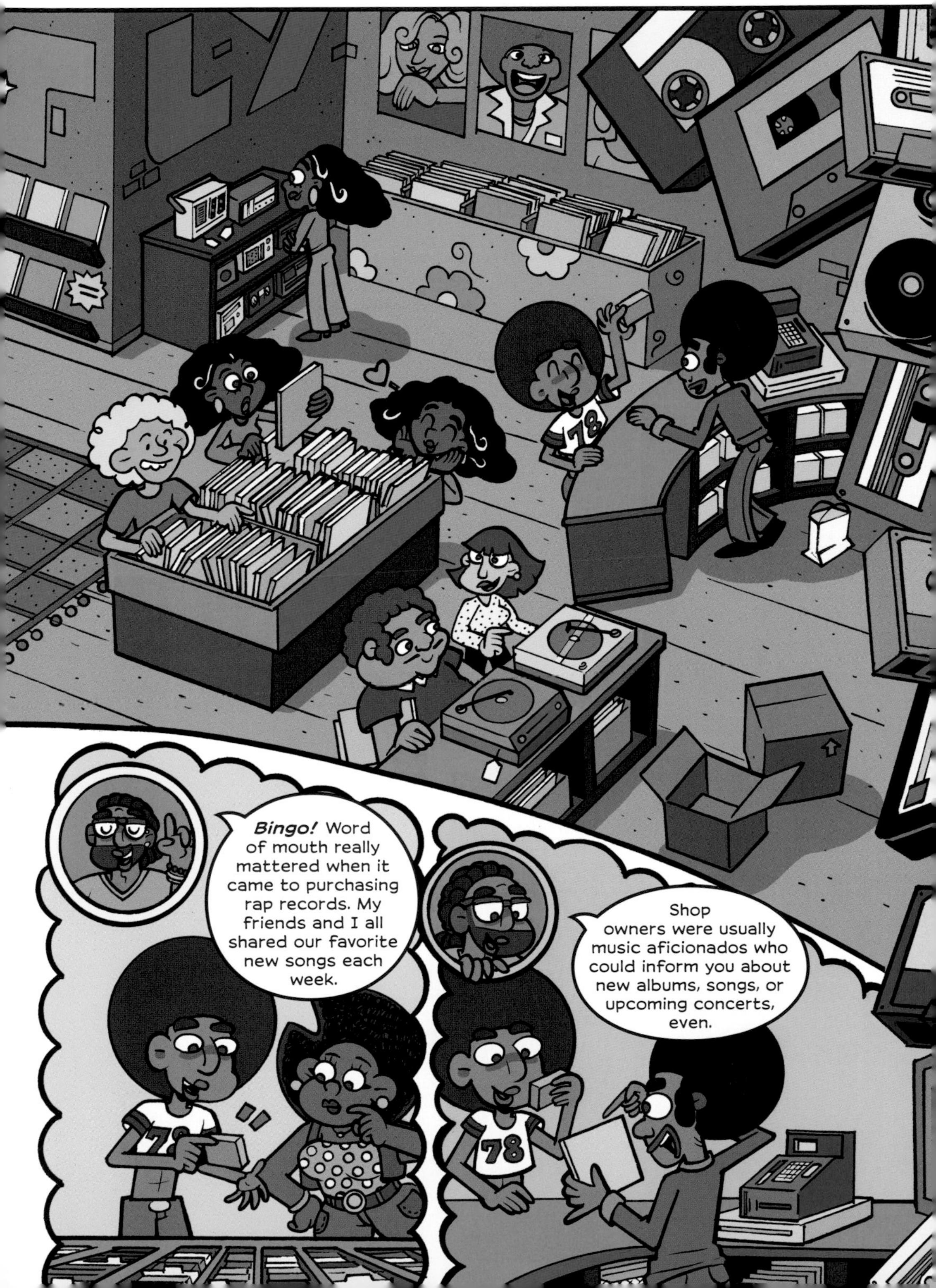
Bingo! Word of mouth really mattered when it came to purchasing rap records. My friends and I all shared our favorite new songs each week.
Shop owners were usually music aficionados who could inform you about new albums, songs, or upcoming concerts, even.

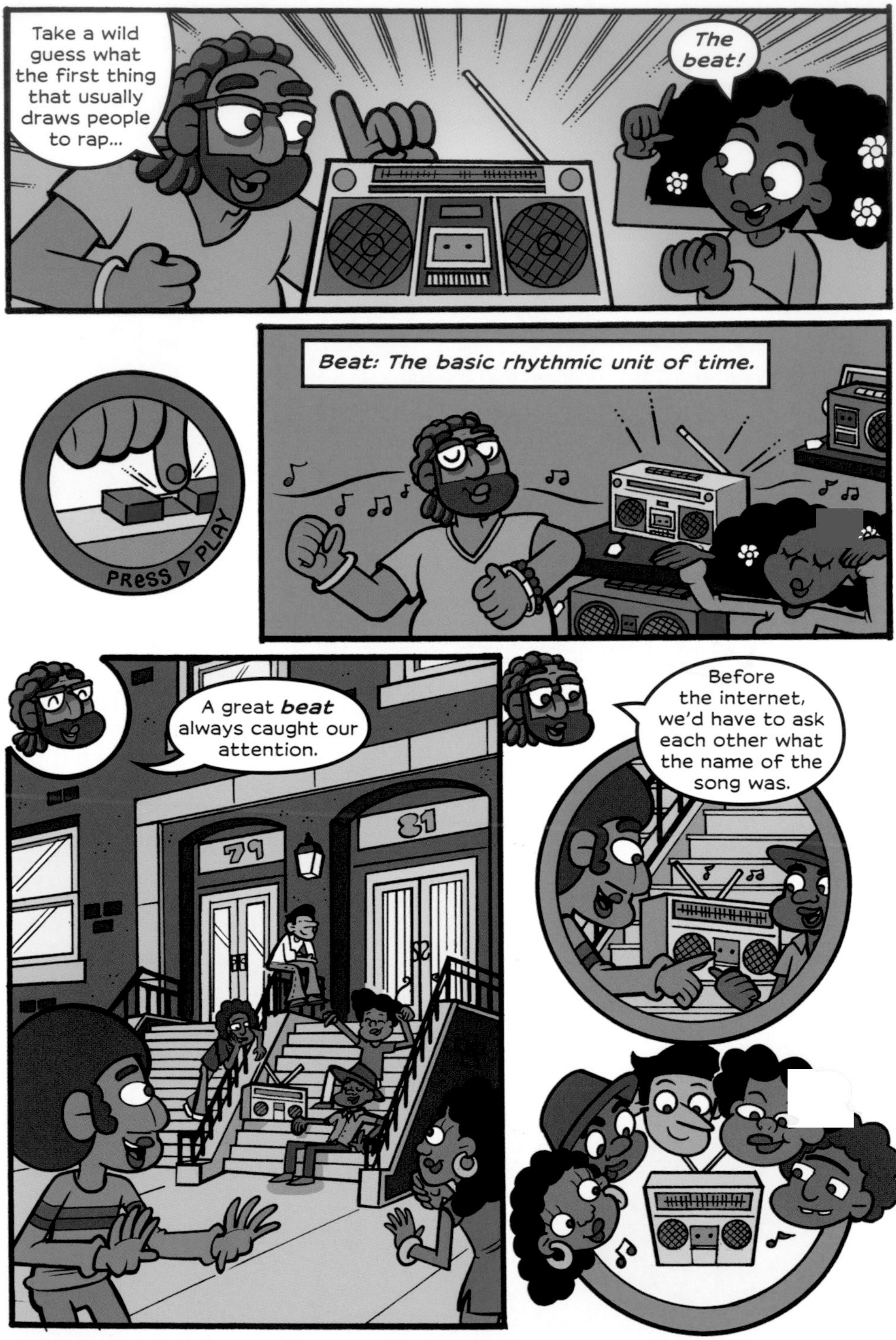
Take a wild guess what the first thing that usually draws people to rap...
The beat!
PRESS ▷ PLAY
Beat: The basic rhythmic unit of time.
A great **beat** always caught our attention.
79
81
Before the internet, we'd have to ask each other what the name of the song was.

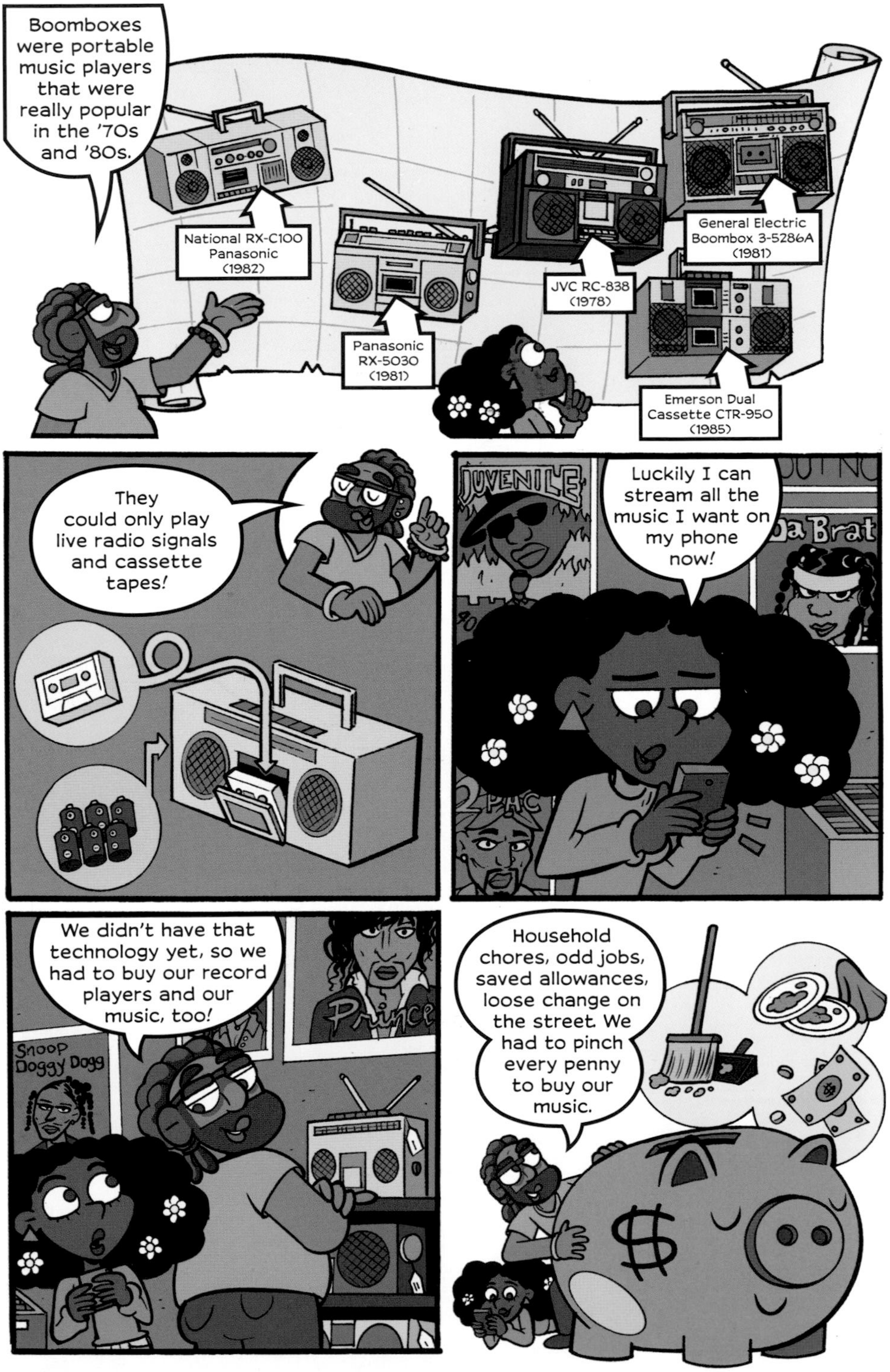
Boomboxes were portable music players that were really popular in the '70s and '80s.
National RX-C100 Panasonic (1982)
Panasonic RX-5030 (1981)
JVC RC-838 (1978)
General Electric Boombox 3-5286A (1981)
Emerson Dual Cassette CTR-950 (1985)
They could only play live radio signals and cassette tapes!
JUVENILE
Da Brat
2PAC
Luckily I can stream all the music I want on my phone now!
We didn't have that technology yet, so we had to buy our record players and our music, too!
Snoop Doggy Dogg
Prince
Household chores, odd jobs, saved allowances, loose change on the street. We had to pinch every penny to buy our music.

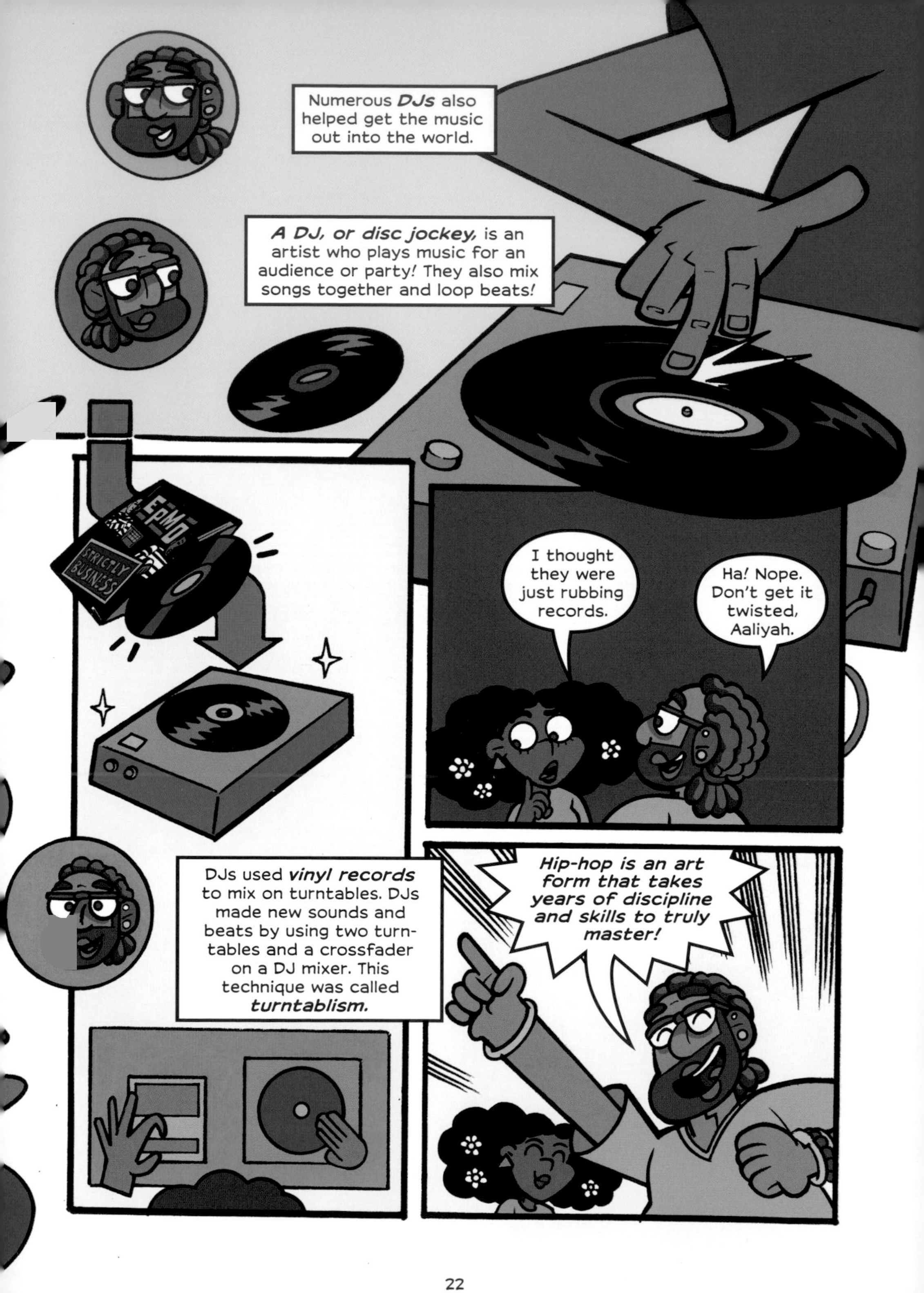

Numerous DJs also helped get the music out into the world.
A DJ, or disc jockey, is an artist who plays music for an audience or party! They also mix songs together and loop beats!
EPMD
STRICTLY BUSINESS
I thought they were just rubbing records.
Ha! Nope. Don't get it twisted, Aaliyah.
DJs used vinyl records to mix on turntables. DJs made new sounds and beats by using two turntables and a crossfader on a DJ mixer. This technique was called turntablism.
Hip-hop is an art form that takes years of discipline and skills to truly master!

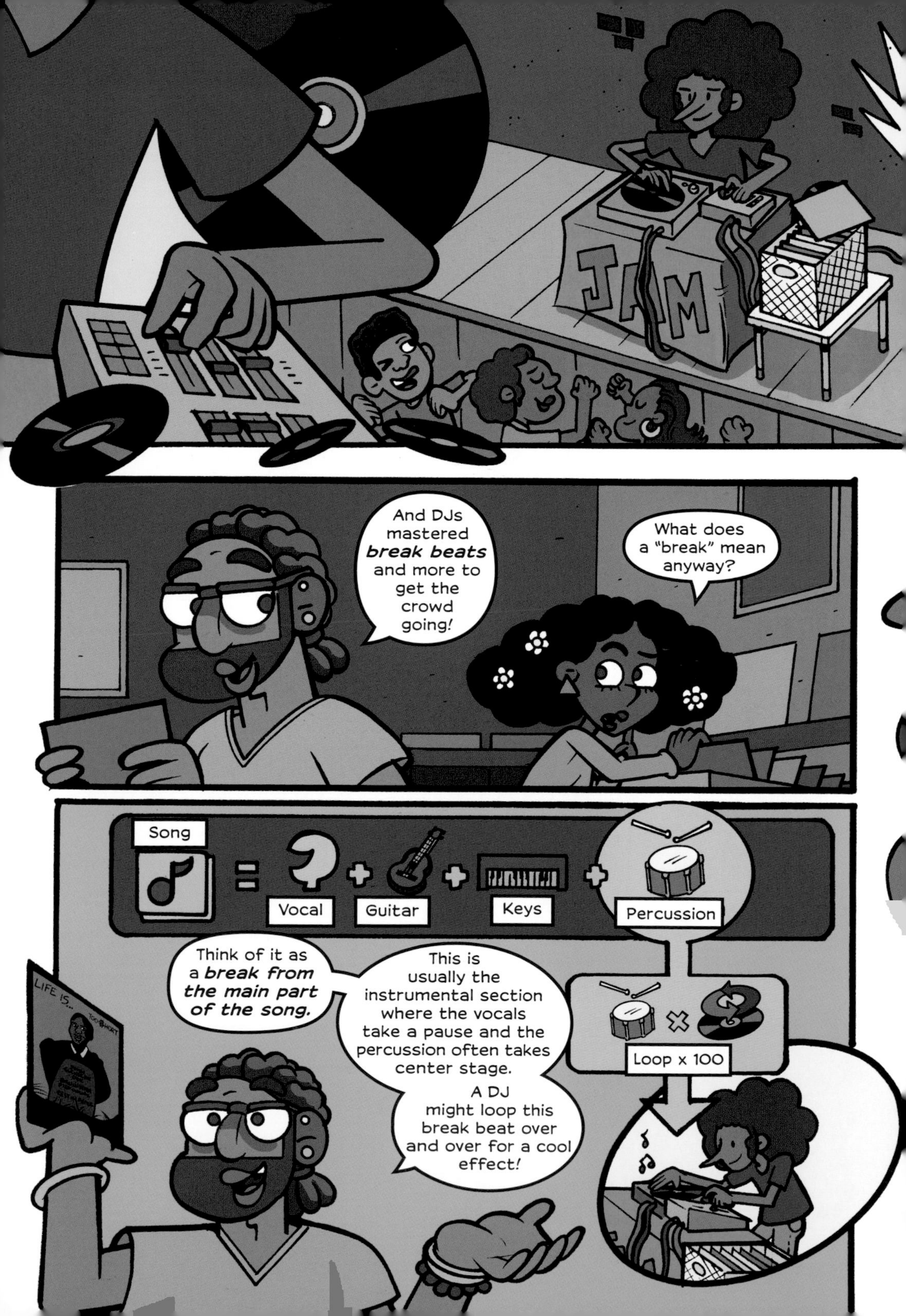

JAM
And DJs mastered ***break beats*** and more to get the crowd going!
What does a "break" mean anyway?
Song
=
Vocal
+
Guitar
+
Keys
+
Percussion
Loop x 100
LIFE IS...
Think of it as a ***break from the main part of the song.***
This is usually the instrumental section where the vocals take a pause and the percussion often takes center stage.
A DJ might loop this break beat over and over for a cool effect!

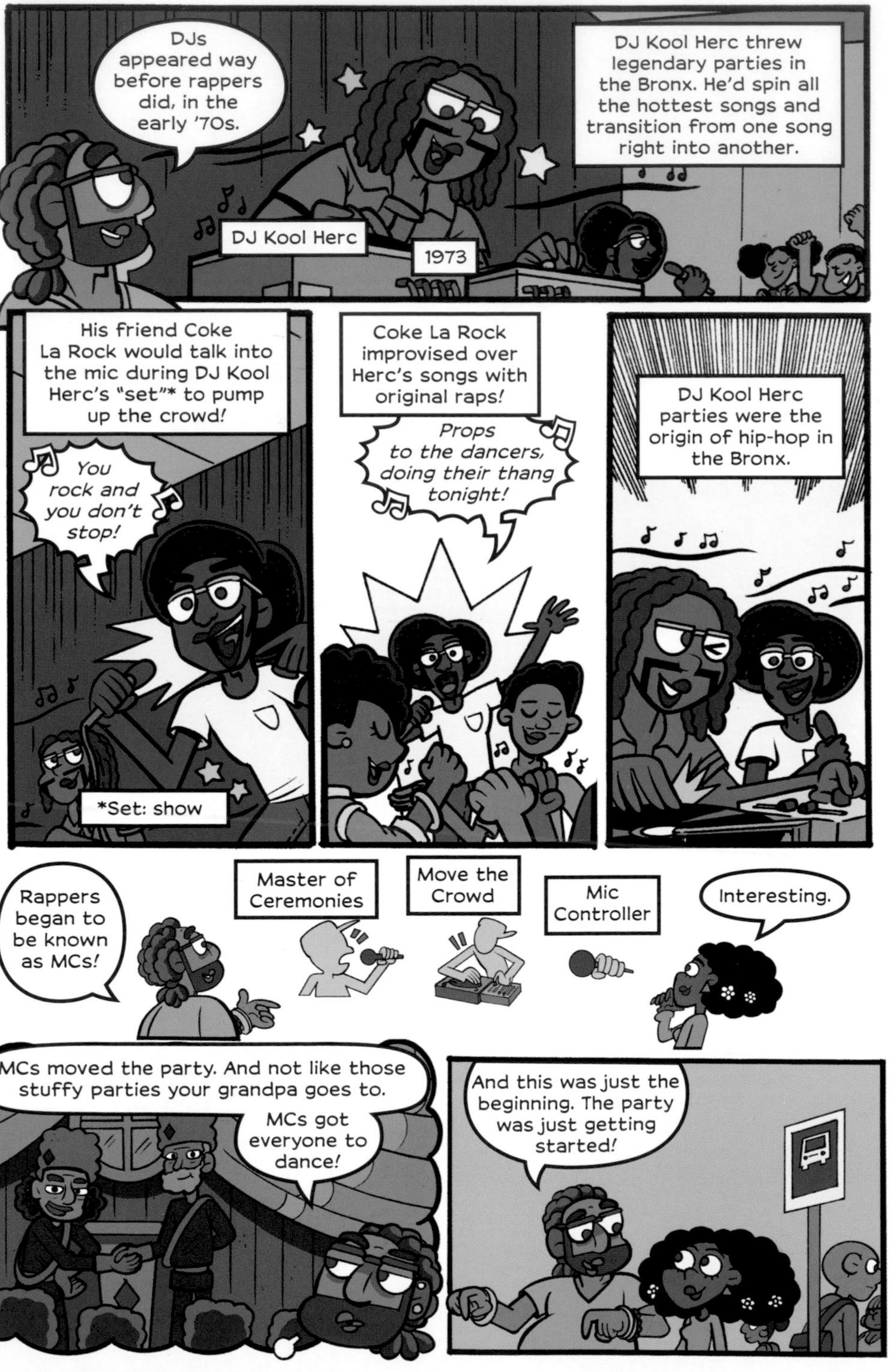
DJs appeared way before rappers did, in the early '70s.
DJ Kool Herc threw legendary parties in the Bronx. He'd spin all the hottest songs and transition from one song right into another.
DJ Kool Herc
1973
His friend Coke La Rock would talk into the mic during DJ Kool Herc's "set"* to pump up the crowd!
You rock and you don't stop!
*Set: show
Coke La Rock improvised over Herc's songs with original raps!
Props to the dancers, doing their thang tonight!
DJ Kool Herc parties were the origin of hip-hop in the Bronx.
Rappers began to be known as MCs!
Master of Ceremonies
Move the Crowd
Mic Controller
Interesting.
MCs moved the party. And not like those stuffy parties your grandpa goes to.
MCs got everyone to dance!
And this was just the beginning. The party was just getting started!

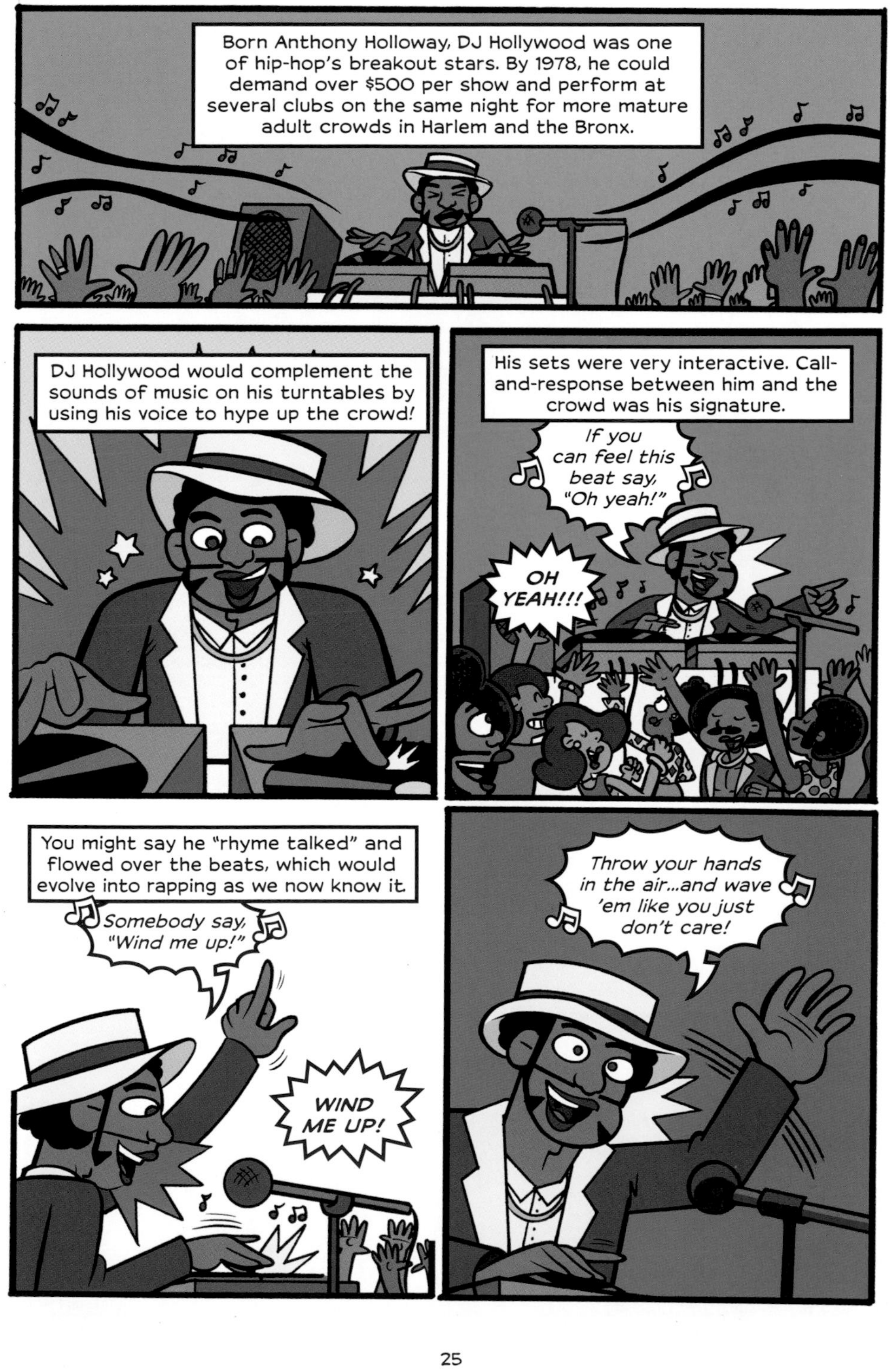
Born Anthony Holloway, DJ Hollywood was one of hip-hop's breakout stars. By 1978, he could demand over $500 per show and perform at several clubs on the same night for more mature adult crowds in Harlem and the Bronx.
DJ Hollywood would complement the sounds of music on his turntables by using his voice to hype up the crowd!
His sets were very interactive. Call-and-response between him and the crowd was his signature.
If you can feel this beat say, "Oh yeah!"
OH YEAH!!!
You might say he "rhyme talked" and flowed over the beats, which would evolve into rapping as we now know it.
Somebody say, "Wind me up!"
WIND ME UP!
Throw your hands in the air...and wave 'em like you just don't care!

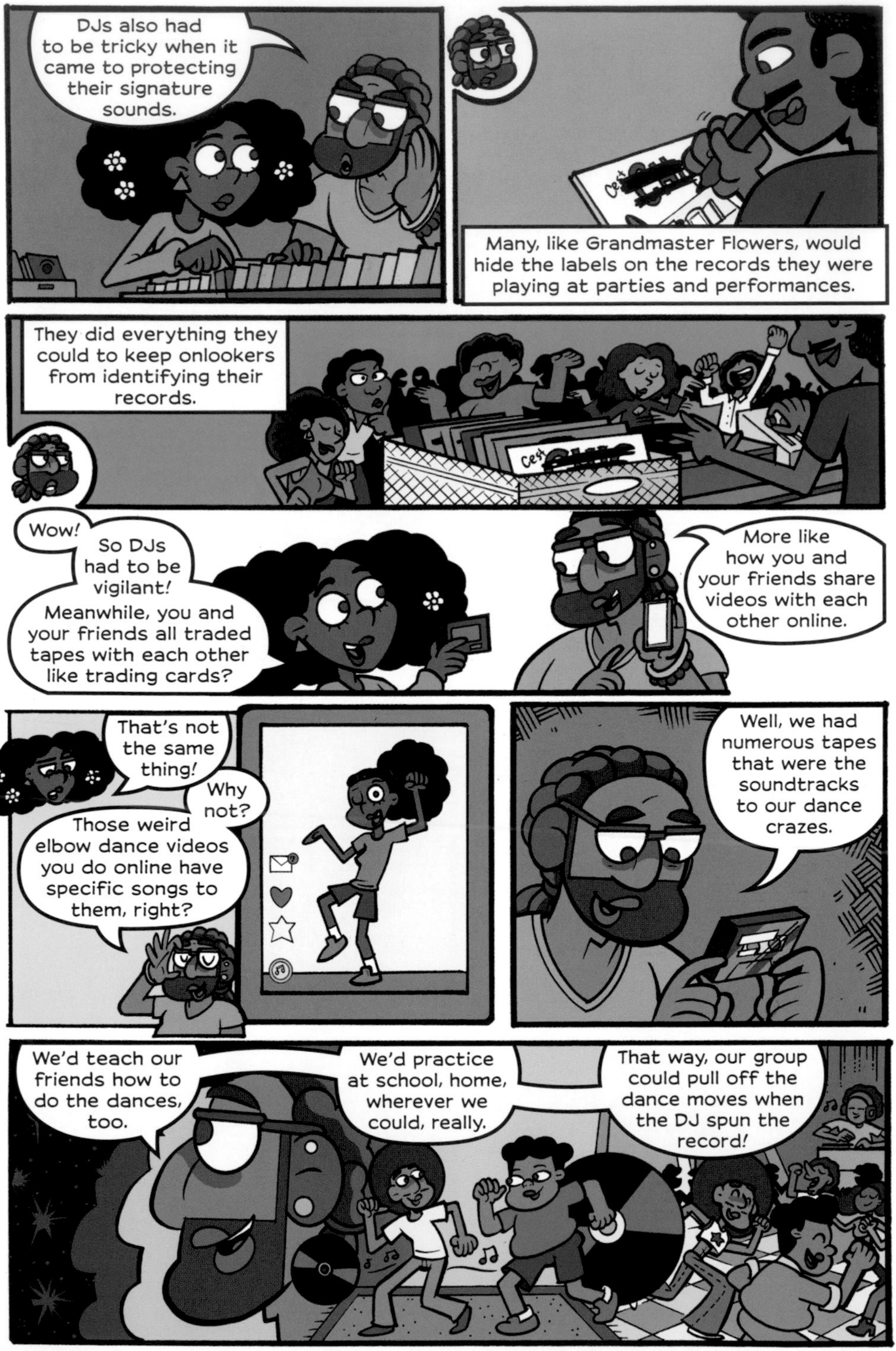
DJs also had to be tricky when it came to protecting their signature sounds.
Many, like Grandmaster Flowers, would hide the labels on the records they were playing at parties and performances.
They did everything they could to keep onlookers from identifying their records.
Wow!
So DJs had to be vigilant!
Meanwhile, you and your friends all traded tapes with each other like trading cards?
More like how you and your friends share videos with each other online.
That's not the same thing!
Why not?
Those weird elbow dance videos you do online have specific songs to them, right?
Well, we had numerous tapes that were the soundtracks to our dance crazes.
We'd teach our friends how to do the dances, too.
We'd practice at school, home, wherever we could, really.
That way, our group could pull off the dance moves when the DJ spun the record!

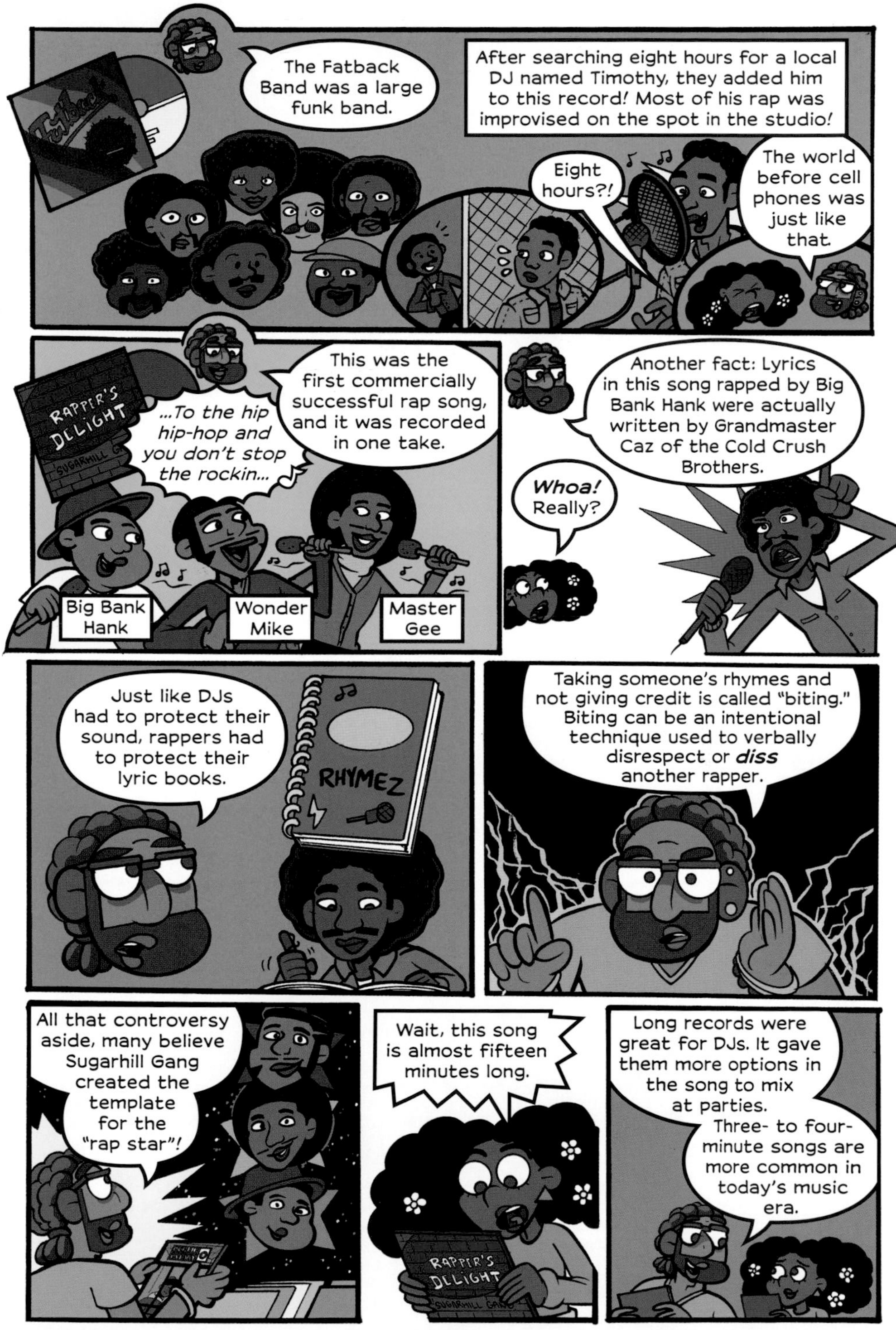

The Fatback Band was a large funk band.
After searching eight hours for a local DJ named Timothy, they added him to this record! Most of his rap was improvised on the spot in the studio!
Eight hours?!
The world before cell phones was just like that.
This was the first commercially successful rap song, and it was recorded in one take.
RAPPER'S DELIGHT
SUGARHILL
...To the hip hip-hop and you don't stop the rockin...
Big Bank Hank
Wonder Mike
Master Gee
Another fact: Lyrics in this song rapped by Big Bank Hank were actually written by Grandmaster Caz of the Cold Crush Brothers.
Whoa! Really?
Just like DJs had to protect their sound, rappers had to protect their lyric books.
RHYMEZ
Taking someone's rhymes and not giving credit is called "biting." Biting can be an intentional technique used to verbally disrespect or ***diss*** another rapper.
All that controversy aside, many believe Sugarhill Gang created the template for the "rap star"!
Wait, this song is almost fifteen minutes long.
RAPPER'S DELIGHT
SUGARHILL GANG
Long records were great for DJs. It gave them more options in the song to mix at parties.
Three- to four-minute songs are more common in today's music era.

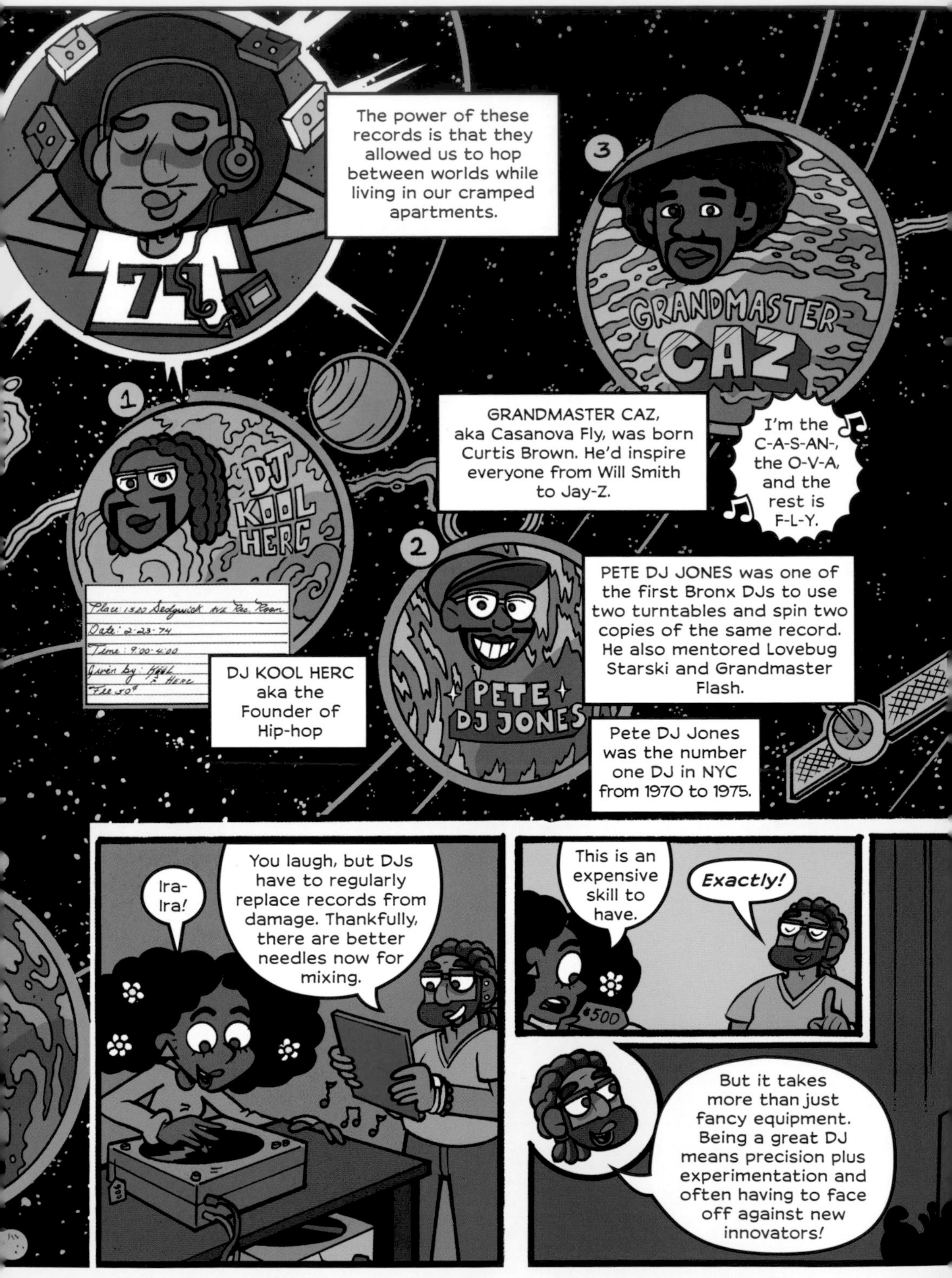

The power of these records is that they allowed us to hop between worlds while living in our cramped apartments.
1
DJ KOOL HERC
Place: 1520 Sedgwick Ave. Rec. Room
Date: 2-23-74
Time: 9:00-4:00
Given by: Kool Herc
Fee 50¢
DJ KOOL HERC aka the Founder of Hip-hop
2
PETE DJ JONES
PETE DJ JONES was one of the first Bronx DJs to use two turntables and spin two copies of the same record. He also mentored Lovebug Starski and Grandmaster Flash.
Pete DJ Jones was the number one DJ in NYC from 1970 to 1975.
3
GRANDMASTER CAZ
GRANDMASTER CAZ, aka Casanova Fly, was born Curtis Brown. He'd inspire everyone from Will Smith to Jay-Z.
I'm the C-A-S-AN-, the O-V-A, and the rest is F-L-Y.
Ira-Ira!
You laugh, but DJs have to regularly replace records from damage. Thankfully, there are better needles now for mixing.
This is an expensive skill to have.
$500
Exactly!
But it takes more than just fancy equipment. Being a great DJ means precision plus experimentation and often having to face off against new innovators!

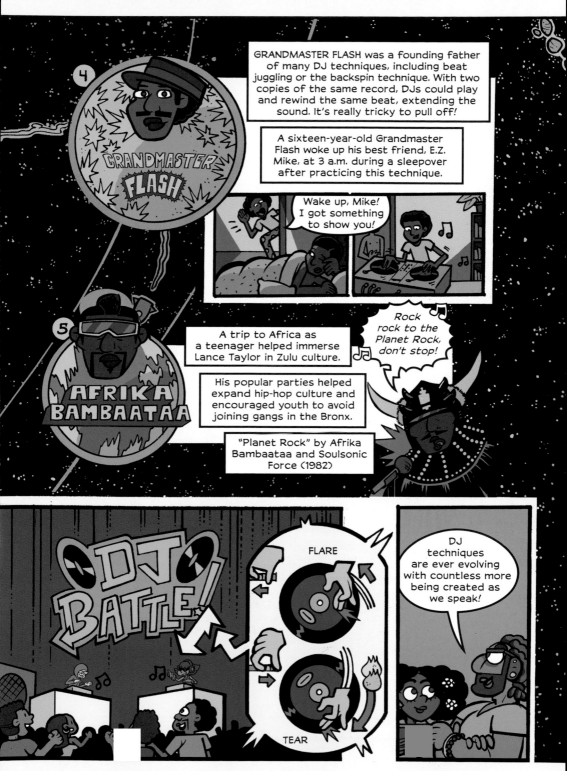

4 GRANDMASTER FLASH

GRANDMASTER FLASH was a founding father of many DJ techniques, including beat juggling or the backspin technique. With two copies of the same record, DJs could play and rewind the same beat, extending the sound. It's really tricky to pull off!

A sixteen-year-old Grandmaster Flash woke up his best friend, E.Z. Mike, at 3 a.m. during a sleepover after practicing this technique.

Wake up, Mike! I got something to show you!

5 AFRIKA BAMBAATAA

A trip to Africa as a teenager helped immerse Lance Taylor in Zulu culture.

His popular parties helped expand hip-hop culture and encouraged youth to avoid joining gangs in the Bronx.

"Planet Rock" by Afrika Bambaataa and Soulsonic Force (1982)

Rock rock to the Planet Rock, don't stop!

DJ BATTLE!

FLARE

TEAR

DJ techniques are ever evolving with countless more being created as we speak!

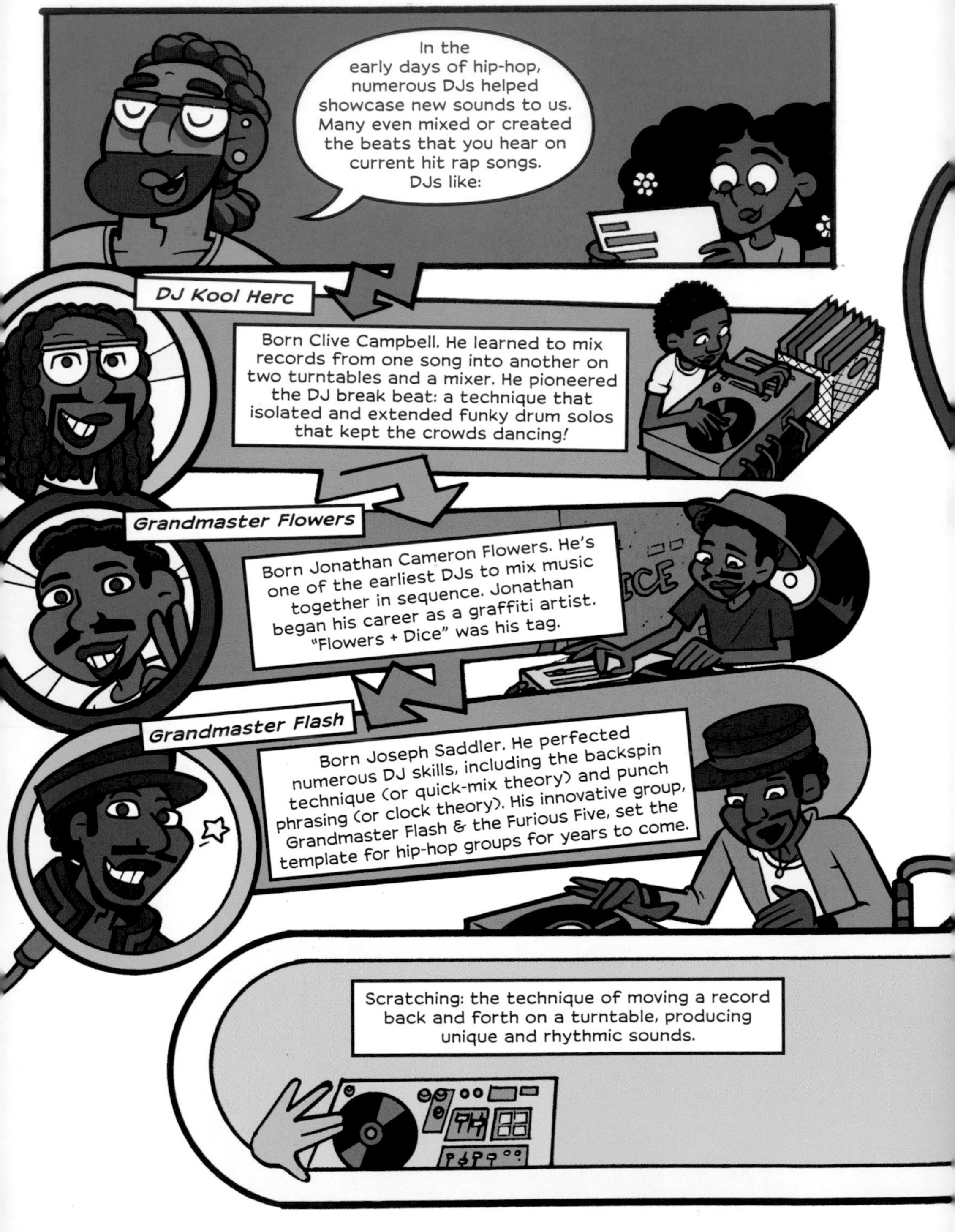

In the early days of hip-hop, numerous DJs helped showcase new sounds to us. Many even mixed or created the beats that you hear on current hit rap songs. DJs like:
DJ Kool Herc
Born Clive Campbell. He learned to mix records from one song into another on two turntables and a mixer. He pioneered the DJ break beat: a technique that isolated and extended funky drum solos that kept the crowds dancing!
Grandmaster Flowers
Born Jonathan Cameron Flowers. He's one of the earliest DJs to mix music together in sequence. Jonathan began his career as a graffiti artist. "Flowers + Dice" was his tag.
Grandmaster Flash
Born Joseph Saddler. He perfected numerous DJ skills, including the backspin technique (or quick-mix theory) and punch phrasing (or clock theory). His innovative group, Grandmaster Flash & the Furious Five, set the template for hip-hop groups for years to come.
Scratching: the technique of moving a record back and forth on a turntable, producing unique and rhythmic sounds.

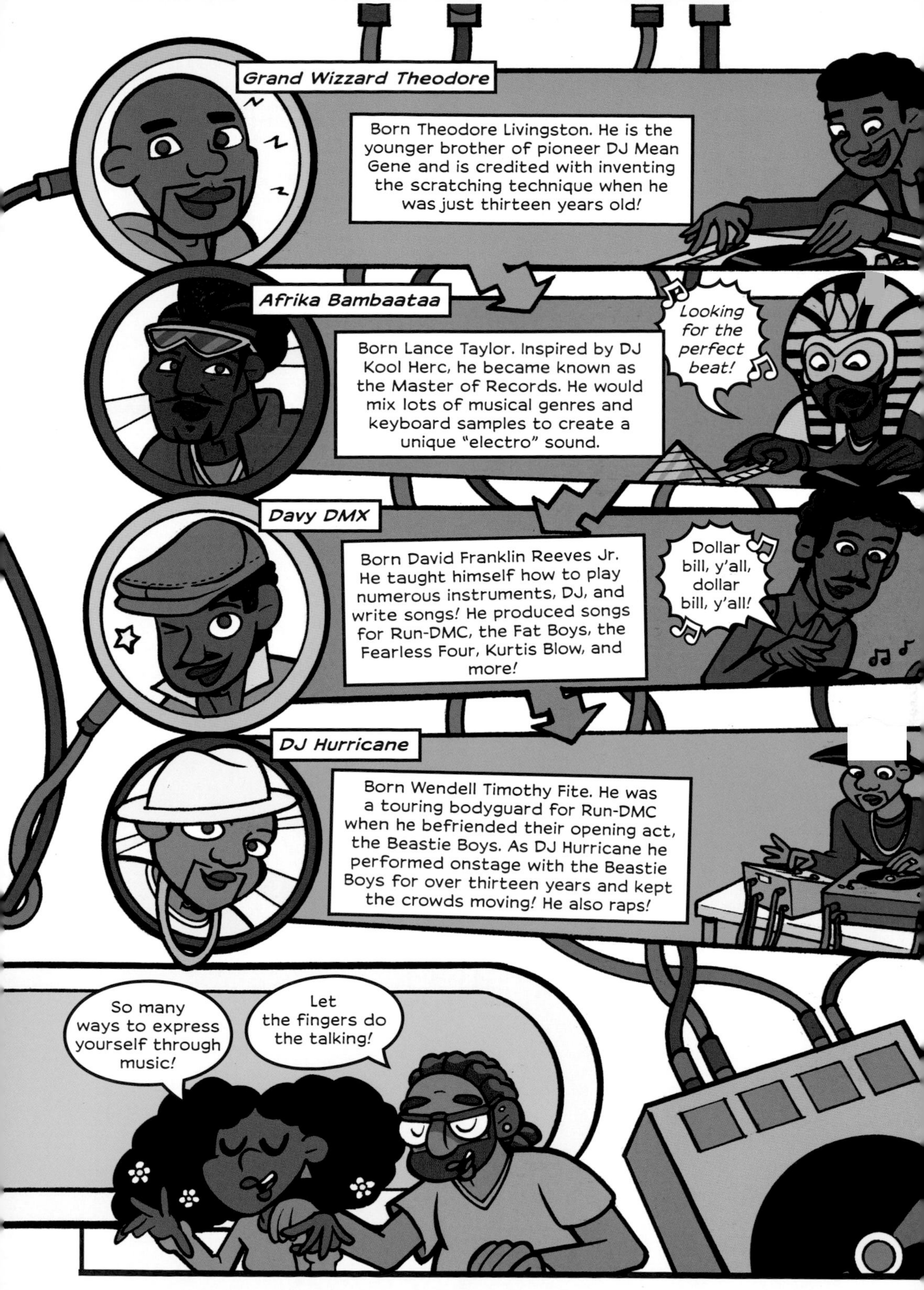
Grand Wizzard Theodore
Born Theodore Livingston. He is the younger brother of pioneer DJ Mean Gene and is credited with inventing the scratching technique when he was just thirteen years old!
Afrika Bambaataa
Born Lance Taylor. Inspired by DJ Kool Herc, he became known as the Master of Records. He would mix lots of musical genres and keyboard samples to create a unique "electro" sound.
Looking for the perfect beat!
Davy DMX
Born David Franklin Reeves Jr. He taught himself how to play numerous instruments, DJ, and write songs! He produced songs for Run-DMC, the Fat Boys, the Fearless Four, Kurtis Blow, and more!
Dollar bill, y'all, dollar bill, y'all!
DJ Hurricane
Born Wendell Timothy Fite. He was a touring bodyguard for Run-DMC when he befriended their opening act, the Beastie Boys. As DJ Hurricane he performed onstage with the Beastie Boys for over thirteen years and kept the crowds moving! He also raps!
So many ways to express yourself through music!
Let the fingers do the talking!

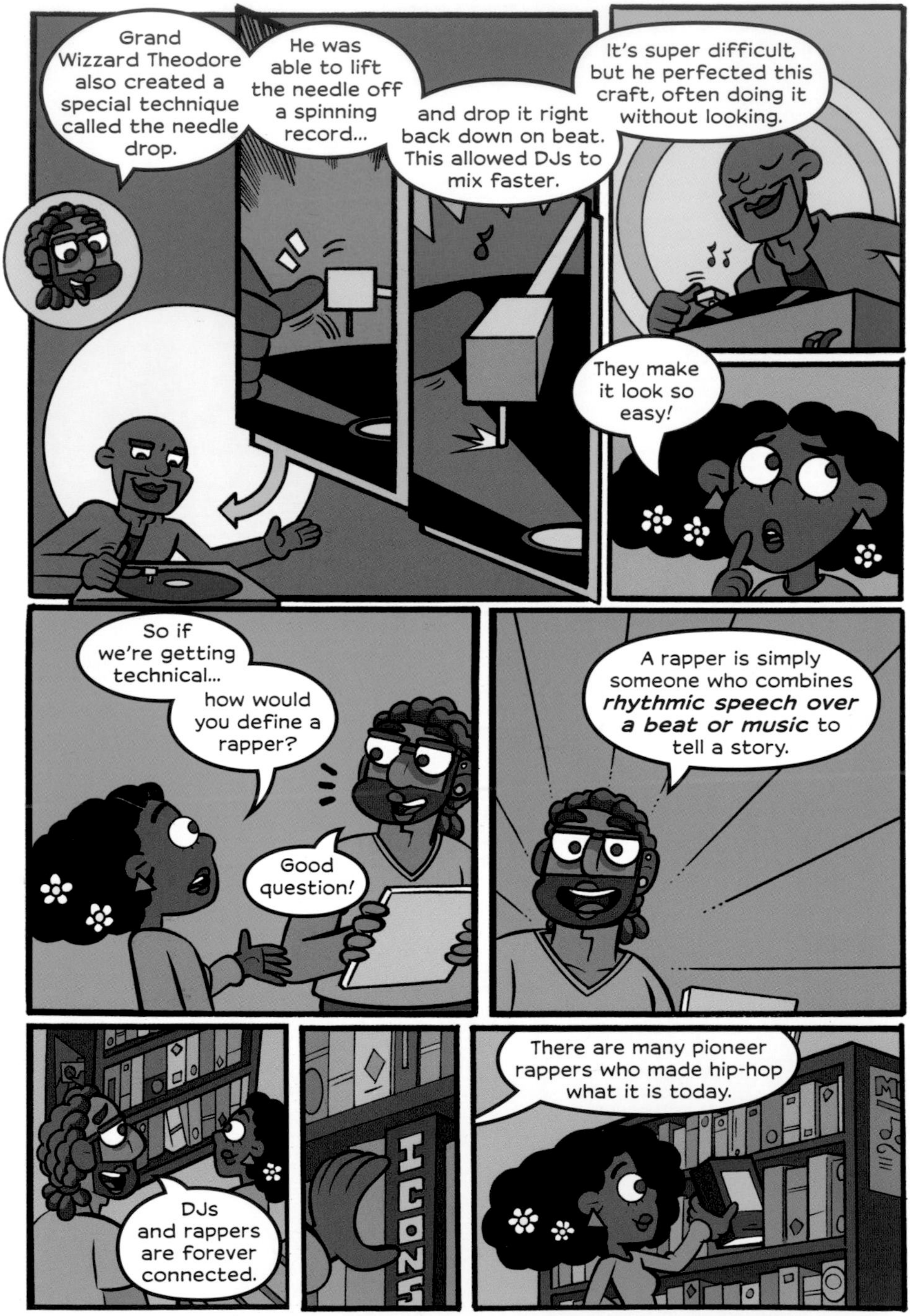
Grand Wizzard Theodore also created a special technique called the needle drop.
He was able to lift the needle off a spinning record...
and drop it right back down on beat. This allowed DJs to mix faster.
It's super difficult but he perfected this craft, often doing it without looking.
They make it look so easy!
So if we're getting technical...
how would you define a rapper?
Good question!
A rapper is simply someone who combines ***rhythmic speech over a beat or music*** to tell a story.
DJs and rappers are forever connected.
ICONS
There are many pioneer rappers who made hip-hop what it is today.

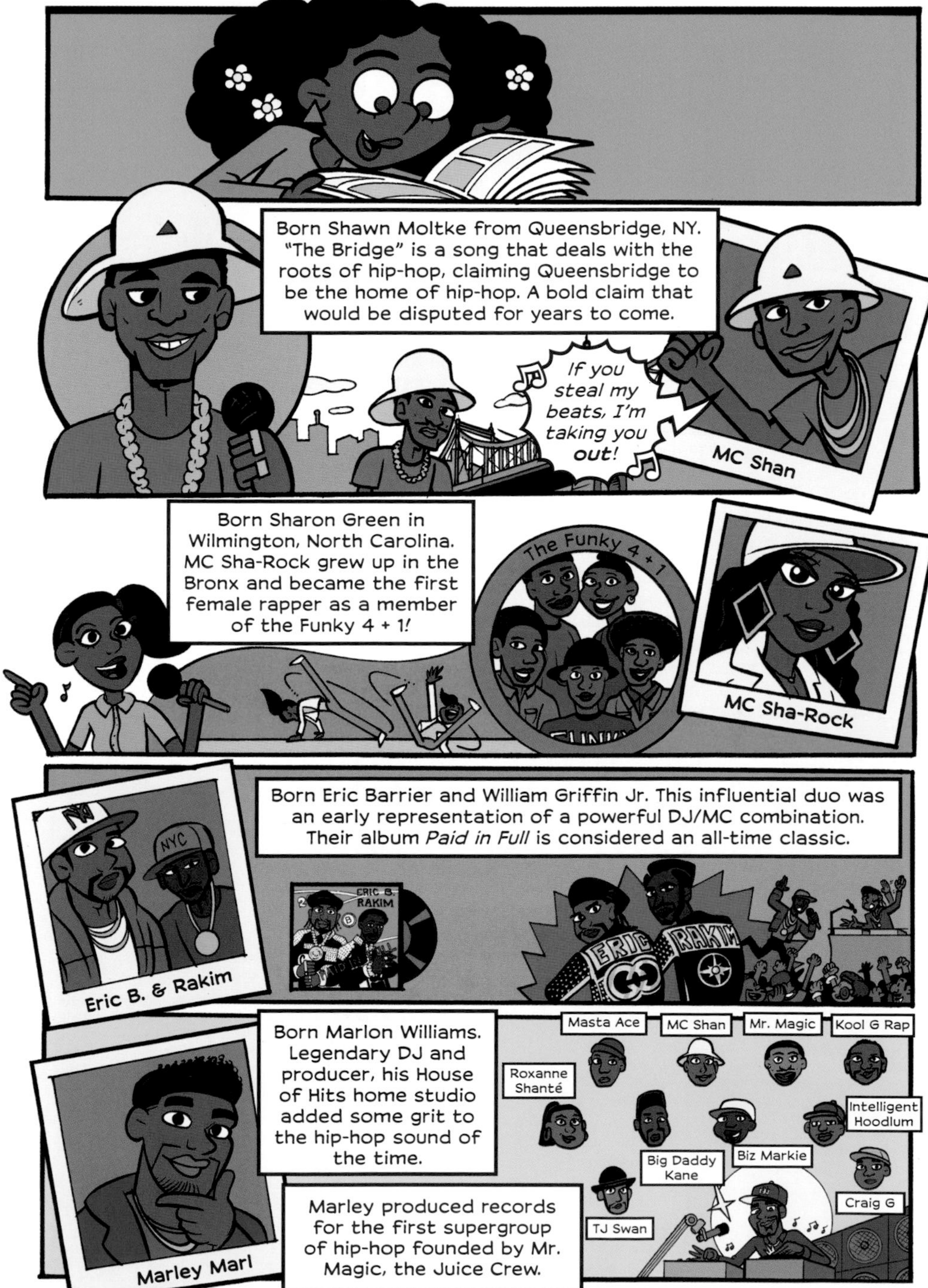
Born Shawn Moltke from Queensbridge, NY. "The Bridge" is a song that deals with the roots of hip-hop, claiming Queensbridge to be the home of hip-hop. A bold claim that would be disputed for years to come.
If you steal my beats, I'm taking you out!
MC Shan
Born Sharon Green in Wilmington, North Carolina. MC Sha-Rock grew up in the Bronx and became the first female rapper as a member of the Funky 4 + 1!
The Funky 4 + 1
MC Sha-Rock
Born Eric Barrier and William Griffin Jr. This influential duo was an early representation of a powerful DJ/MC combination. Their album *Paid in Full* is considered an all-time classic.
Eric B. & Rakim
Born Marlon Williams. Legendary DJ and producer, his House of Hits home studio added some grit to the hip-hop sound of the time.
Masta Ace
MC Shan
Mr. Magic
Kool G Rap
Roxanne Shanté
Intelligent Hoodlum
Big Daddy Kane
Biz Markie
Craig G
TJ Swan
Marley Marl
Marley produced records for the first supergroup of hip-hop founded by Mr. Magic, the Juice Crew.

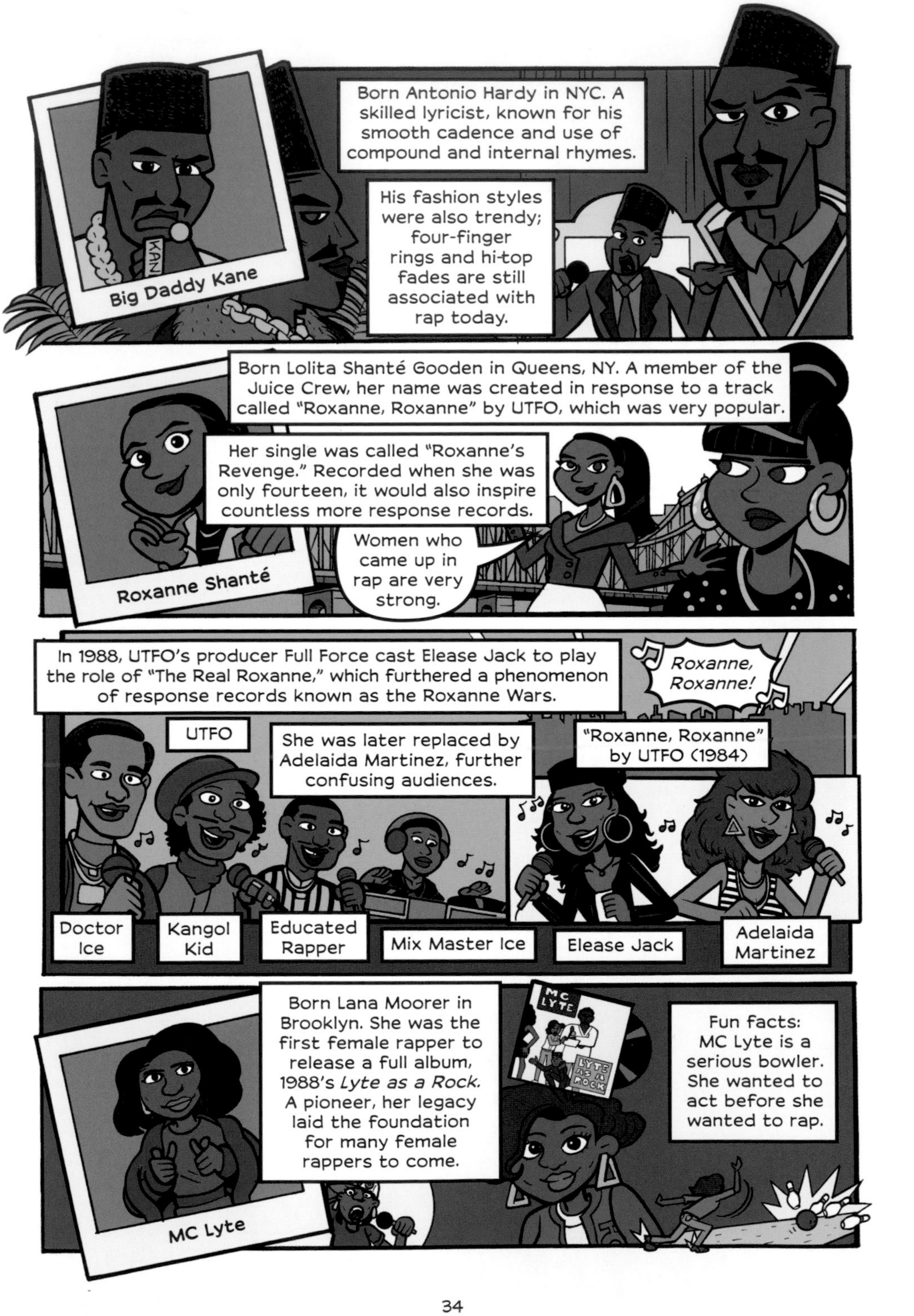
Born Antonio Hardy in NYC. A skilled lyricist, known for his smooth cadence and use of compound and internal rhymes.
His fashion styles were also trendy; four-finger rings and hi-top fades are still associated with rap today.
Big Daddy Kane
Born Lolita Shanté Gooden in Queens, NY. A member of the Juice Crew, her name was created in response to a track called "Roxanne, Roxanne" by UTFO, which was very popular.
Her single was called "Roxanne's Revenge." Recorded when she was only fourteen, it would also inspire countless more response records.
Women who came up in rap are very strong.
Roxanne Shanté
In 1988, UTFO's producer Full Force cast Elease Jack to play the role of "The Real Roxanne," which furthered a phenomenon of response records known as the Roxanne Wars.
Roxanne, Roxanne!
UTFO
She was later replaced by Adelaida Martinez, further confusing audiences.
"Roxanne, Roxanne" by UTFO (1984)
Doctor Ice
Kangol Kid
Educated Rapper
Mix Master Ice
Elease Jack
Adelaida Martinez
Born Lana Moorer in Brooklyn. She was the first female rapper to release a full album, 1988's *Lyte as a Rock*. A pioneer, her legacy laid the foundation for many female rappers to come.
MC LYTE
LYTE AS A ROCK
Fun facts: MC Lyte is a serious bowler. She wanted to act before she wanted to rap.
MC Lyte

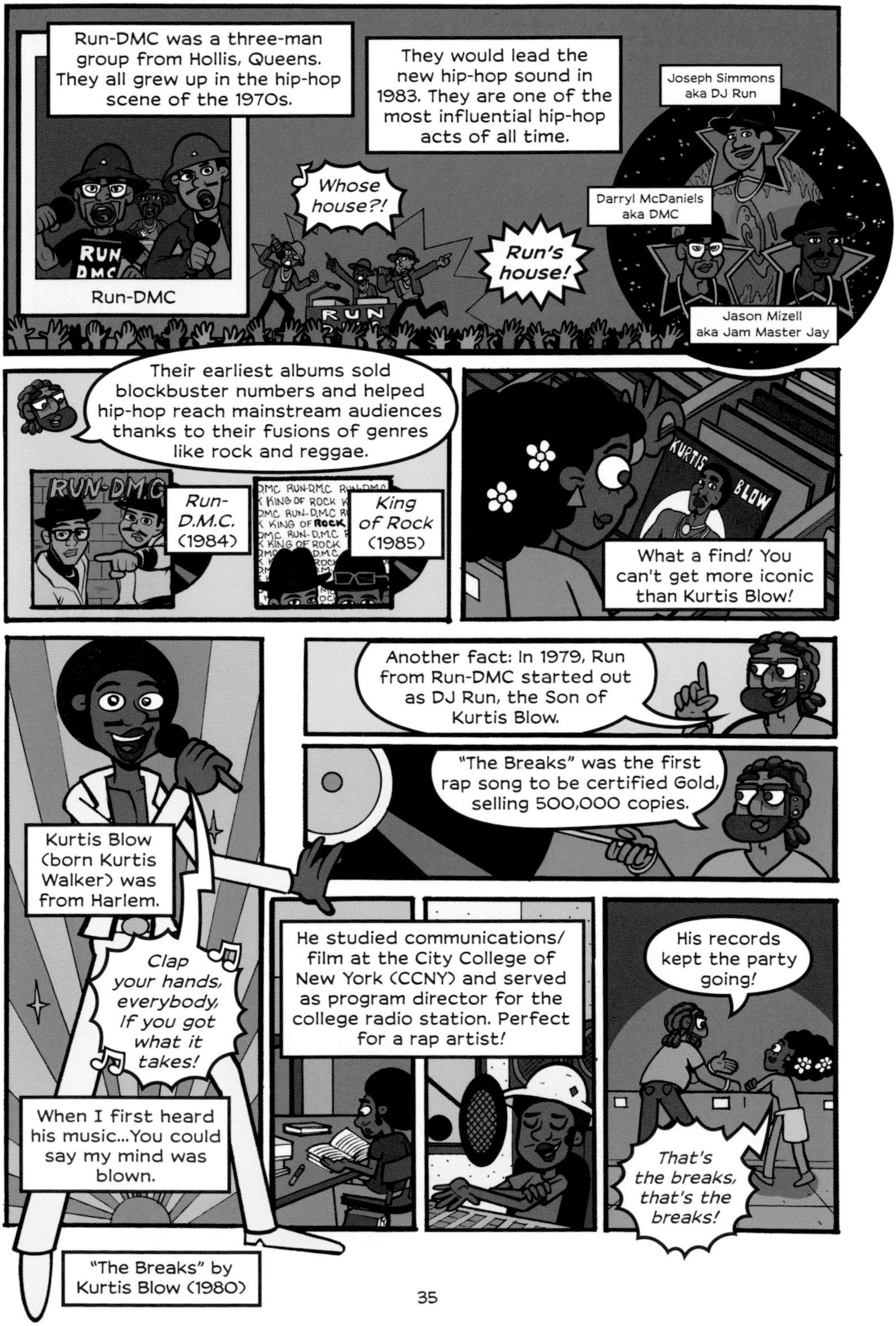

Run-DMC was a three-man group from Hollis, Queens. They all grew up in the hip-hop scene of the 1970s.
Run-DMC
RUN DMC
They would lead the new hip-hop sound in 1983. They are one of the most influential hip-hop acts of all time.
Whose house?!
Run's house!
RUN
Joseph Simmons aka DJ Run
Darryl McDaniels aka DMC
Jason Mizell aka Jam Master Jay
Their earliest albums sold blockbuster numbers and helped hip-hop reach mainstream audiences thanks to their fusions of genres like rock and reggae.
RUN-DMC
Run-D.M.C. (1984)
King of Rock (1985)
KURTIS BLOW
What a find! You can't get more iconic than Kurtis Blow!
Another fact: In 1979, Run from Run-DMC started out as DJ Run, the Son of Kurtis Blow.
"The Breaks" was the first rap song to be certified Gold, selling 500,000 copies.
Kurtis Blow (born Kurtis Walker) was from Harlem.
Clap your hands, everybody, If you got what it takes!
When I first heard his music...You could say my mind was blown.
"The Breaks" by Kurtis Blow (1980)
He studied communications/film at the City College of New York (CCNY) and served as program director for the college radio station. Perfect for a rap artist!
His records kept the party going!
That's the breaks, that's the breaks!

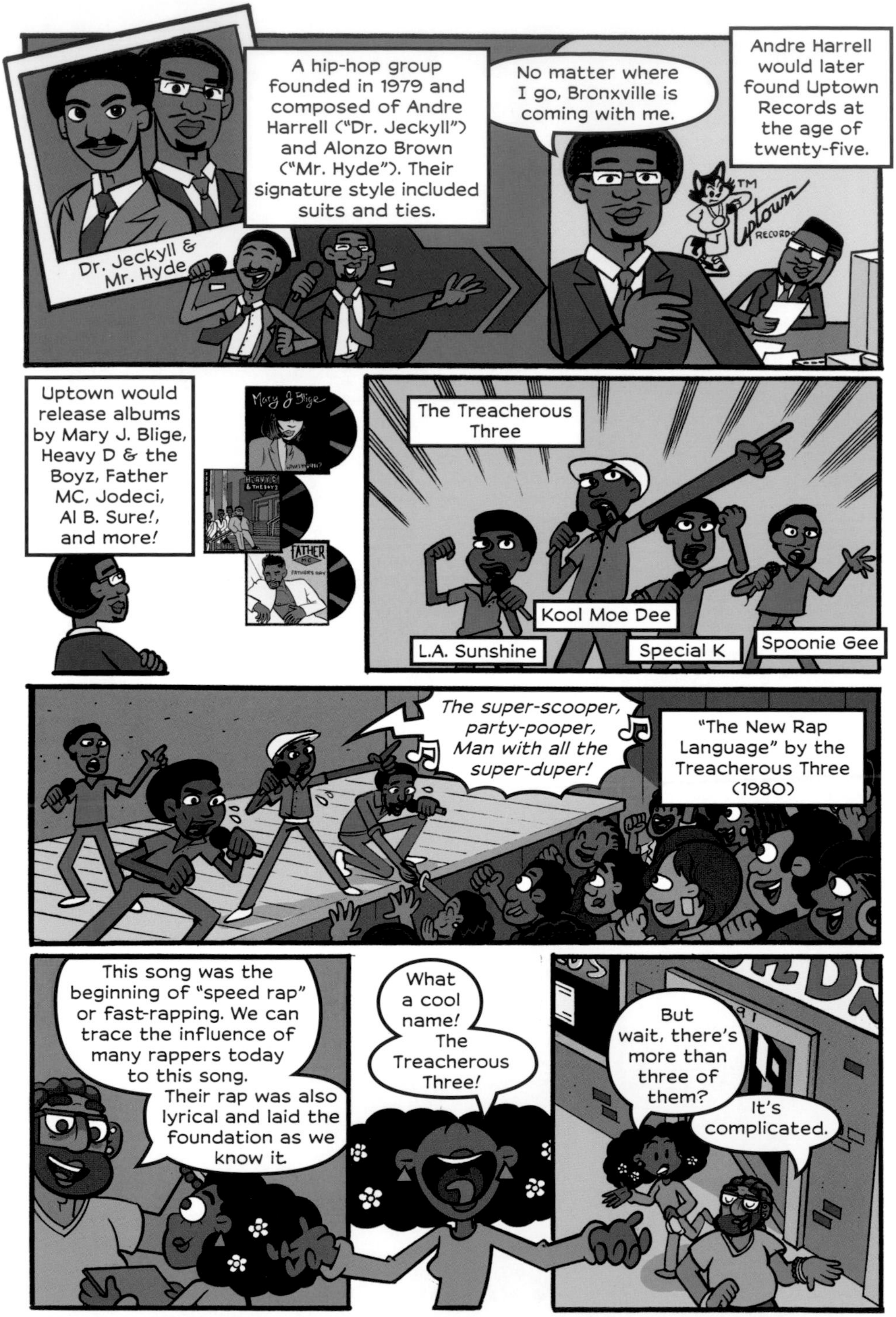

Dr. Jeckyll & Mr. Hyde
A hip-hop group founded in 1979 and composed of Andre Harrell ("Dr. Jeckyll") and Alonzo Brown ("Mr. Hyde"). Their signature style included suits and ties.
No matter where I go, Bronxville is coming with me.
Andre Harrell would later found Uptown Records at the age of twenty-five.
Uptown Records
Uptown would release albums by Mary J. Blige, Heavy D & the Boyz, Father MC, Jodeci, Al B. Sure!, and more!
Mary J. Blige
Heavy D & The Boyz
Father MC
The Treacherous Three
Kool Moe Dee
L.A. Sunshine
Special K
Spoonie Gee
The super-scooper, party-pooper, Man with all the super-duper!
"The New Rap Language" by the Treacherous Three (1980)
This song was the beginning of "speed rap" or fast-rapping. We can trace the influence of many rappers today to this song.
Their rap was also lyrical and laid the foundation as we know it.
What a cool name! The Treacherous Three!
But wait, there's more than three of them?
It's complicated.

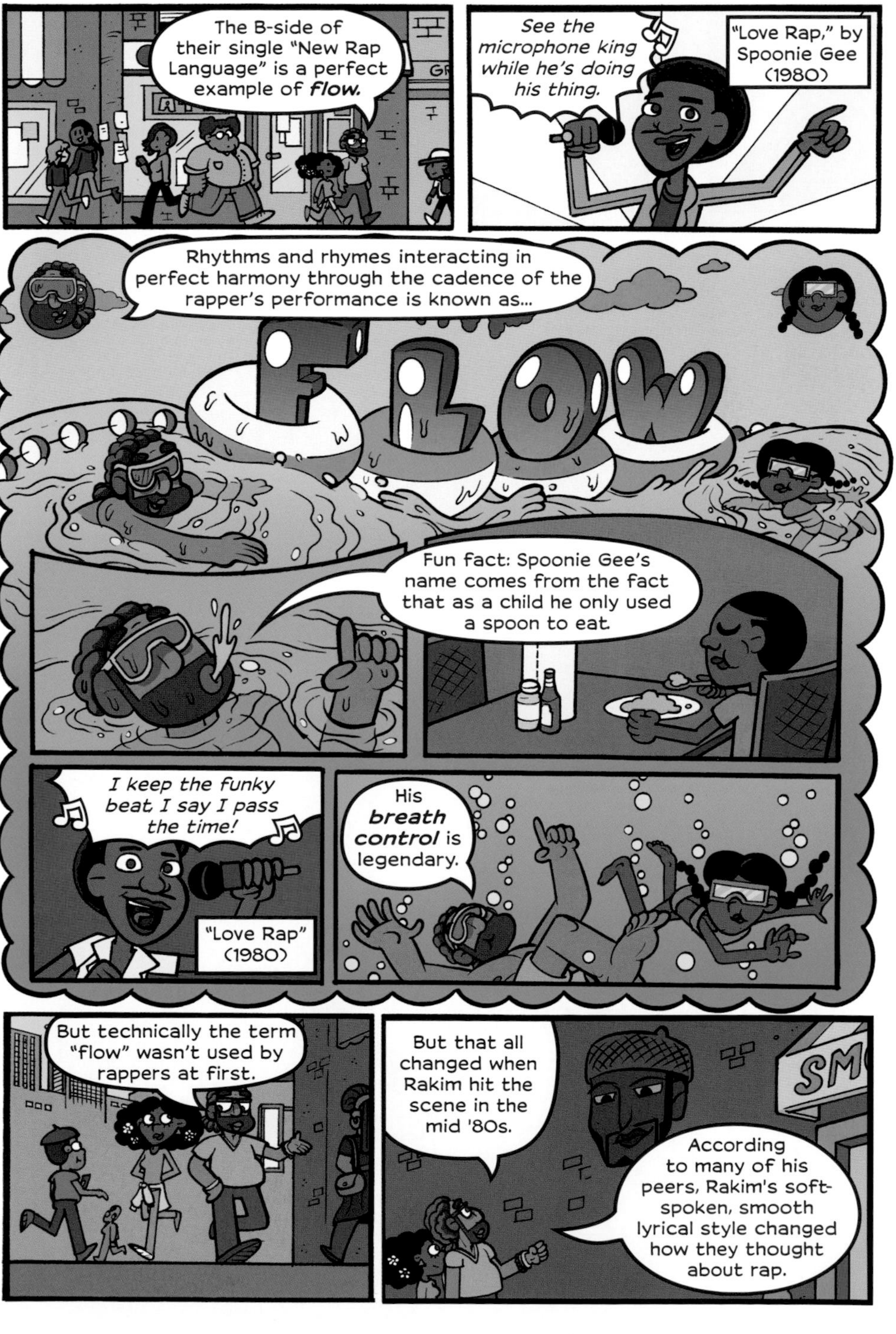
The B-side of their single "New Rap Language" is a perfect example of *flow.*
See the microphone king while he's doing his thing.
"Love Rap," by Spoonie Gee (1980)
Rhythms and rhymes interacting in perfect harmony through the cadence of the rapper's performance is known as...
FLOW
Fun fact: Spoonie Gee's name comes from the fact that as a child he only used a spoon to eat.
I keep the funky beat, I say I pass the time!
"Love Rap" (1980)
His **breath control** is legendary.
But technically the term "flow" wasn't used by rappers at first.
But that all changed when Rakim hit the scene in the mid '80s.
According to many of his peers, Rakim's soft-spoken, smooth lyrical style changed how they thought about rap.

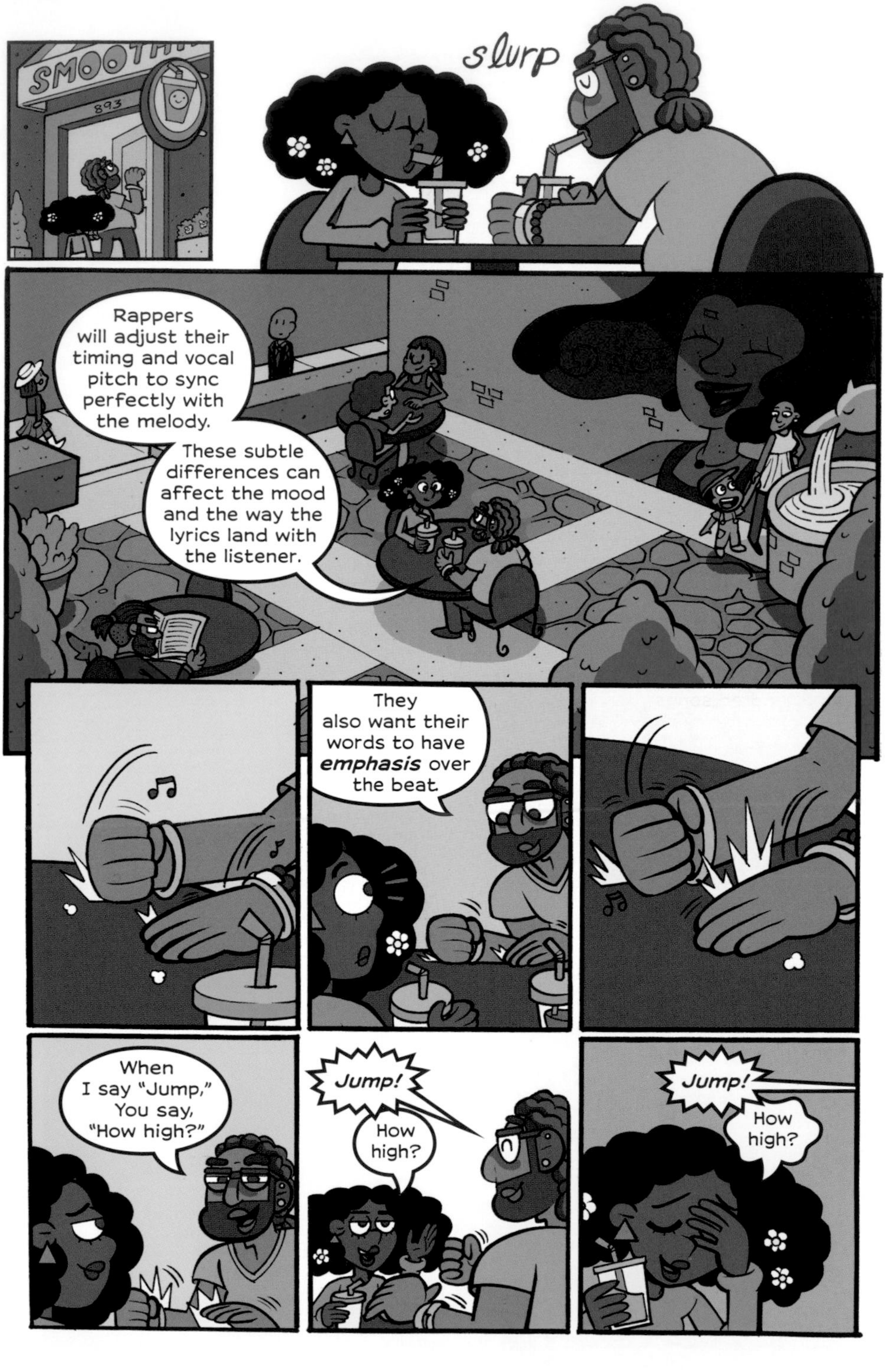

SMOOTH
893
slurp
Rappers will adjust their timing and vocal pitch to sync perfectly with the melody.
These subtle differences can affect the mood and the way the lyrics land with the listener.
They also want their words to have *emphasis* over the beat.
When I say "Jump," You say, "How high?"
Jump!
How high?
Jump!
How high?

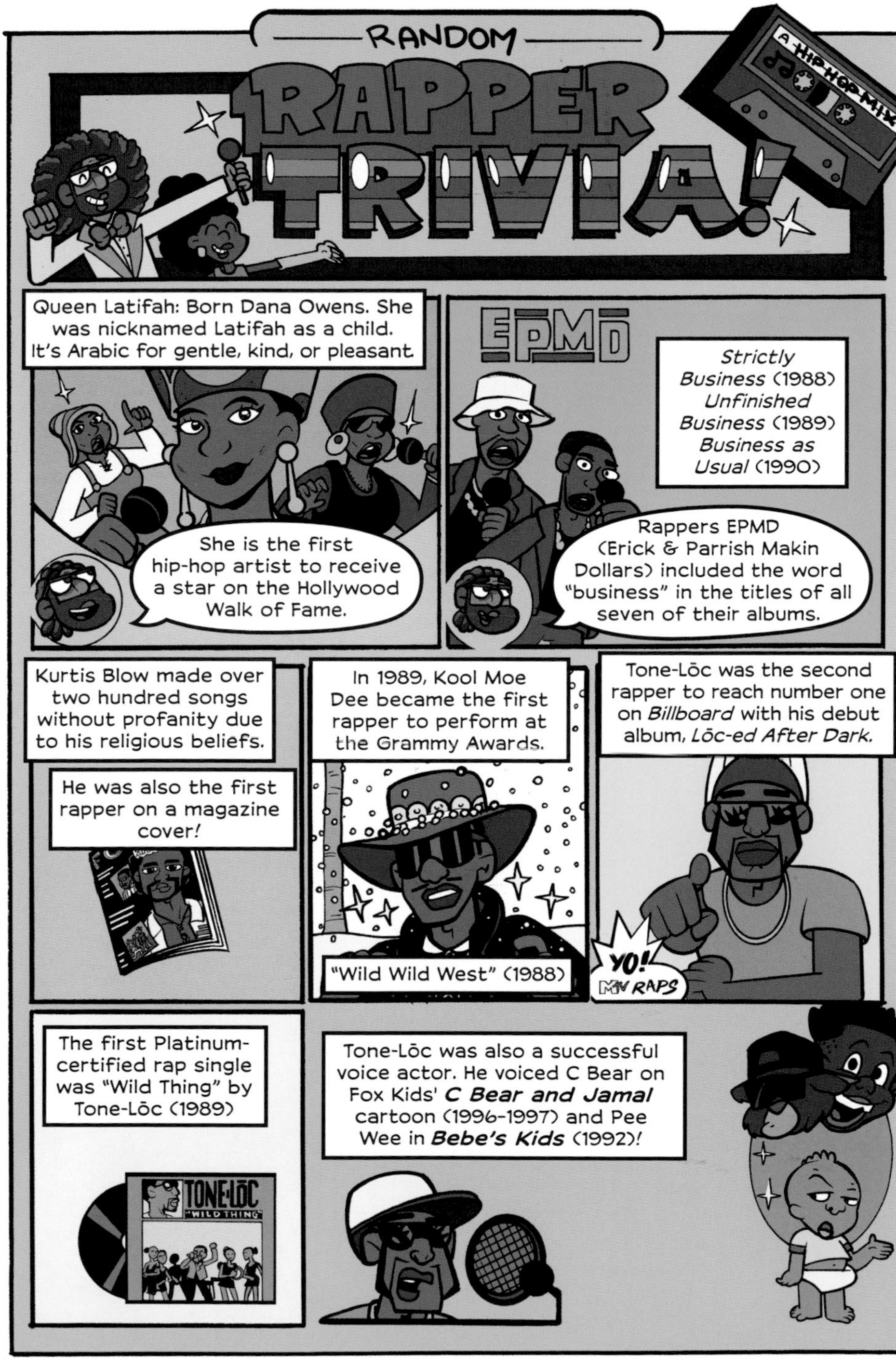
RANDOM
RAPPER TRIVIA!
A HIP-HOP MIX
Queen Latifah: Born Dana Owens. She was nicknamed Latifah as a child. It's Arabic for gentle, kind, or pleasant.
She is the first hip-hop artist to receive a star on the Hollywood Walk of Fame.
EPMD
Strictly Business (1988)
Unfinished Business (1989)
Business as Usual (1990)
Rappers EPMD (Erick & Parrish Makin Dollars) included the word "business" in the titles of all seven of their albums.
Kurtis Blow made over two hundred songs without profanity due to his religious beliefs.
He was also the first rapper on a magazine cover!
In 1989, Kool Moe Dee became the first rapper to perform at the Grammy Awards.
"Wild Wild West" (1988)
Tone-Lōc was the second rapper to reach number one on *Billboard* with his debut album, *Lōc-ed After Dark.*
YO! MTV RAPS
The first Platinum-certified rap single was "Wild Thing" by Tone-Lōc (1989)
TONE-LŌC
"WILD THING"
Tone-Lōc was also a successful voice actor. He voiced C Bear on Fox Kids' ***C Bear and Jamal*** cartoon (1996-1997) and Pee Wee in ***Bebe's Kids*** (1992)!

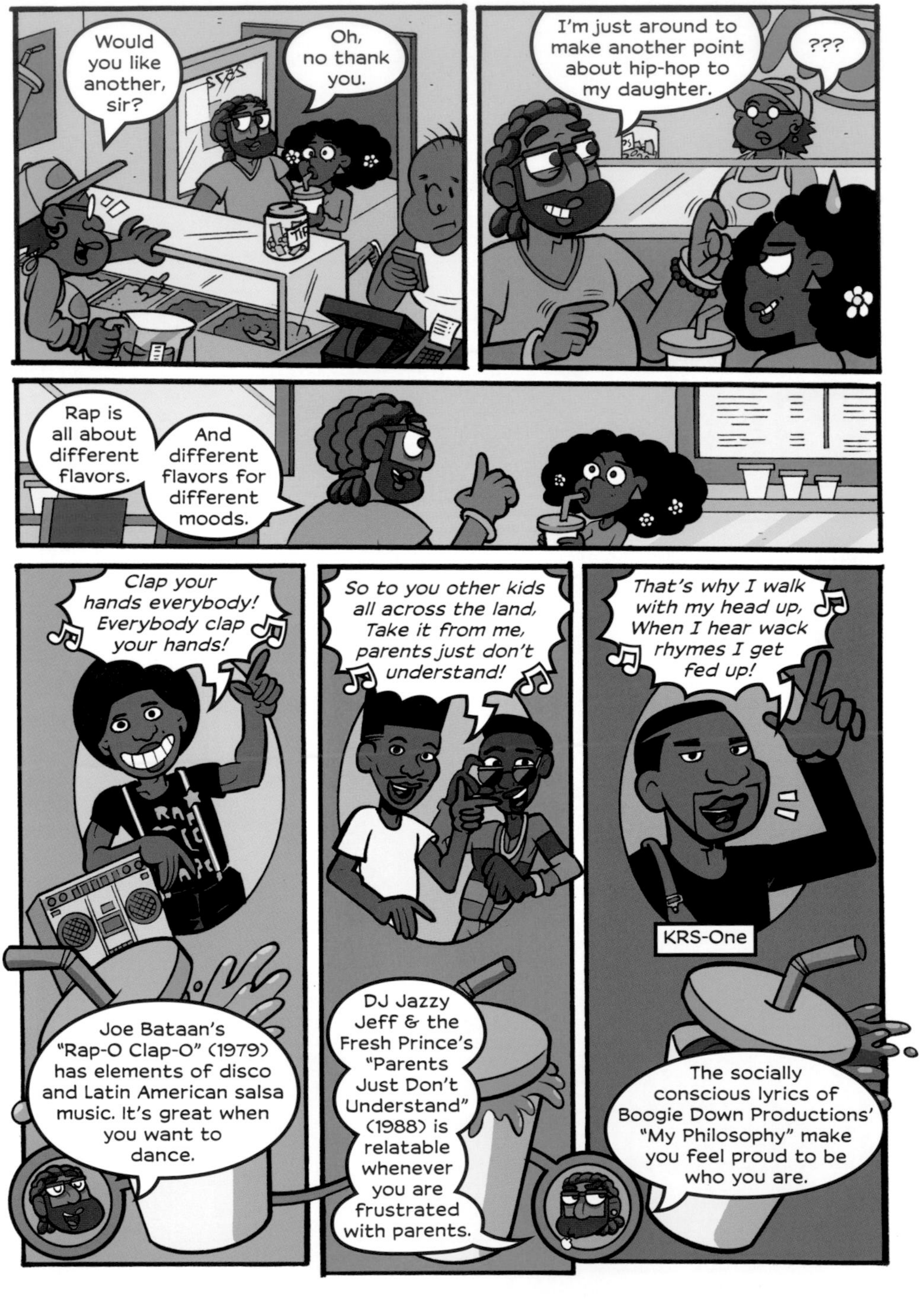
Would you like another, sir?
Oh, no thank you.
I'm just around to make another point about hip-hop to my daughter.
???
Rap is all about different flavors.
And different flavors for different moods.
Clap your hands everybody! Everybody clap your hands!
Joe Bataan's "Rap-O Clap-O" (1979) has elements of disco and Latin American salsa music. It's great when you want to dance.
So to you other kids all across the land, Take it from me, parents just don't understand!
DJ Jazzy Jeff & the Fresh Prince's "Parents Just Don't Understand" (1988) is relatable whenever you are frustrated with parents.
That's why I walk with my head up, When I hear wack rhymes I get fed up!
KRS-One
The socially conscious lyrics of Boogie Down Productions' "My Philosophy" make you feel proud to be who you are.

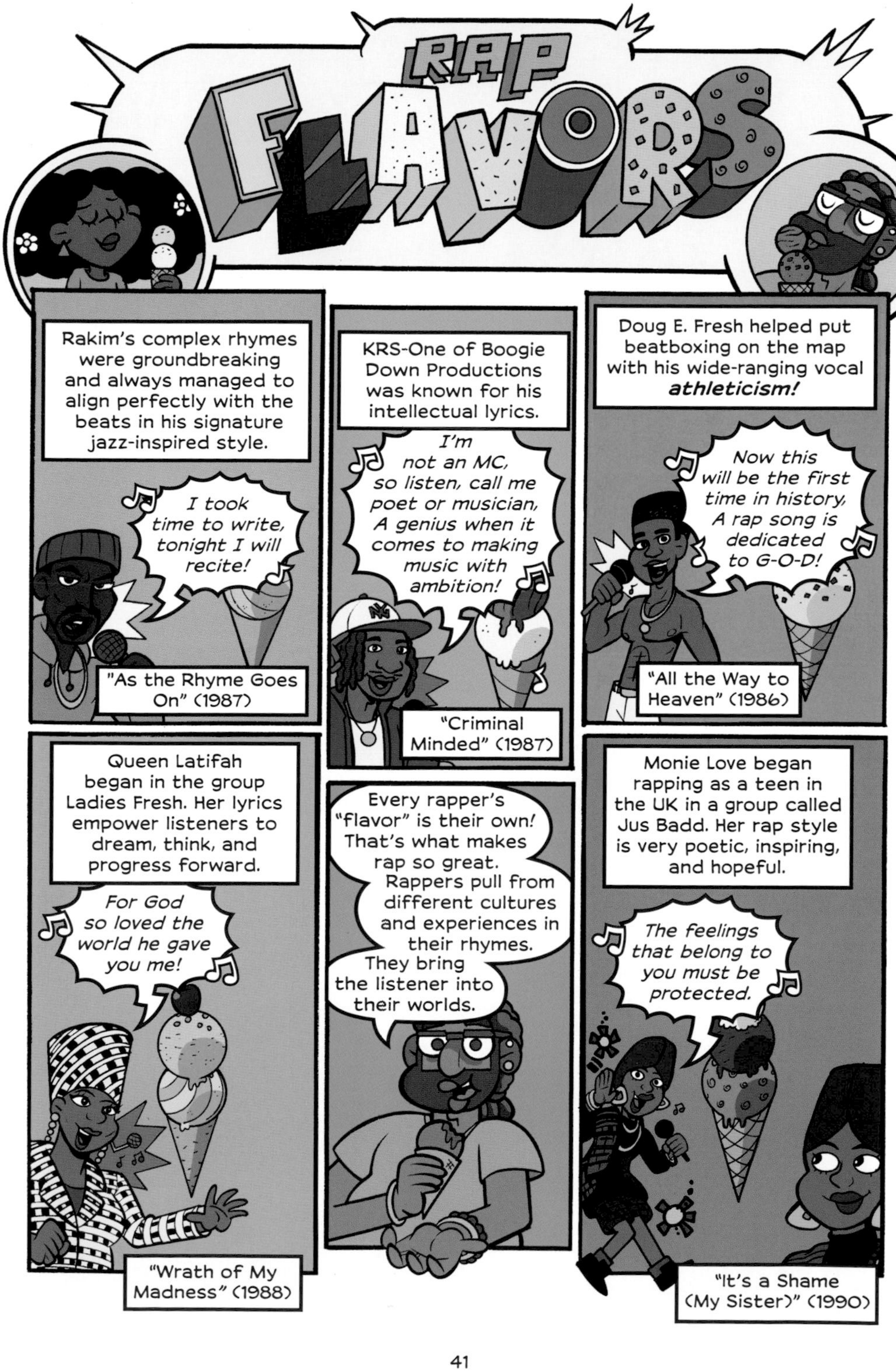
RAP FLAVORS
Rakim's complex rhymes were groundbreaking and always managed to align perfectly with the beats in his signature jazz-inspired style.
I took time to write, tonight I will recite!
"As the Rhyme Goes On" (1987)
KRS-One of Boogie Down Productions was known for his intellectual lyrics.
I'm not an MC, so listen, call me poet or musician, A genius when it comes to making music with ambition!
"Criminal Minded" (1987)
Doug E. Fresh helped put beatboxing on the map with his wide-ranging vocal athleticism!
Now this will be the first time in history, A rap song is dedicated to G-O-D!
"All the Way to Heaven" (1986)
Queen Latifah began in the group Ladies Fresh. Her lyrics empower listeners to dream, think, and progress forward.
For God so loved the world he gave you me!
"Wrath of My Madness" (1988)
Every rapper's "flavor" is their own! That's what makes rap so great.
Rappers pull from different cultures and experiences in their rhymes.
They bring the listener into their worlds.
Monie Love began rapping as a teen in the UK in a group called Jus Badd. Her rap style is very poetic, inspiring, and hopeful.
The feelings that belong to you must be protected.
"It's a Shame (My Sister)" (1990)

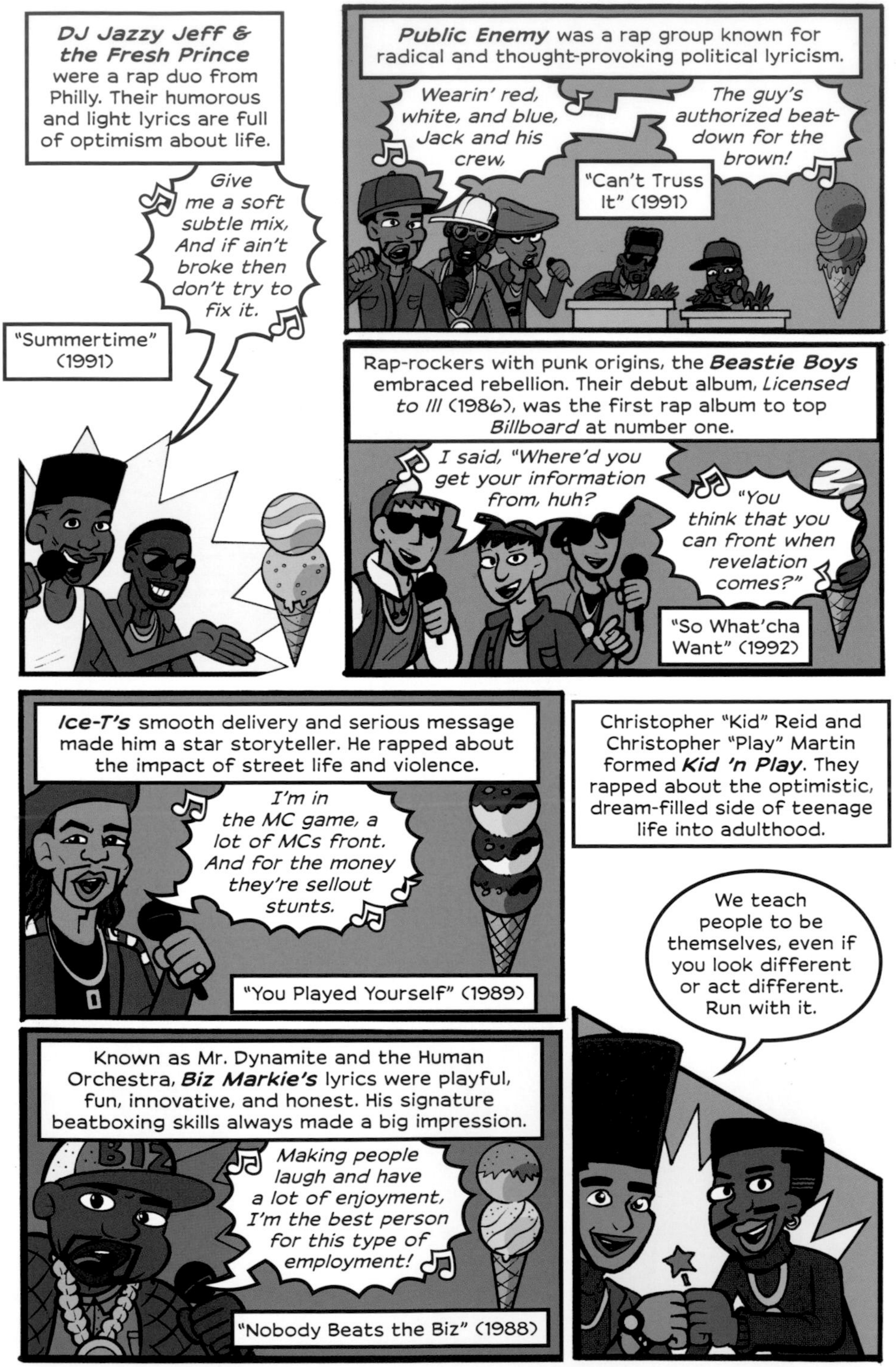
DJ Jazzy Jeff & the Fresh Prince were a rap duo from Philly. Their humorous and light lyrics are full of optimism about life.
Give me a soft subtle mix, And if ain't broke then don't try to fix it.
"Summertime" (1991)
Public Enemy was a rap group known for radical and thought-provoking political lyricism.
Wearin' red, white, and blue, Jack and his crew,
The guy's authorized beat-down for the brown!
"Can't Truss It" (1991)
Rap-rockers with punk origins, the Beastie Boys embraced rebellion. Their debut album, Licensed to Ill (1986), was the first rap album to top Billboard at number one.
I said, "Where'd you get your information from, huh?
"You think that you can front when revelation comes?"
"So What'cha Want" (1992)
Ice-T's smooth delivery and serious message made him a star storyteller. He rapped about the impact of street life and violence.
I'm in the MC game, a lot of MCs front. And for the money they're sellout stunts.
"You Played Yourself" (1989)
Christopher "Kid" Reid and Christopher "Play" Martin formed Kid 'n Play. They rapped about the optimistic, dream-filled side of teenage life into adulthood.
We teach people to be themselves, even if you look different or act different. Run with it.
Known as Mr. Dynamite and the Human Orchestra, Biz Markie's lyrics were playful, fun, innovative, and honest. His signature beatboxing skills always made a big impression.
Making people laugh and have a lot of enjoyment, I'm the best person for this type of employment!
"Nobody Beats the Biz" (1988)

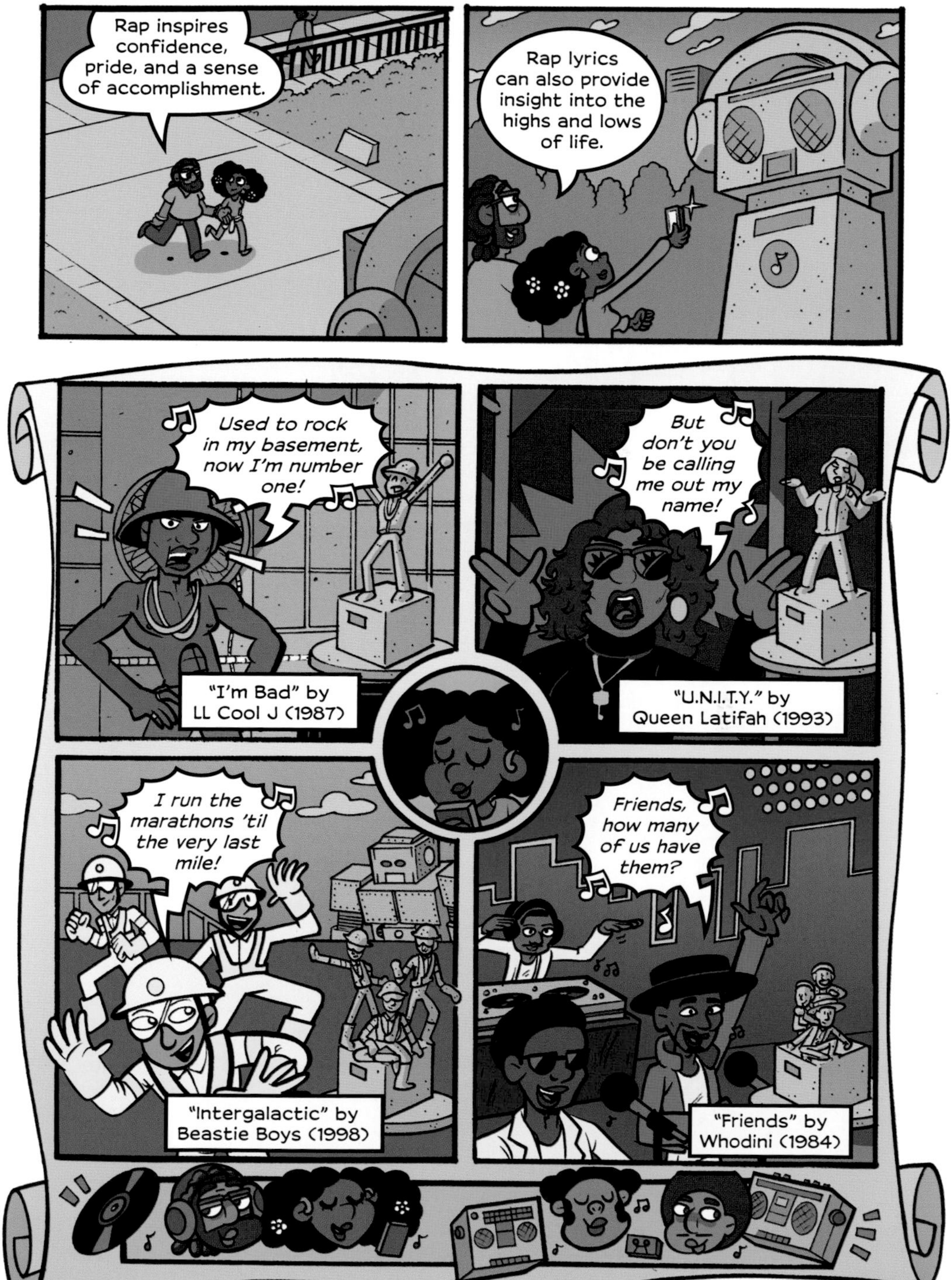
Rap inspires confidence, pride, and a sense of accomplishment.
Rap lyrics can also provide insight into the highs and lows of life.
Used to rock in my basement, now I'm number one!
"I'm Bad" by LL Cool J (1987)
But don't you be calling me out my name!
"U.N.I.T.Y." by Queen Latifah (1993)
I run the marathons 'til the very last mile!
"Intergalactic" by Beastie Boys (1998)
Friends, how many of us have them?
"Friends" by Whodini (1984)

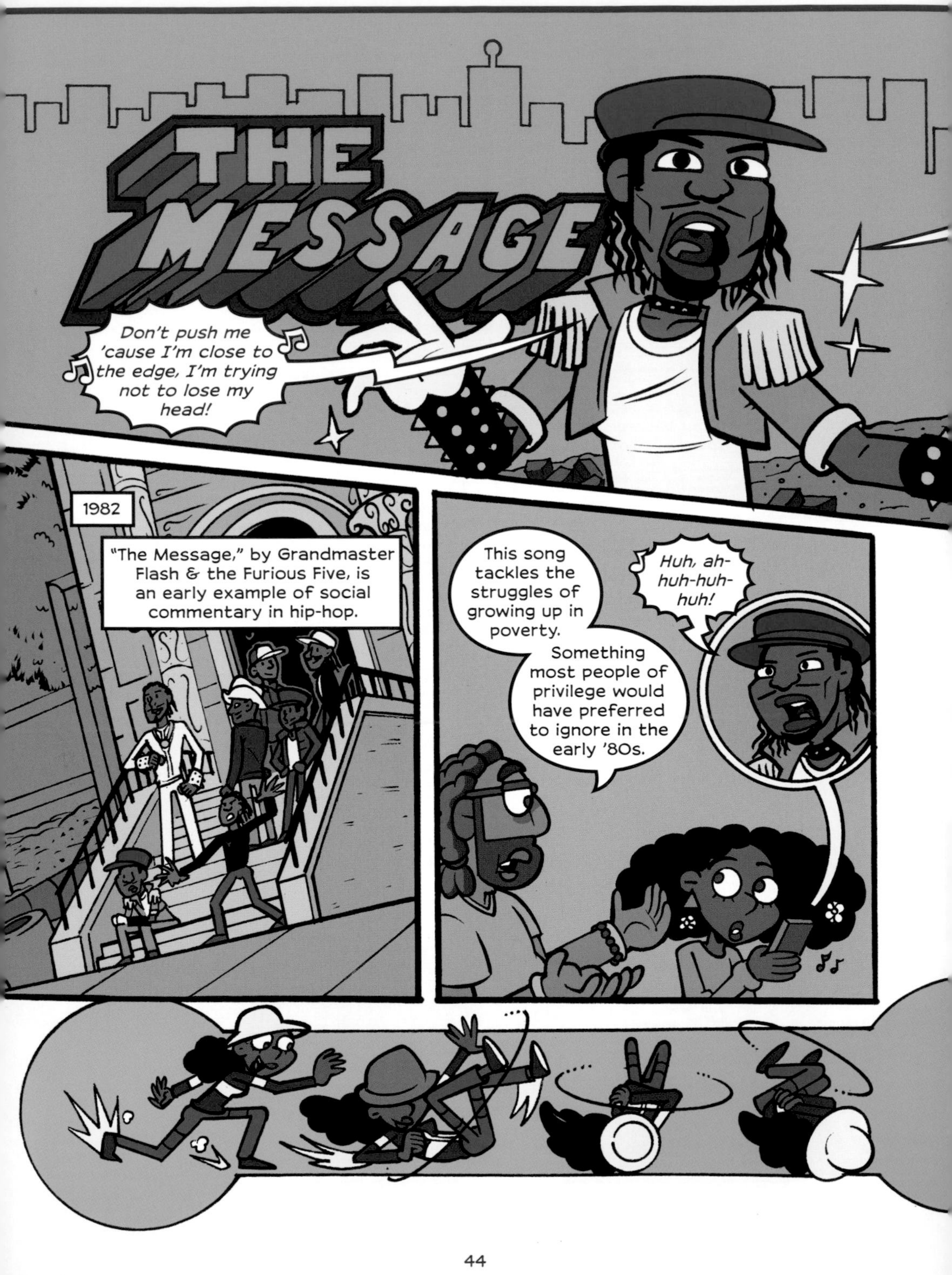
THE MESSAGE
Don't push me 'cause I'm close to the edge, I'm trying not to lose my head!
1982
"The Message," by Grandmaster Flash & the Furious Five, is an early example of social commentary in hip-hop.
This song tackles the struggles of growing up in poverty.
Something most people of privilege would have preferred to ignore in the early '80s.
Huh, ah-huh-huh-huh!

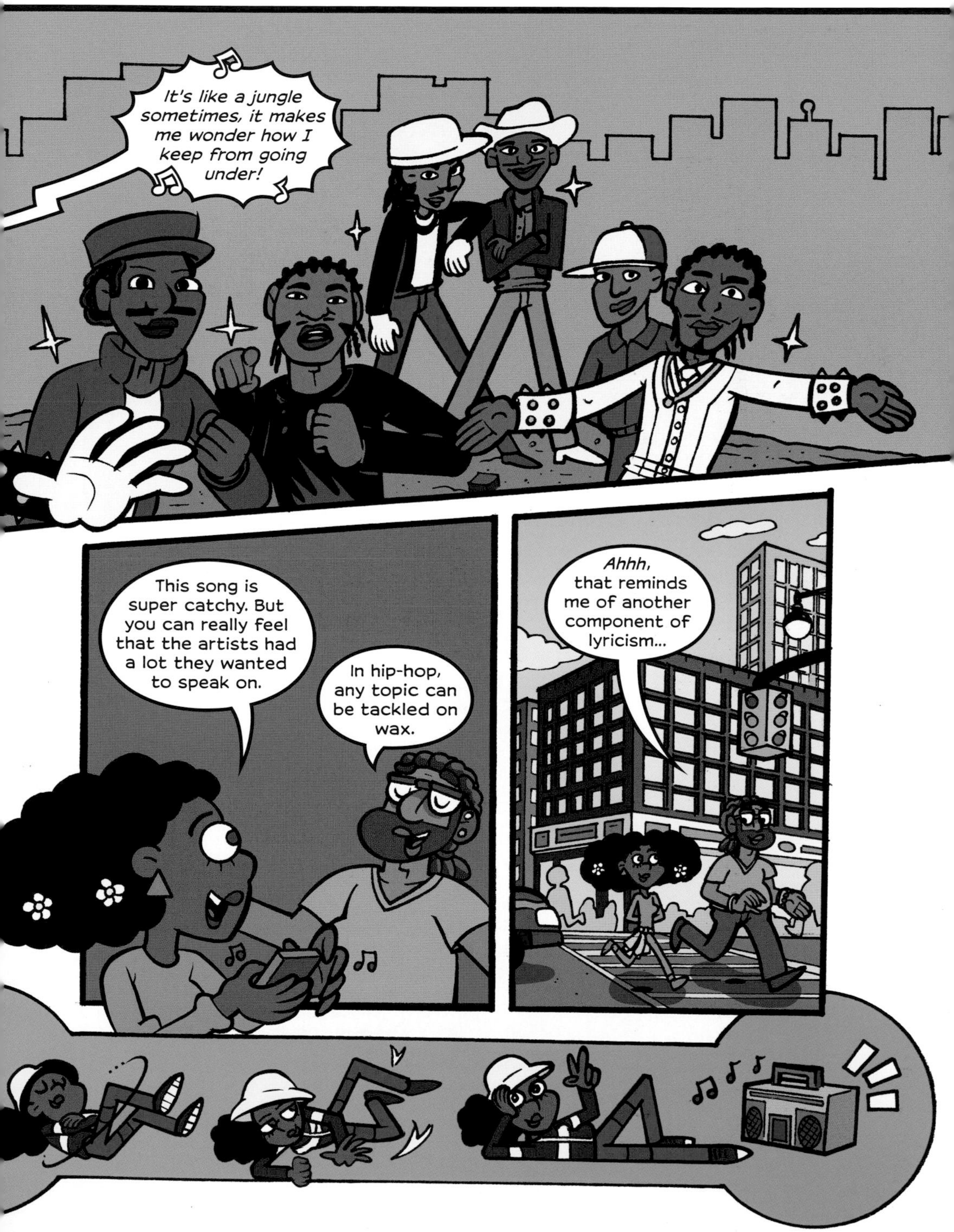
It's like a jungle sometimes, it makes me wonder how I keep from going under!
This song is super catchy. But you can really feel that the artists had a lot they wanted to speak on.
In hip-hop, any topic can be tackled on wax.
Ahhh, that reminds me of another component of lyricism...

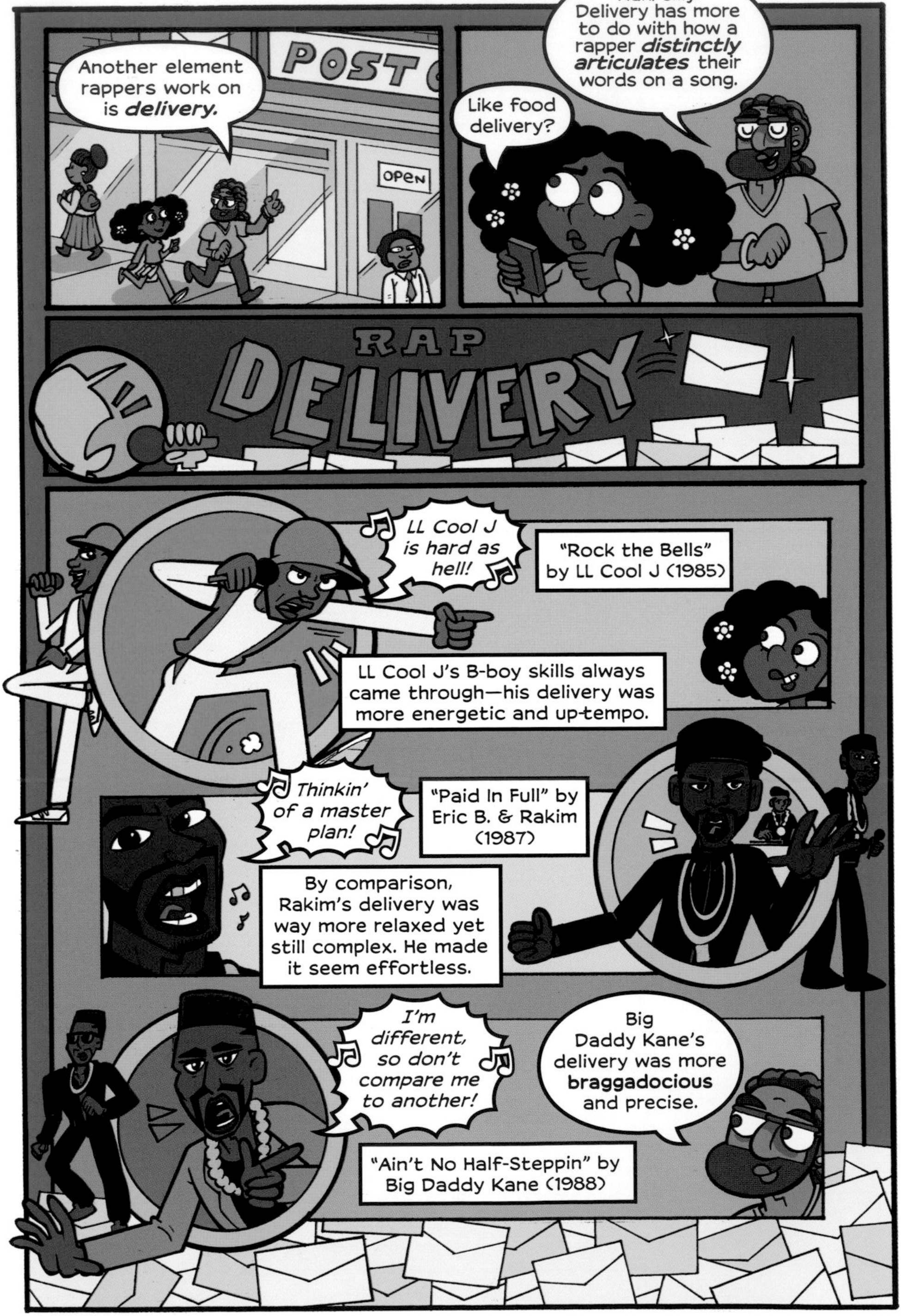

Another element rappers work on is *delivery.*
POST
OPEN
Like food delivery?
Nah, silly. Delivery has more to do with how a rapper *distinctly articulates* their words on a song.
RAP
DELIVERY
LL Cool J is hard as hell!
"Rock the Bells" by LL Cool J (1985)
LL Cool J's B-boy skills always came through—his delivery was more energetic and up-tempo.
Thinkin' of a master plan!
"Paid In Full" by Eric B. & Rakim (1987)
By comparison, Rakim's delivery was way more relaxed yet still complex. He made it seem effortless.
I'm different, so don't compare me to another!
Big Daddy Kane's delivery was more **braggadocious** and precise.
"Ain't No Half-Steppin" by Big Daddy Kane (1988)

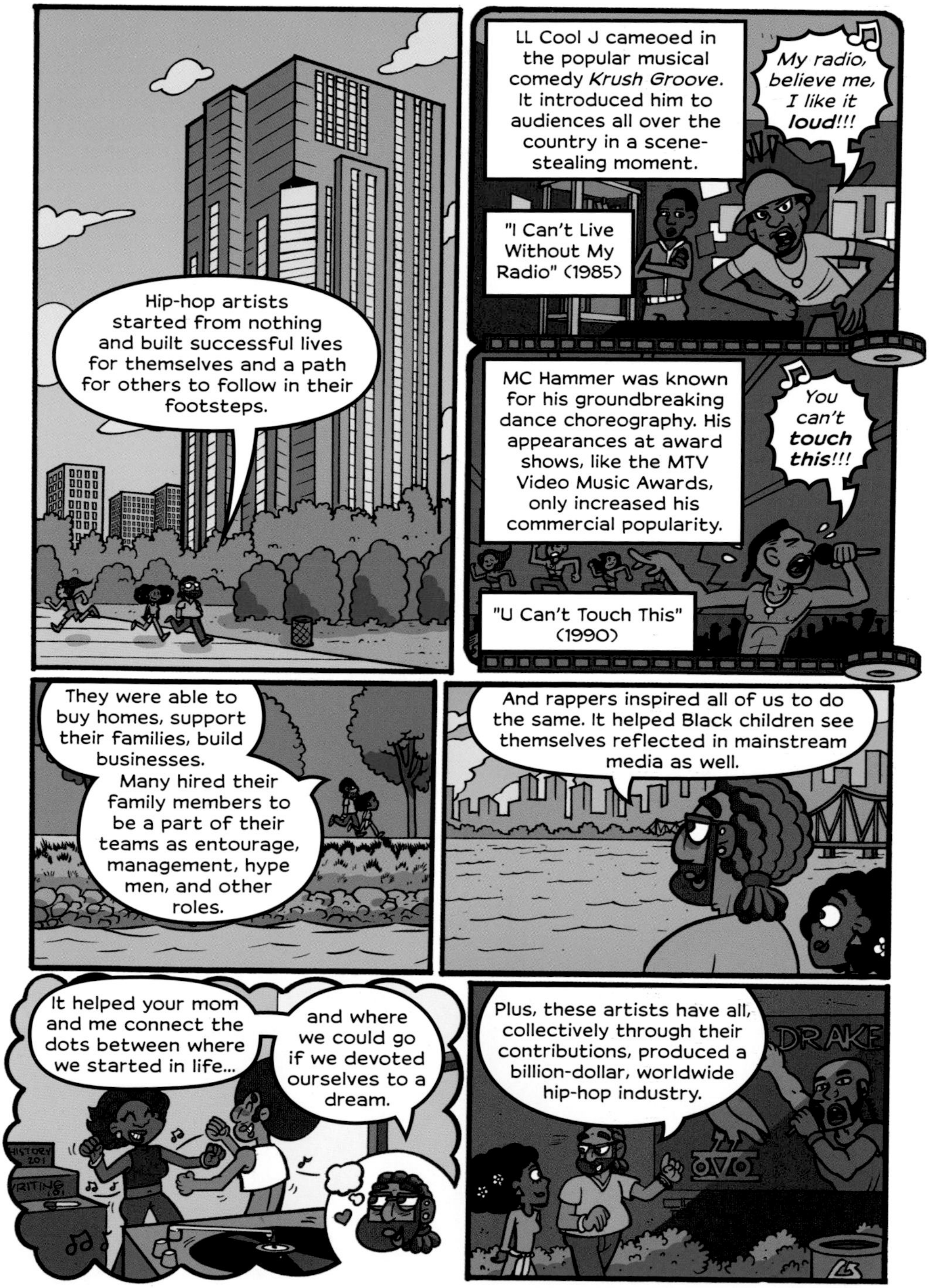

Hip-hop artists started from nothing and built successful lives for themselves and a path for others to follow in their footsteps.
LL Cool J cameoed in the popular musical comedy *Krush Groove*. It introduced him to audiences all over the country in a scene-stealing moment.
My radio, believe me, I like it ***loud***!!!
"I Can't Live Without My Radio" (1985)
MC Hammer was known for his groundbreaking dance choreography. His appearances at award shows, like the MTV Video Music Awards, only increased his commercial popularity.
You can't ***touch this***!!!
"U Can't Touch This" (1990)
They were able to buy homes, support their families, build businesses.
Many hired their family members to be a part of their teams as entourage, management, hype men, and other roles.
And rappers inspired all of us to do the same. It helped Black children see themselves reflected in mainstream media as well.
It helped your mom and me connect the dots between where we started in life...
and where we could go if we devoted ourselves to a dream.
Plus, these artists have all, collectively through their contributions, produced a billion-dollar, worldwide hip-hop industry.
DRAKE

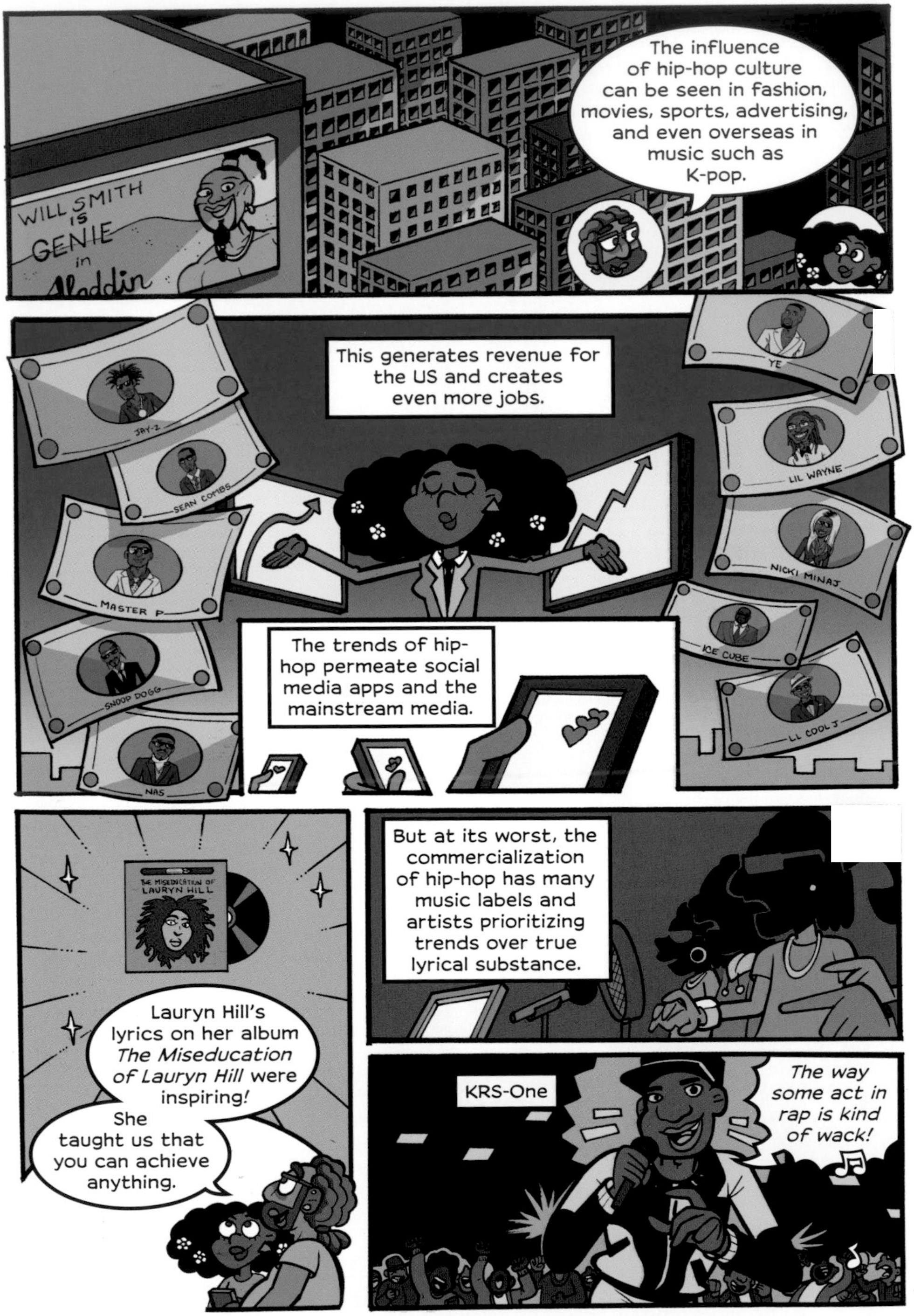
WILL SMITH IS GENIE in Aladdin
The influence of hip-hop culture can be seen in fashion, movies, sports, advertising, and even overseas in music such as K-pop.
This generates revenue for the US and creates even more jobs.
JAY-Z
SEAN COMBS
MASTER P
SNOOP DOGG
NAS
YE
LIL WAYNE
NICKI MINAJ
ICE CUBE
LL COOL J
The trends of hip-hop permeate social media apps and the mainstream media.
THE MISEDUCATION OF LAURYN HILL
Lauryn Hill's lyrics on her album *The Miseducation of Lauryn Hill* were inspiring!
She taught us that you can achieve anything.
But at its worst, the commercialization of hip-hop has many music labels and artists prioritizing trends over true lyrical substance.
KRS-One
The way some act in rap is kind of wack!

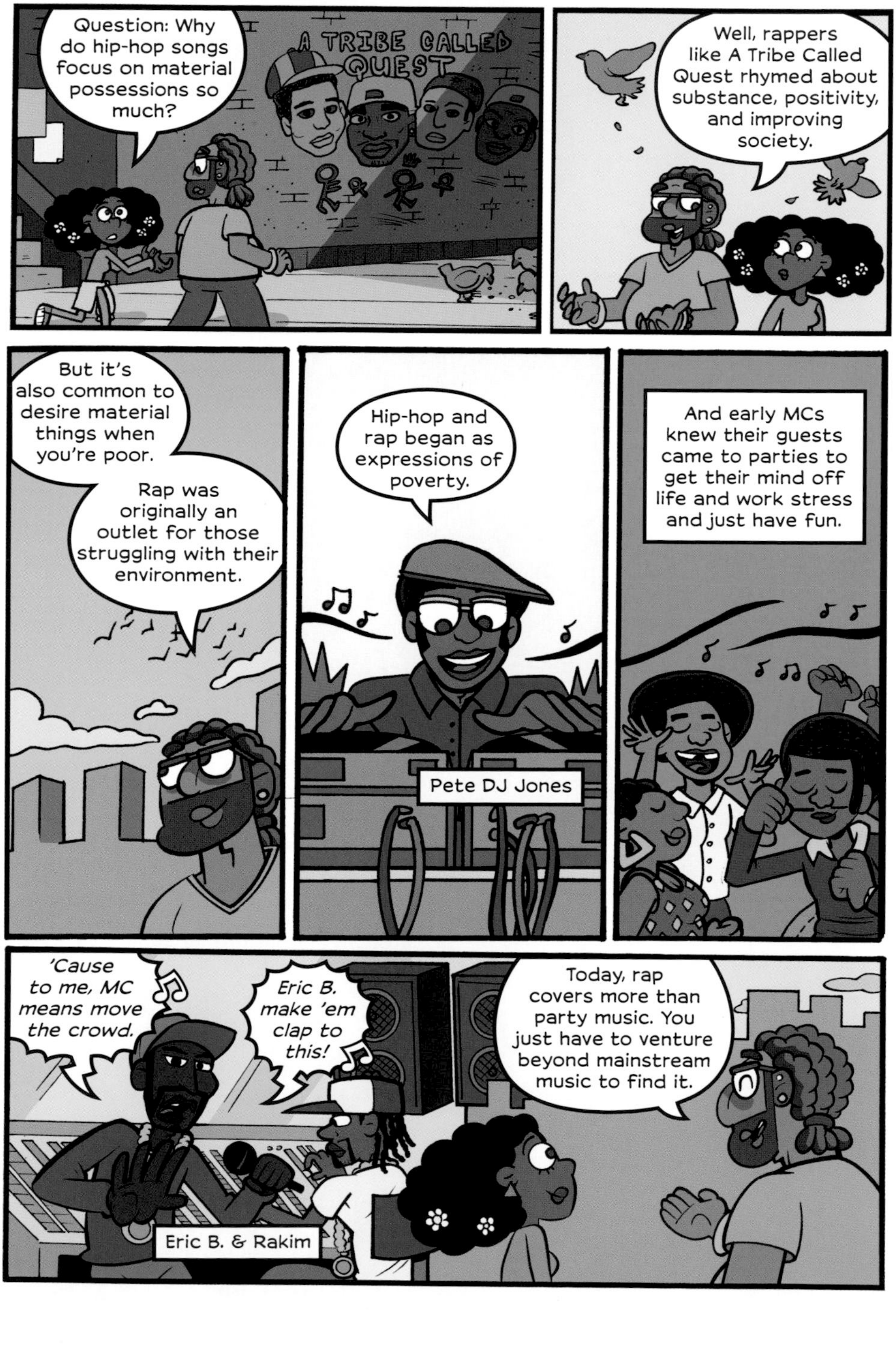
Question: Why do hip-hop songs focus on material possessions so much?
A TRIBE CALLED QUEST
Well, rappers like A Tribe Called Quest rhymed about substance, positivity, and improving society.
But it's also common to desire material things when you're poor.
Rap was originally an outlet for those struggling with their environment.
Hip-hop and rap began as expressions of poverty.
Pete DJ Jones
And early MCs knew their guests came to parties to get their mind off life and work stress and just have fun.
'Cause to me, MC means move the crowd.
Eric B. make 'em clap to this!
Eric B. & Rakim
Today, rap covers more than party music. You just have to venture beyond mainstream music to find it.

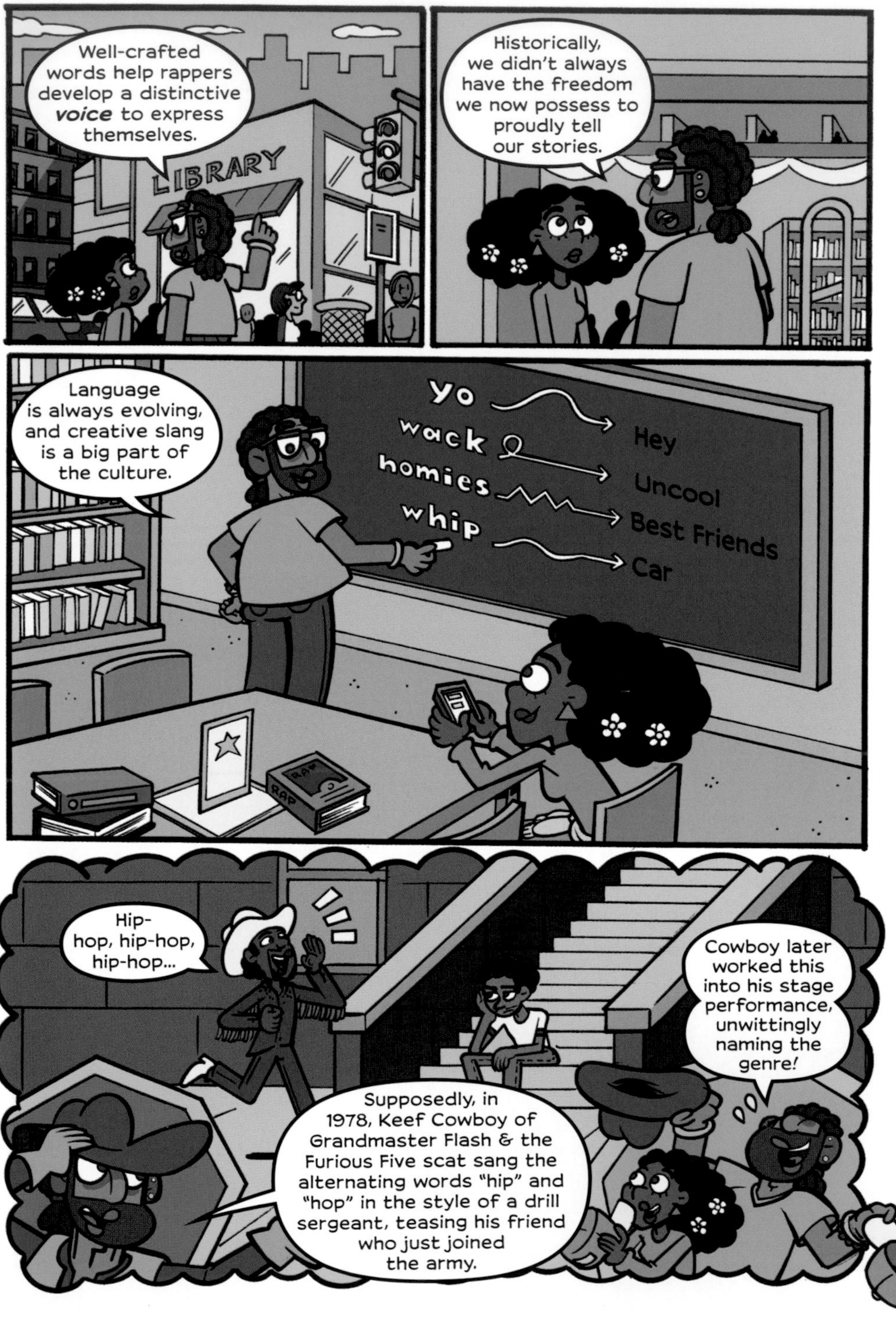
Well-crafted words help rappers develop a distinctive ***voice*** to express themselves.
LIBRARY
Historically, we didn't always have the freedom we now possess to proudly tell our stories.
Language is always evolving, and creative slang is a big part of the culture.
yo → Hey
wack → Uncool
homies → Best Friends
whip → Car
RAP
Hip-hop, hip-hop, hip-hop...
Cowboy later worked this into his stage performance, unwittingly naming the genre!
Supposedly, in 1978, Keef Cowboy of Grandmaster Flash & the Furious Five scat sang the alternating words "hip" and "hop" in the style of a drill sergeant, teasing his friend who just joined the army.

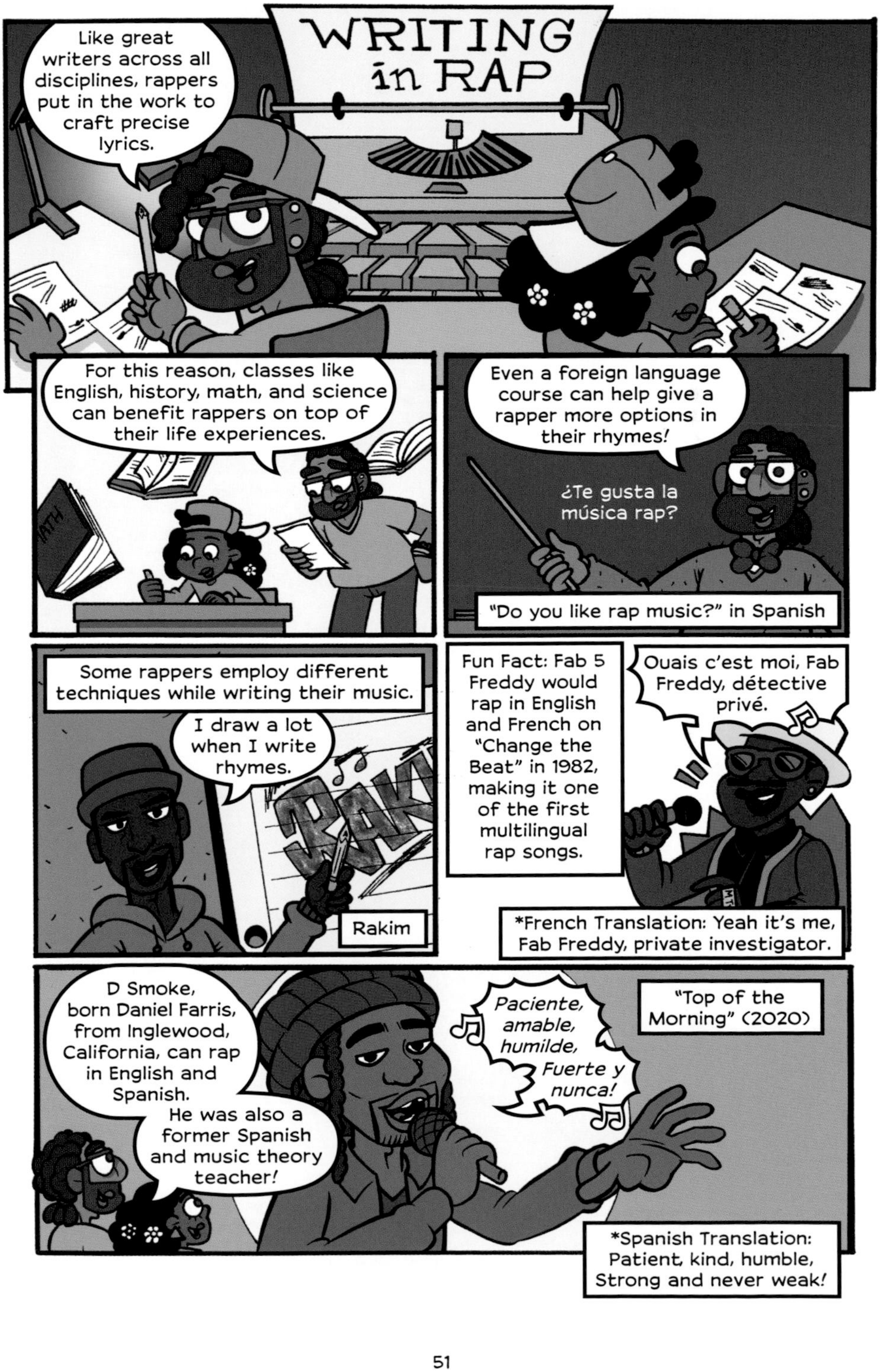
WRITING in RAP
Like great writers across all disciplines, rappers put in the work to craft precise lyrics.
For this reason, classes like English, history, math, and science can benefit rappers on top of their life experiences.
Even a foreign language course can help give a rapper more options in their rhymes!
¿Te gusta la música rap?
"Do you like rap music?" in Spanish
Some rappers employ different techniques while writing their music.
I draw a lot when I write rhymes.
Rakim
Fun Fact: Fab 5 Freddy would rap in English and French on "Change the Beat" in 1982, making it one of the first multilingual rap songs.
Ouais c'est moi, Fab Freddy, détective privé.
*French Translation: Yeah it's me, Fab Freddy, private investigator.
D Smoke, born Daniel Farris, from Inglewood, California, can rap in English and Spanish.
He was also a former Spanish and music theory teacher!
Paciente, amable, humilde,
Fuerte y nunca!
"Top of the Morning" (2020)
*Spanish Translation: Patient, kind, humble, Strong and never weak!

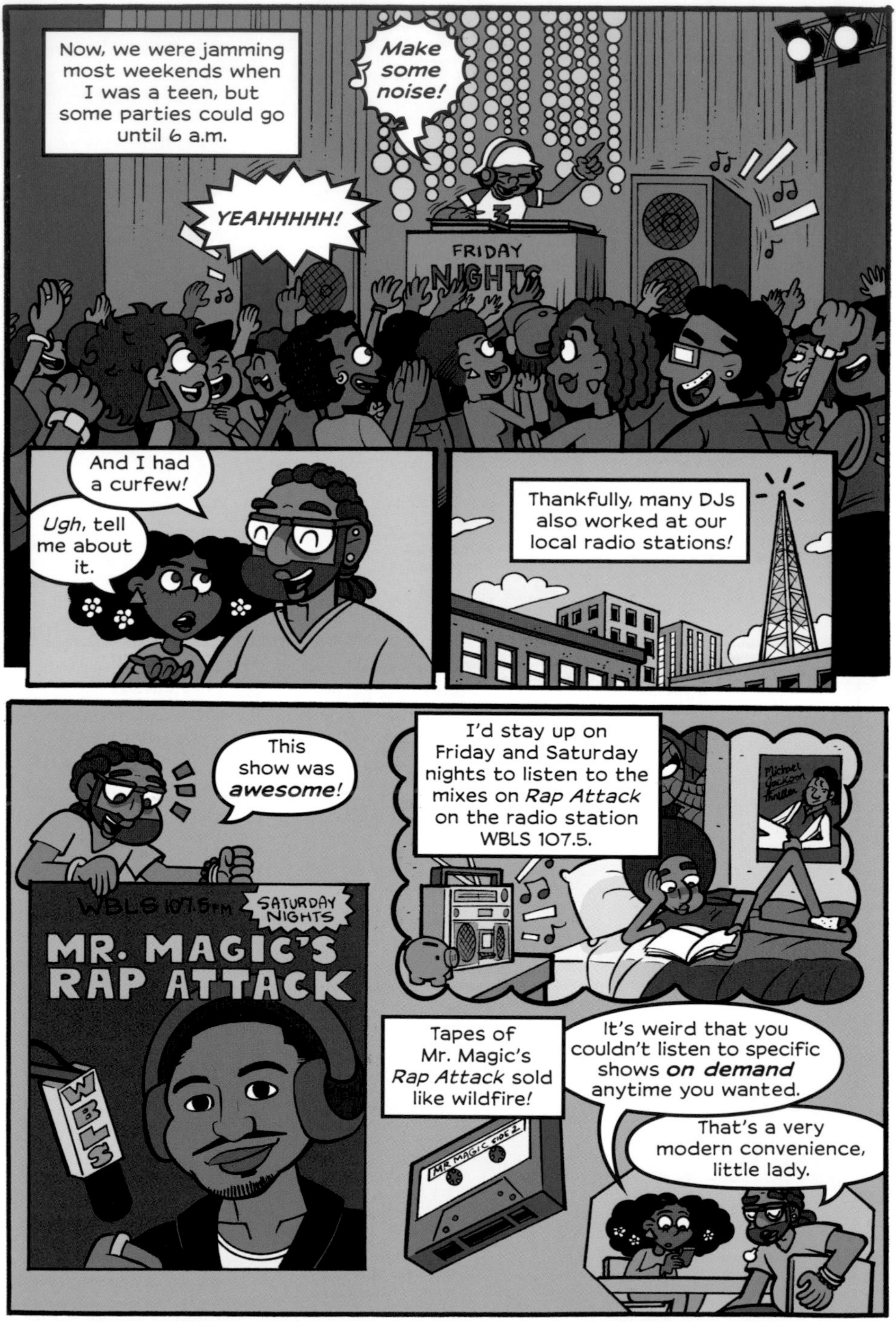
Now, we were jamming most weekends when I was a teen, but some parties could go until 6 a.m.
Make some noise!
YEAHHHHH!
FRIDAY NIGHTS
And I had a curfew!
Ugh, tell me about it.
Thankfully, many DJs also worked at our local radio stations!
This show was awesome!
WBLS 107.5 FM
SATURDAY NIGHTS
MR. MAGIC'S RAP ATTACK
WBLS
I'd stay up on Friday and Saturday nights to listen to the mixes on Rap Attack on the radio station WBLS 107.5.
Tapes of Mr. Magic's Rap Attack sold like wildfire!
MR MAGIC SIDE 2
It's weird that you couldn't listen to specific shows on demand anytime you wanted.
That's a very modern convenience, little lady.

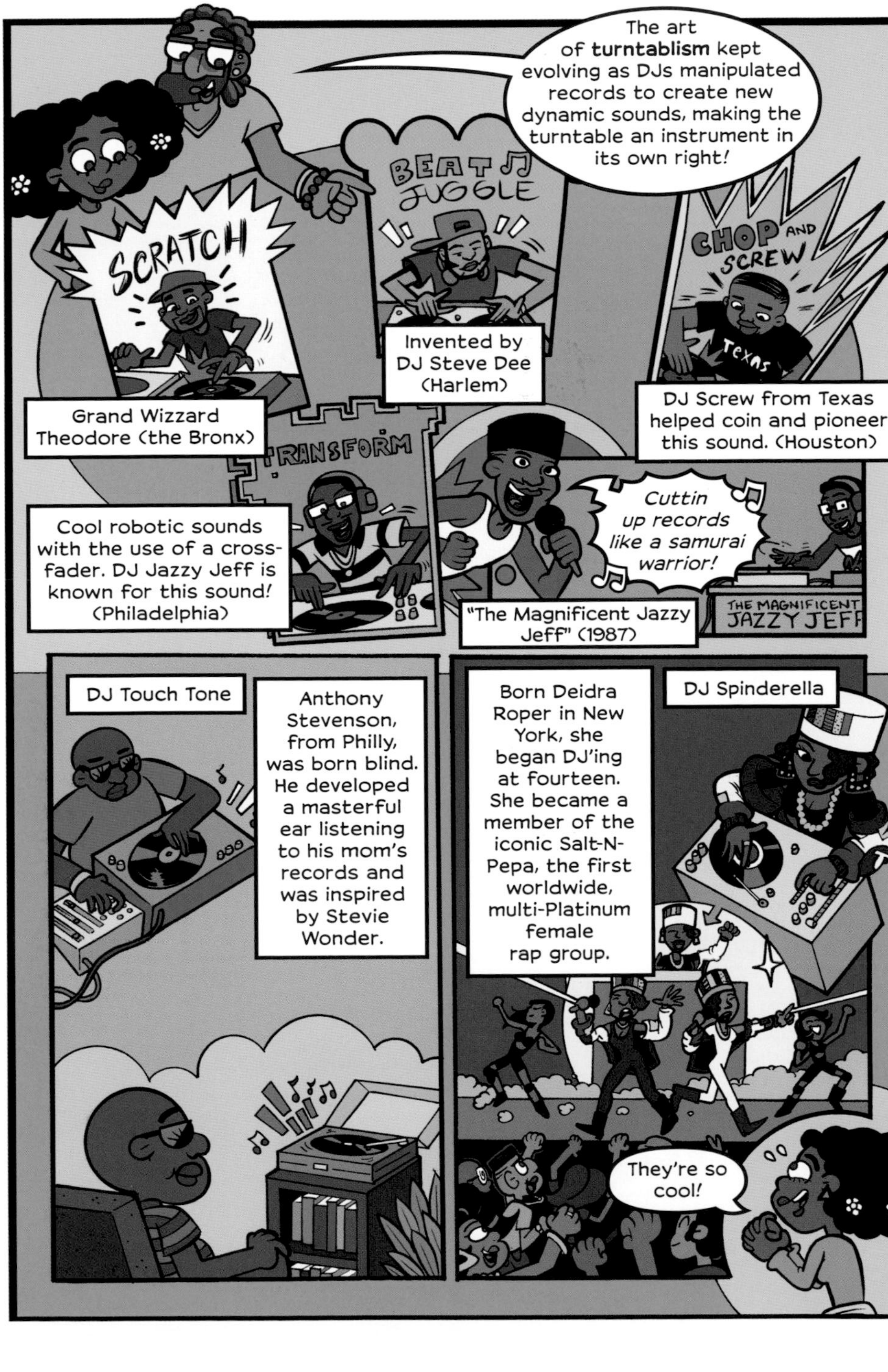

The art of **turntablism** kept evolving as DJs manipulated records to create new dynamic sounds, making the turntable an instrument in its own right!
SCRATCH
Grand Wizzard Theodore (the Bronx)
BEAT JUGGLE
Invented by DJ Steve Dee (Harlem)
CHOP AND SCREW
TEXAS
DJ Screw from Texas helped coin and pioneer this sound. (Houston)
TRANSFORM
Cool robotic sounds with the use of a cross-fader. DJ Jazzy Jeff is known for this sound! (Philadelphia)
Cuttin up records like a samurai warrior!
THE MAGNIFICENT JAZZY JEFF
"The Magnificent Jazzy Jeff" (1987)
DJ Touch Tone
Anthony Stevenson, from Philly, was born blind. He developed a masterful ear listening to his mom's records and was inspired by Stevie Wonder.
Born Deidra Roper in New York, she began DJ'ing at fourteen. She became a member of the iconic Salt-N-Pepa, the first worldwide, multi-Platinum female rap group.
DJ Spinderella
They're so cool!

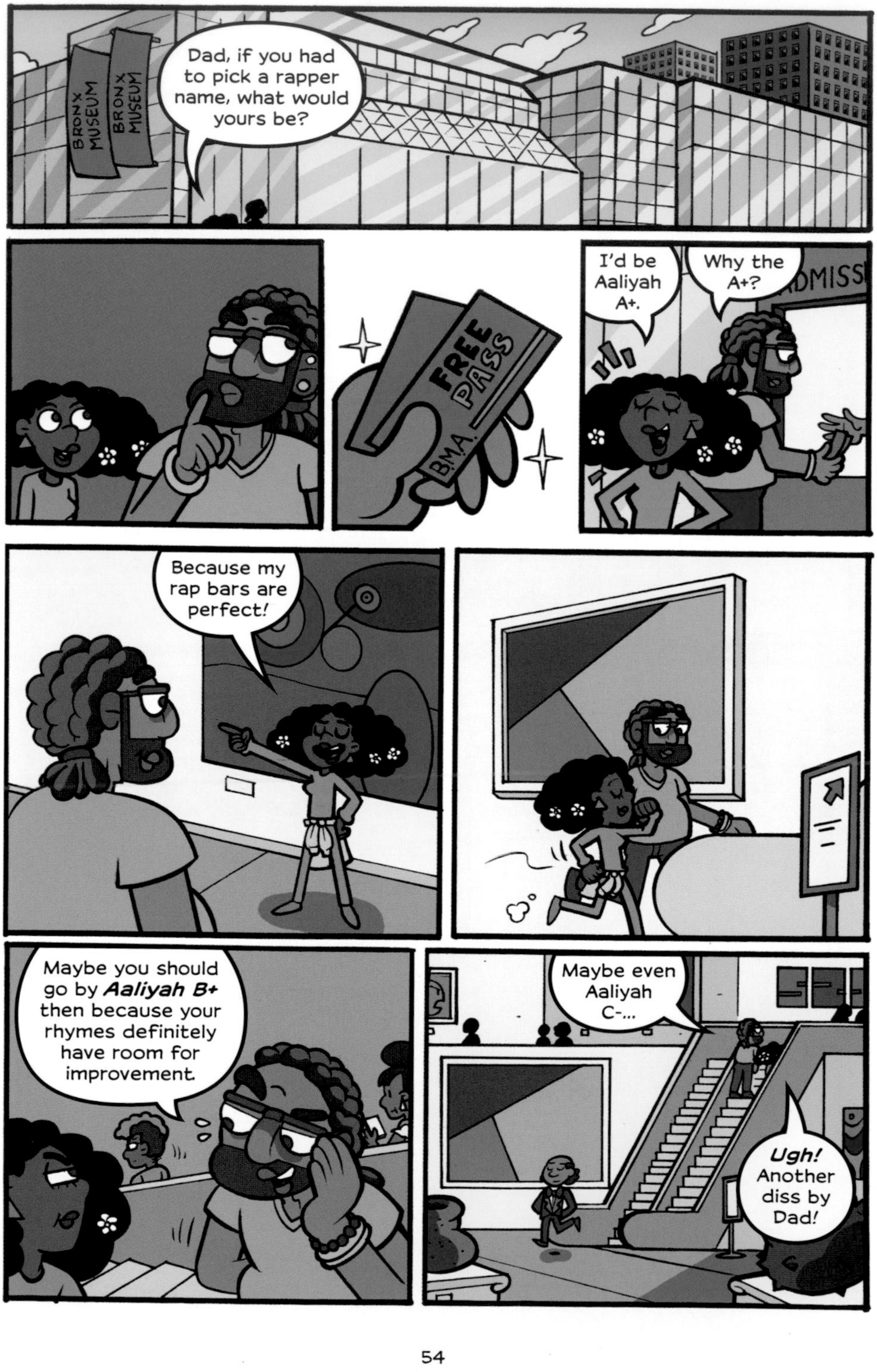
BRONX MUSEUM
BRONX MUSEUM
Dad, if you had to pick a rapper name, what would yours be?
FREE PASS
B.M.A.
I'd be Aaliyah A+.
Why the A+?
ADMISS
Because my rap bars are perfect!
Maybe you should go by ***Aaliyah B+*** then because your rhymes definitely have room for improvement.
Maybe even Aaliyah C-...
Ugh! Another diss by Dad!

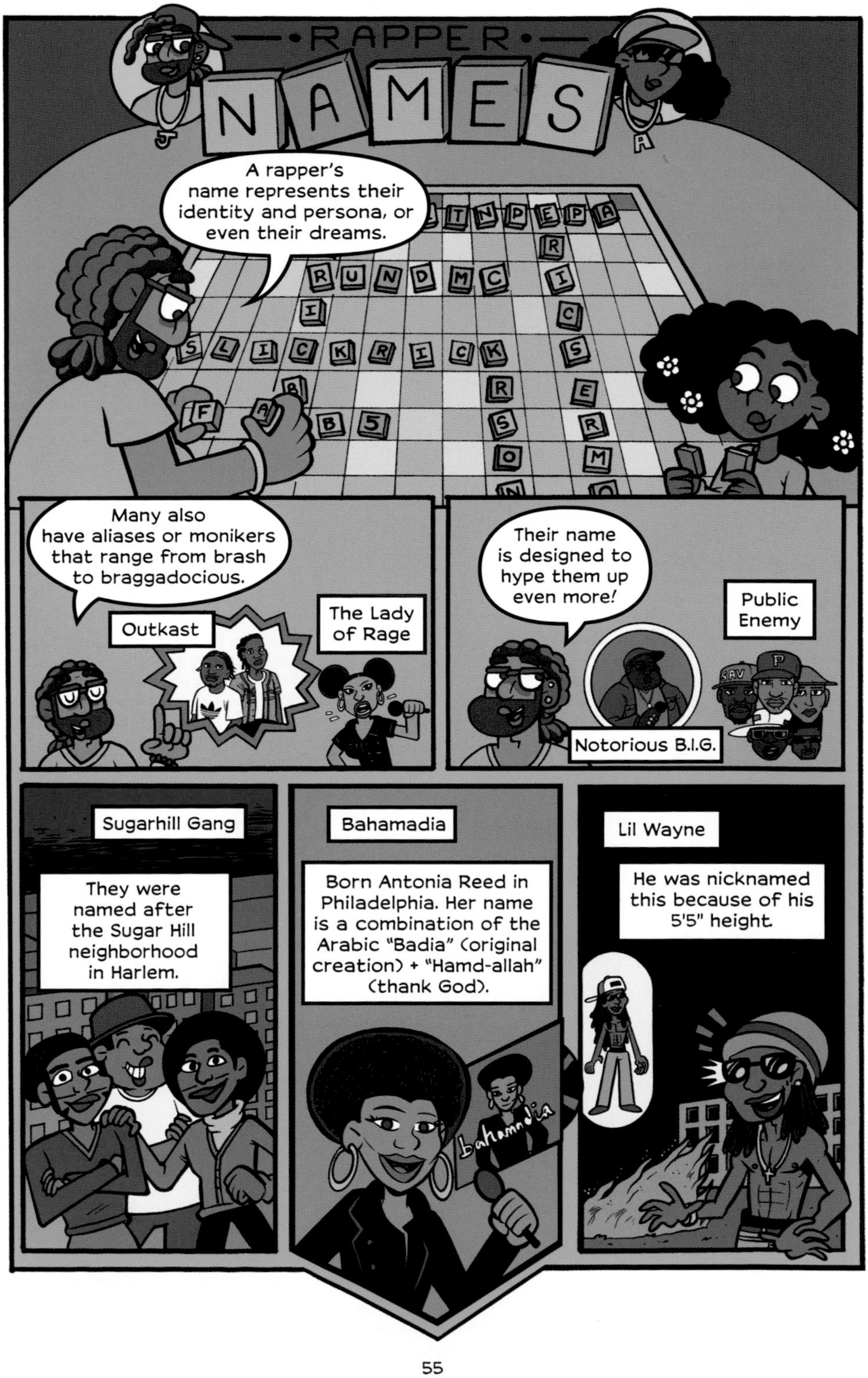
RAPPER
NAMES
A rapper's name represents their identity and persona, or even their dreams.
Many also have aliases or monikers that range from brash to braggadocious.
Outkast
The Lady of Rage
Their name is designed to hype them up even more!
Public Enemy
Notorious B.I.G.
Sugarhill Gang
They were named after the Sugar Hill neighborhood in Harlem.
Bahamadia
Born Antonia Reed in Philadelphia. Her name is a combination of the Arabic "Badia" (original creation) + "Hamd-allah" (thank God).
bahamadia
Lil Wayne
He was nicknamed this because of his 5'5" height.

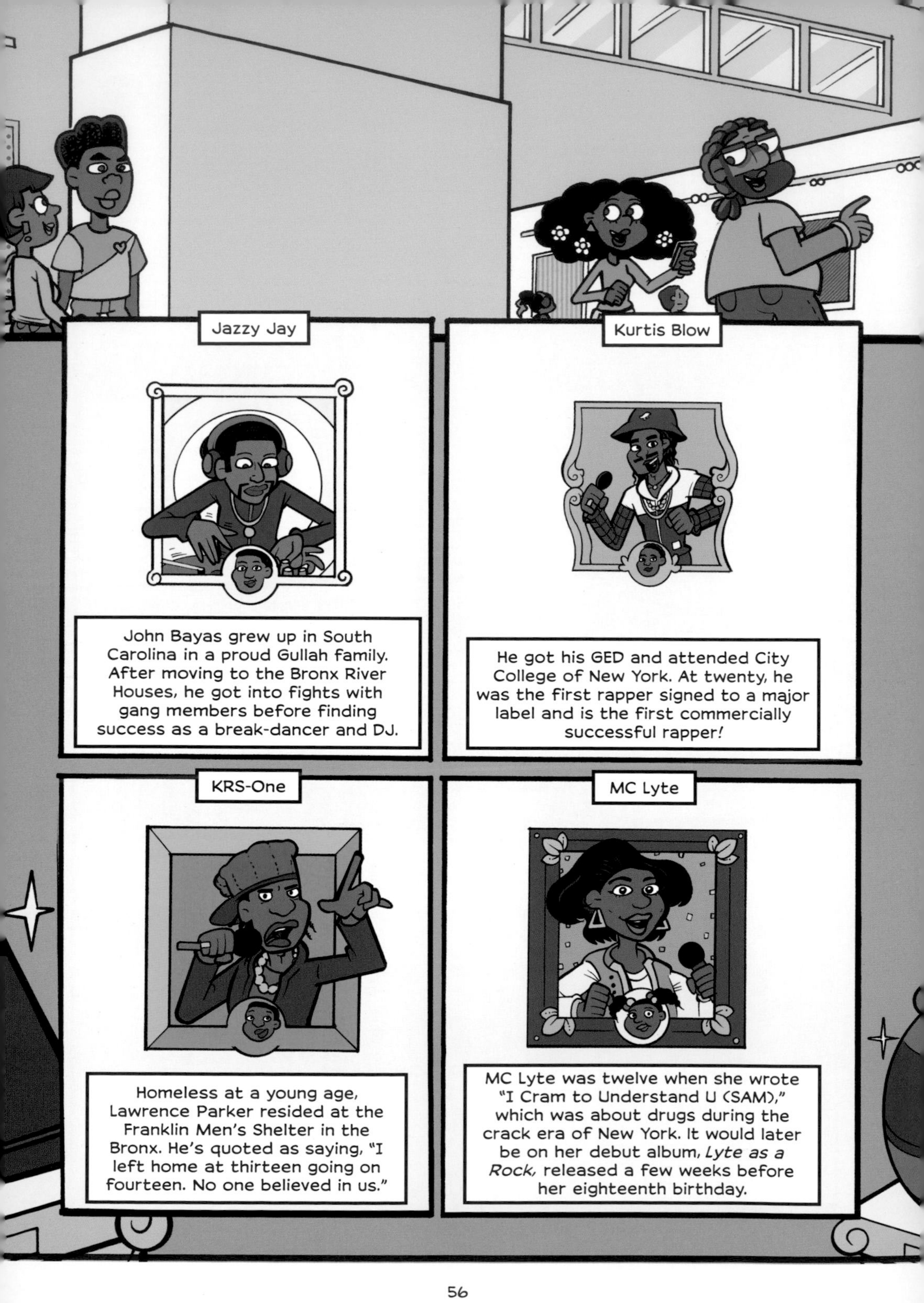

Jazzy Jay
John Bayas grew up in South Carolina in a proud Gullah family. After moving to the Bronx River Houses, he got into fights with gang members before finding success as a break-dancer and DJ.
Kurtis Blow
He got his GED and attended City College of New York. At twenty, he was the first rapper signed to a major label and is the first commercially successful rapper!
KRS-One
Homeless at a young age, Lawrence Parker resided at the Franklin Men's Shelter in the Bronx. He's quoted as saying, "I left home at thirteen going on fourteen. No one believed in us."
MC Lyte
MC Lyte was twelve when she wrote "I Cram to Understand U (SAM)," which was about drugs during the crack era of New York. It would later be on her debut album, *Lyte as a Rock,* released a few weeks before her eighteenth birthday.

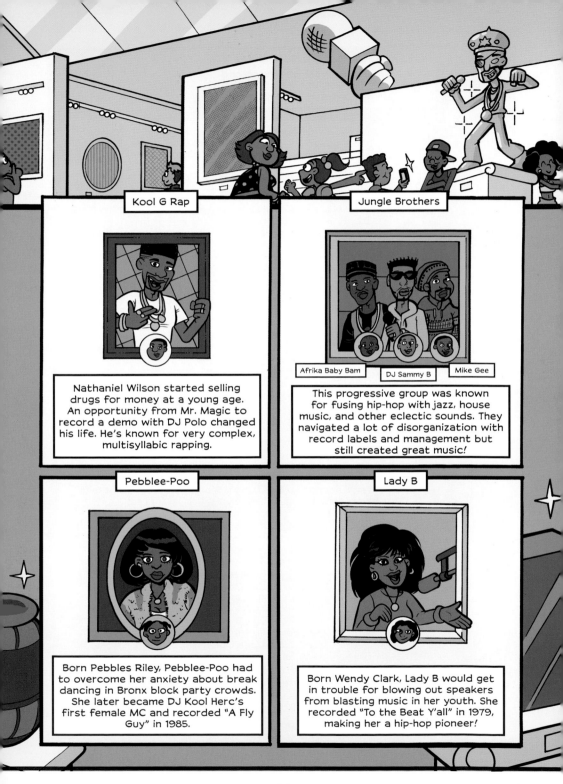

Kool G Rap

Nathaniel Wilson started selling drugs for money at a young age. An opportunity from Mr. Magic to record a demo with DJ Polo changed his life. He's known for very complex, multisyllabic rapping.

Jungle Brothers

Afrika Baby Bam

DJ Sammy B

Mike Gee

This progressive group was known for fusing hip-hop with jazz, house music, and other eclectic sounds. They navigated a lot of disorganization with record labels and management but still created great music!

Pebblee-Poo

Born Pebbles Riley, Pebblee-Poo had to overcome her anxiety about break dancing in Bronx block party crowds. She later became DJ Kool Herc's first female MC and recorded "A Fly Guy" in 1985.

Lady B

Born Wendy Clark, Lady B would get in trouble for blowing out speakers from blasting music in her youth. She recorded "To the Beat Y'all" in 1979, making her a hip-hop pioneer!

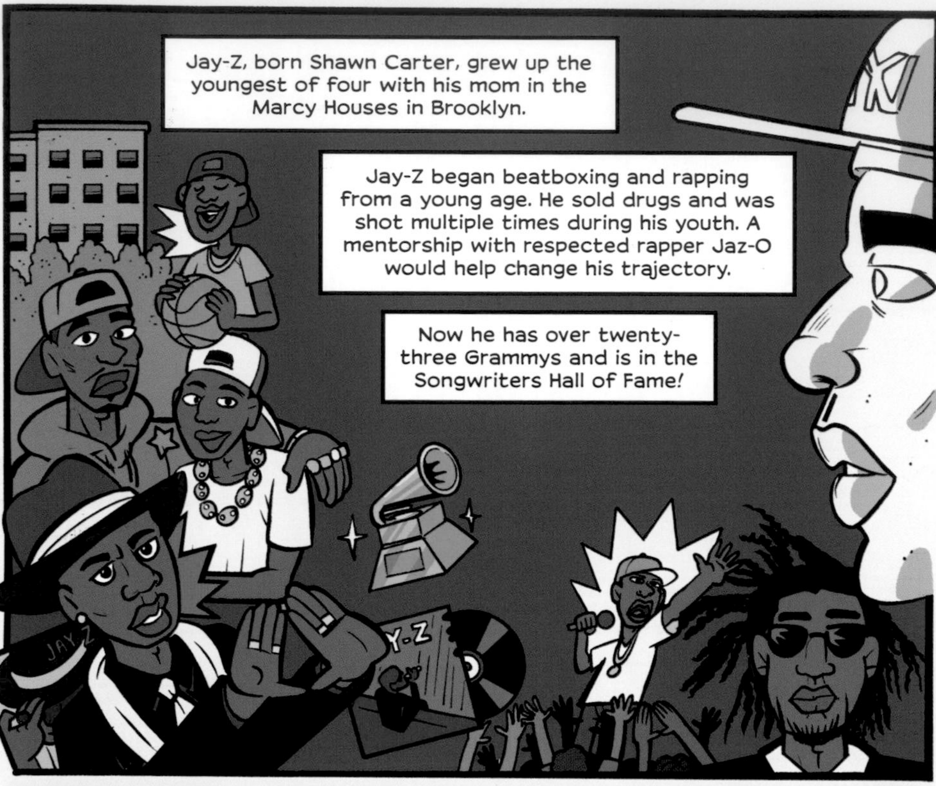
Jay-Z, born Shawn Carter, grew up the youngest of four with his mom in the Marcy Houses in Brooklyn.
Jay-Z began beatboxing and rapping from a young age. He sold drugs and was shot multiple times during his youth. A mentorship with respected rapper Jaz-O would help change his trajectory.
Now he has over twenty-three Grammys and is in the Songwriters Hall of Fame!
JAY-Z

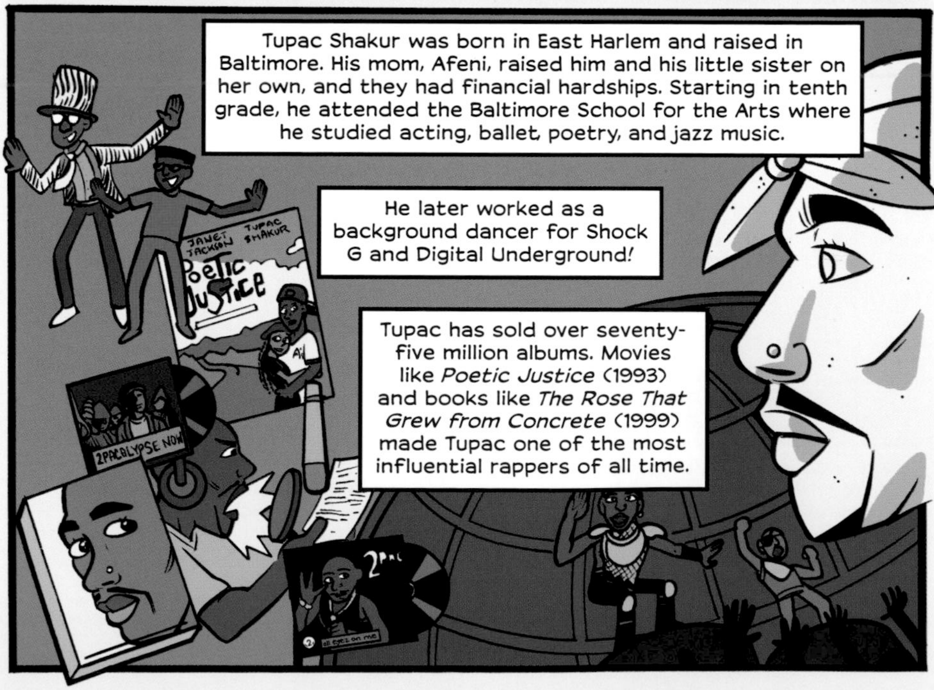
Tupac Shakur was born in East Harlem and raised in Baltimore. His mom, Afeni, raised him and his little sister on her own, and they had financial hardships. Starting in tenth grade, he attended the Baltimore School for the Arts where he studied acting, ballet, poetry, and jazz music.
He later worked as a background dancer for Shock G and Digital Underground!
JANET JACKSON
TUPAC SHAKUR
Poetic Justice
Tupac has sold over seventy-five million albums. Movies like *Poetic Justice* (1993) and books like *The Rose That Grew from Concrete* (1999) made Tupac one of the most influential rappers of all time.
2PACALYPSE NOW
2PAC

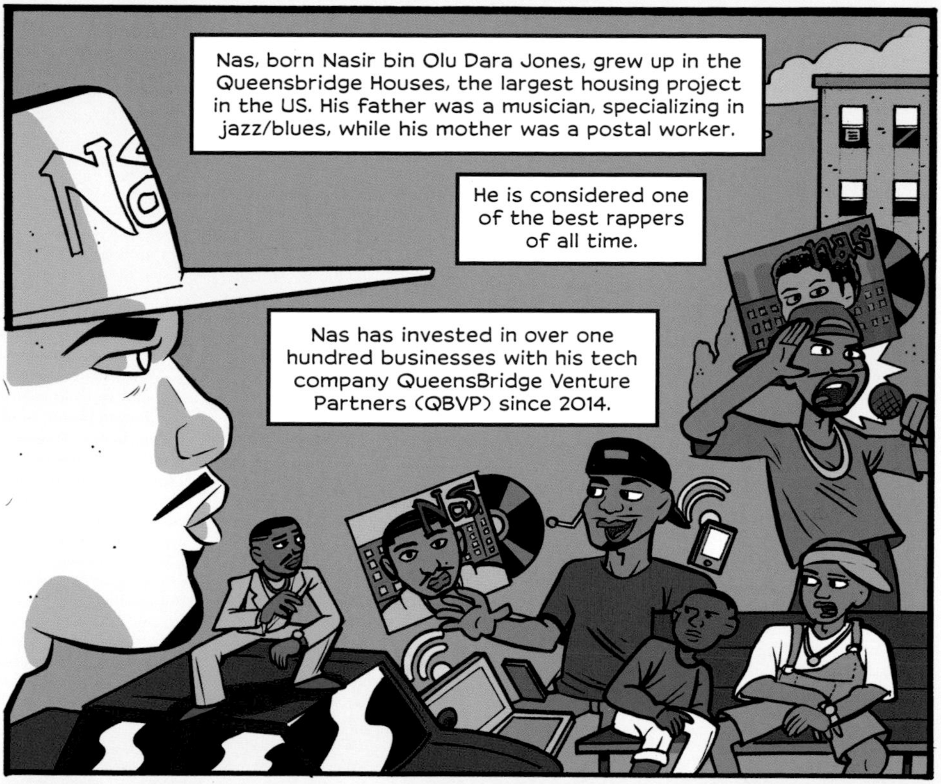
Nas, born Nasir bin Olu Dara Jones, grew up in the Queensbridge Houses, the largest housing project in the US. His father was a musician, specializing in jazz/blues, while his mother was a postal worker.
He is considered one of the best rappers of all time.
Nas has invested in over one hundred businesses with his tech company QueensBridge Venture Partners (QBVP) since 2014.

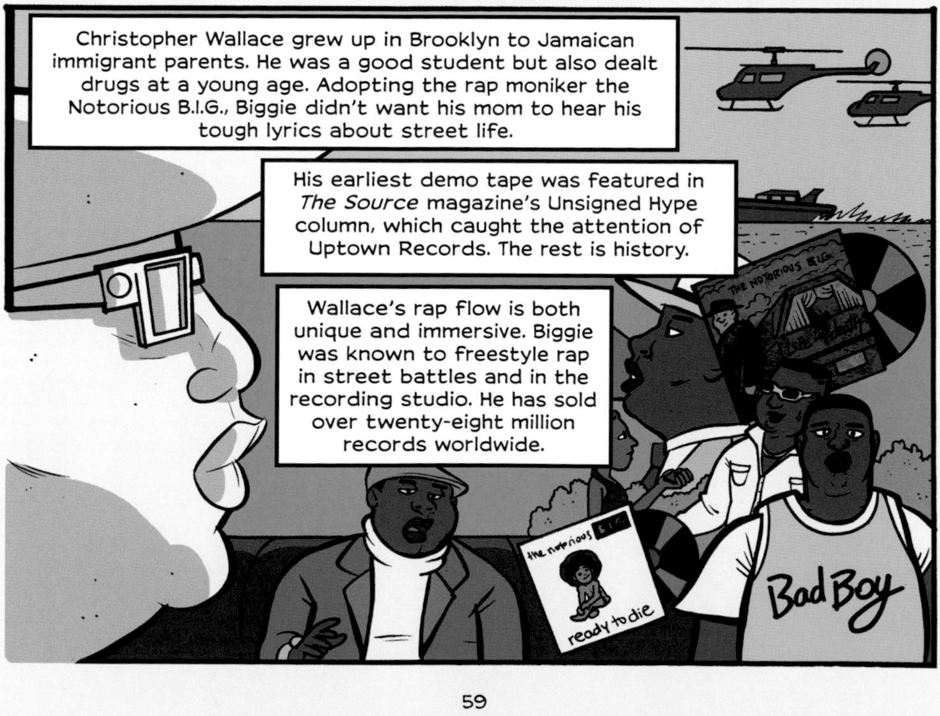
Christopher Wallace grew up in Brooklyn to Jamaican immigrant parents. He was a good student but also dealt drugs at a young age. Adopting the rap moniker the Notorious B.I.G., Biggie didn't want his mom to hear his tough lyrics about street life.
His earliest demo tape was featured in *The Source* magazine's Unsigned Hype column, which caught the attention of Uptown Records. The rest is history.
Wallace's rap flow is both unique and immersive. Biggie was known to freestyle rap in street battles and in the recording studio. He has sold over twenty-eight million records worldwide.
the notorious B.I.G.
ready to die
Bad Boy

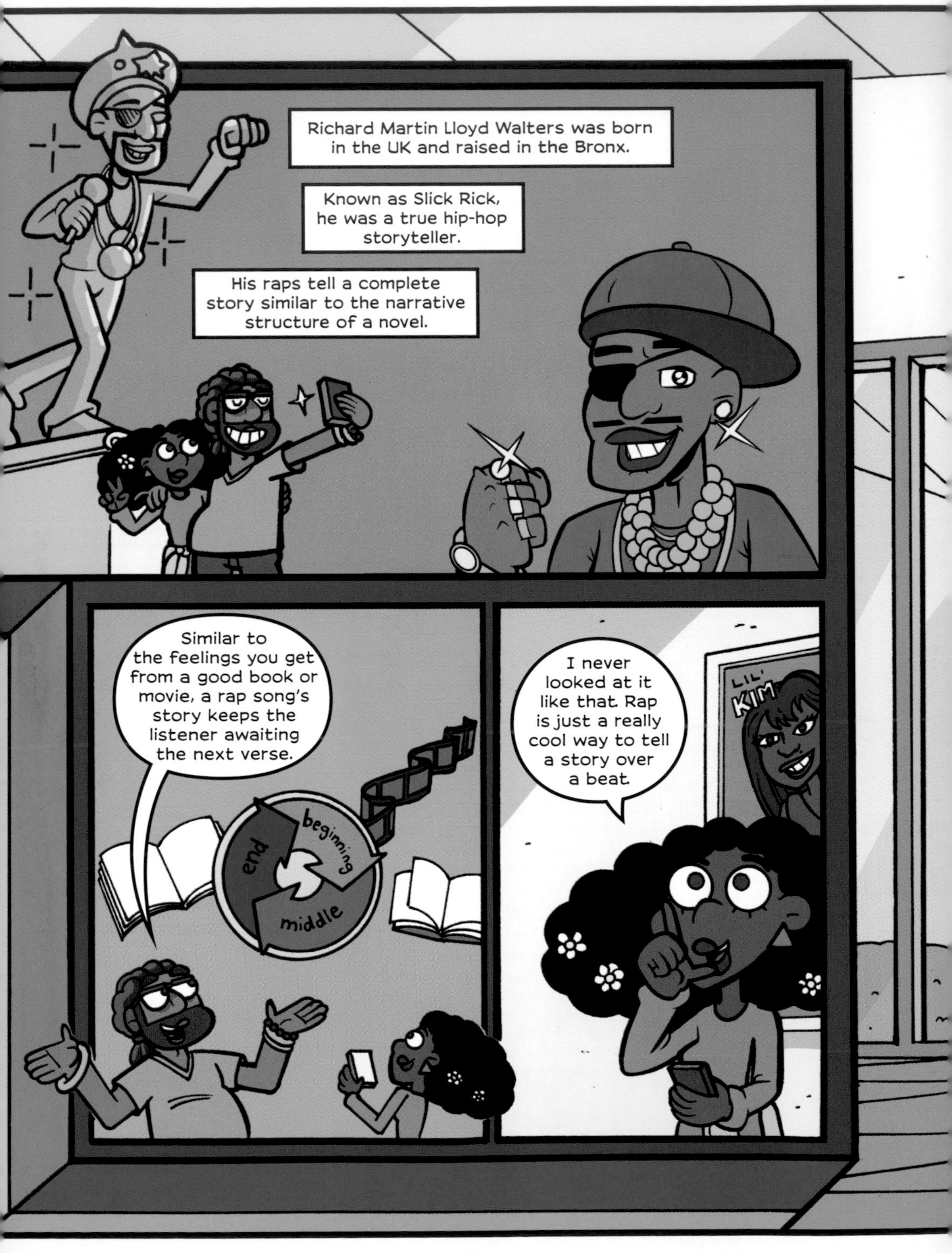
Richard Martin Lloyd Walters was born in the UK and raised in the Bronx.
Known as Slick Rick, he was a true hip-hop storyteller.
His raps tell a complete story similar to the narrative structure of a novel.
Similar to the feelings you get from a good book or movie, a rap song's story keeps the listener awaiting the next verse.
beginning
middle
end
I never looked at it like that. Rap is just a really cool way to tell a story over a beat.
LIL' KIM

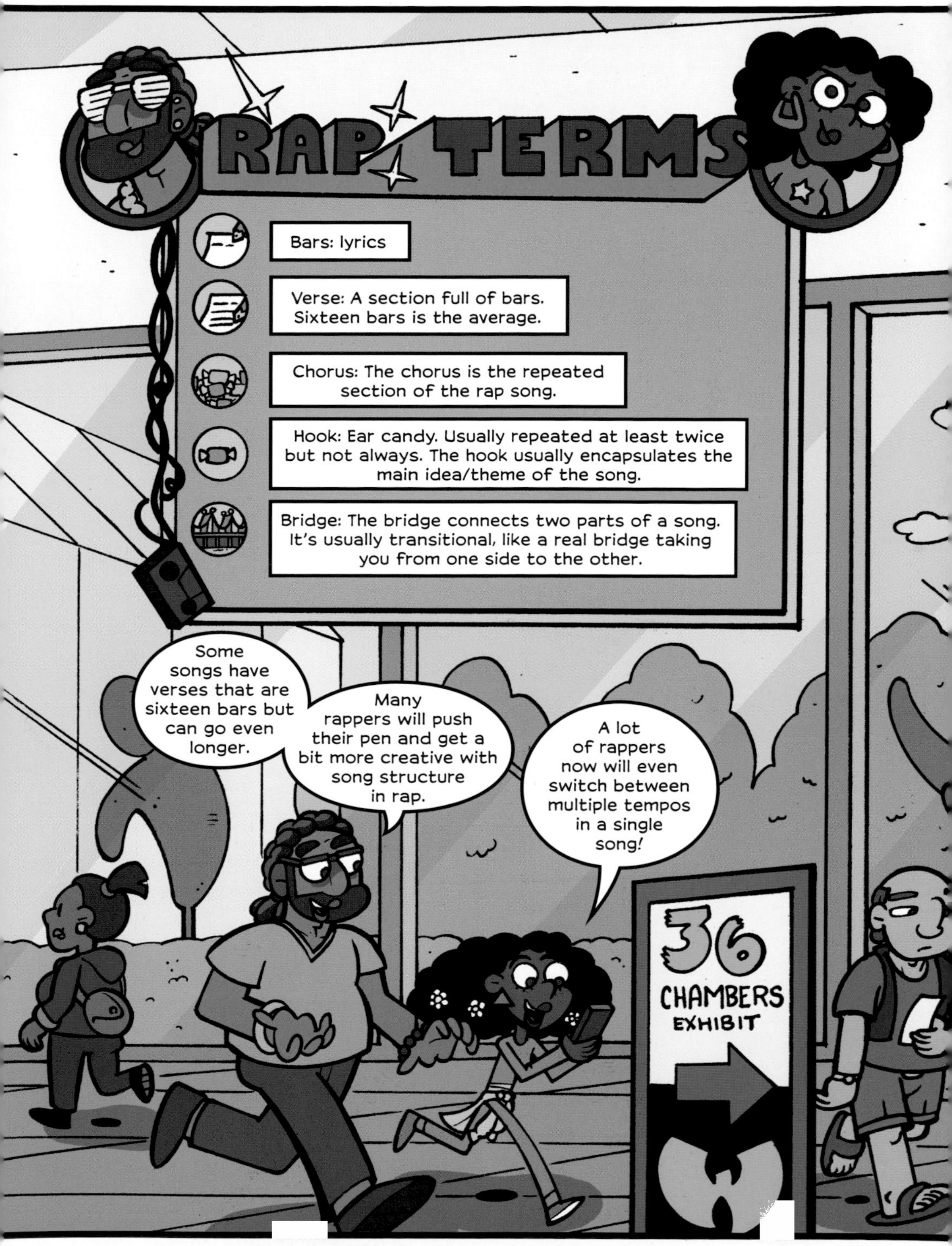
RAP TERMS
Bars: lyrics
Verse: A section full of bars. Sixteen bars is the average.
Chorus: The chorus is the repeated section of the rap song.
Hook: Ear candy. Usually repeated at least twice but not always. The hook usually encapsulates the main idea/theme of the song.
Bridge: The bridge connects two parts of a song. It's usually transitional, like a real bridge taking you from one side to the other.
Some songs have verses that are sixteen bars but can go even longer.
Many rappers will push their pen and get a bit more creative with song structure in rap.
A lot of rappers now will even switch between multiple tempos in a single song!
36 CHAMBERS EXHIBIT

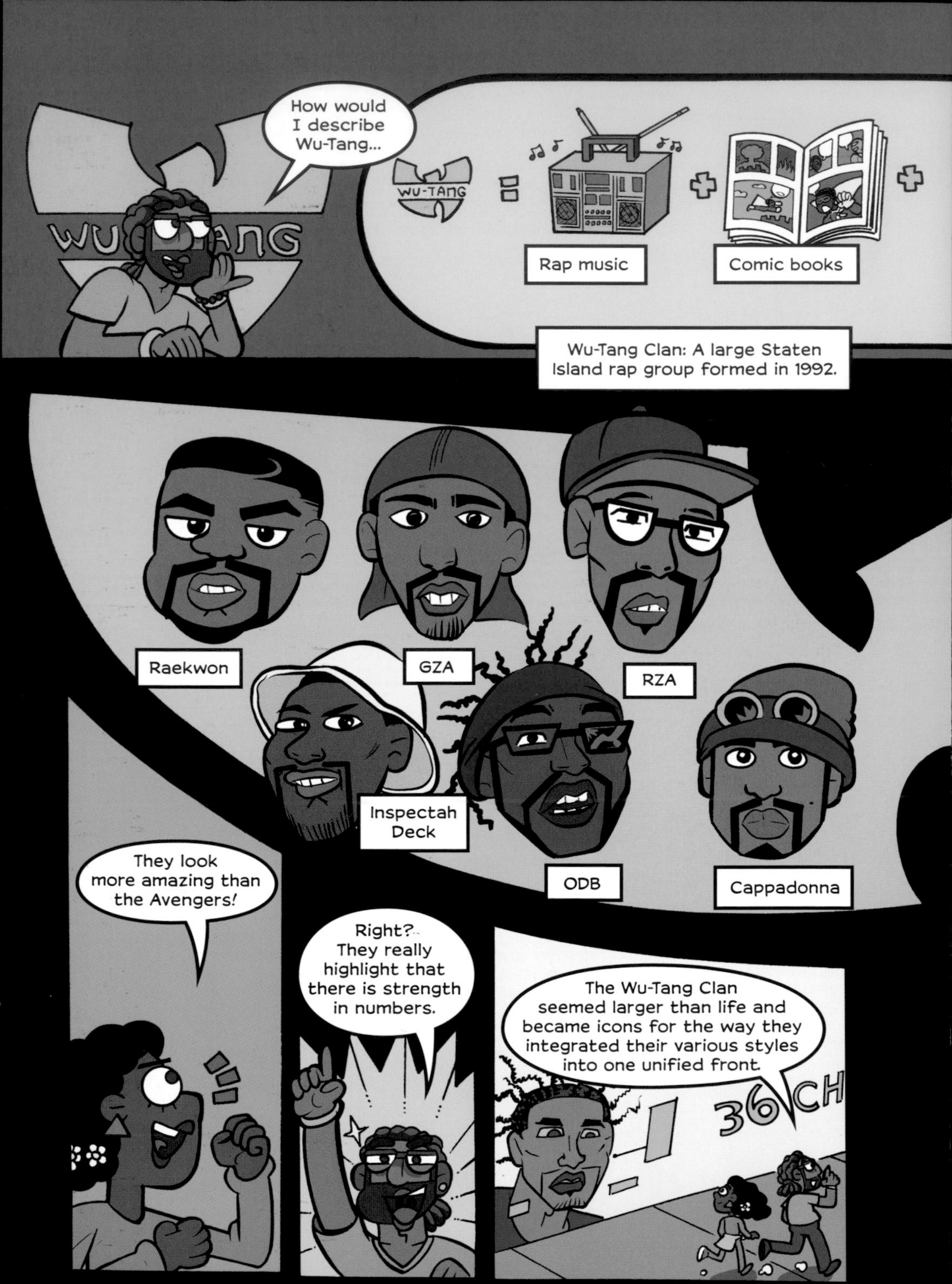

How would I describe Wu-Tang...
WU-TANG
WU-TANG
=
+
+
Rap music
Comic books
Wu-Tang Clan: A large Staten Island rap group formed in 1992.
Raekwon
GZA
RZA
Inspectah Deck
ODB
Cappadonna
They look more amazing than the Avengers!
Right? They really highlight that there is strength in numbers.
The Wu-Tang Clan seemed larger than life and became icons for the way they integrated their various styles into one unified front.
36 CH

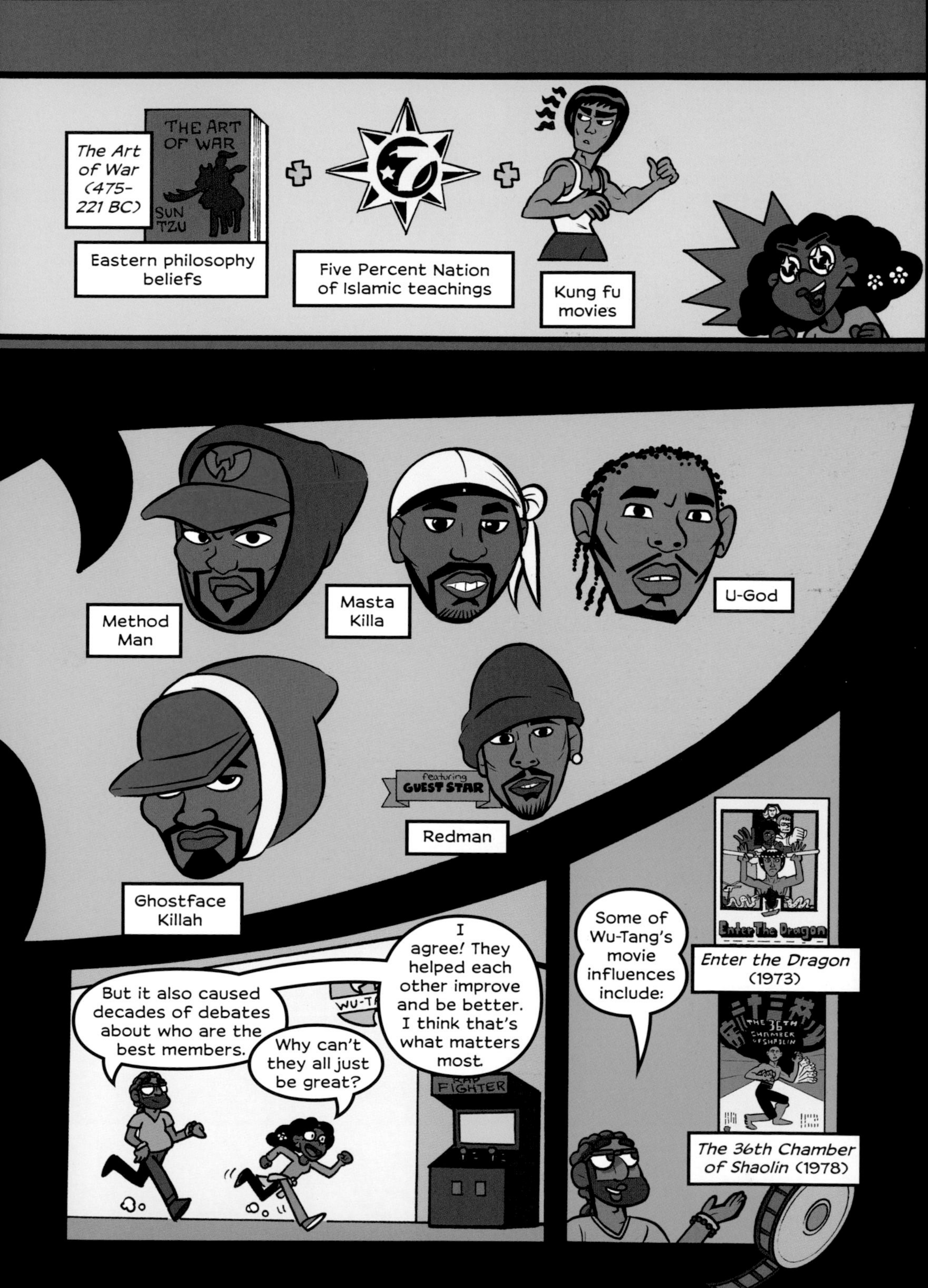

THE ART OF WAR SUN TZU
The Art of War (475–221 BC)
Eastern philosophy beliefs
Five Percent Nation of Islamic teachings
Kung fu movies
Method Man
Masta Killa
U-God
Ghostface Killah
featuring GUEST STAR
Redman
But it also caused decades of debates about who are the best members.
Why can't they all just be great?
I agree! They helped each other improve and be better. I think that's what matters most.
RAP FIGHTER
Some of Wu-Tang's movie influences include:
Enter The Dragon
Enter the Dragon (1973)
THE 36TH CHAMBER OF SHAOLIN
The 36th Chamber of Shaolin (1978)

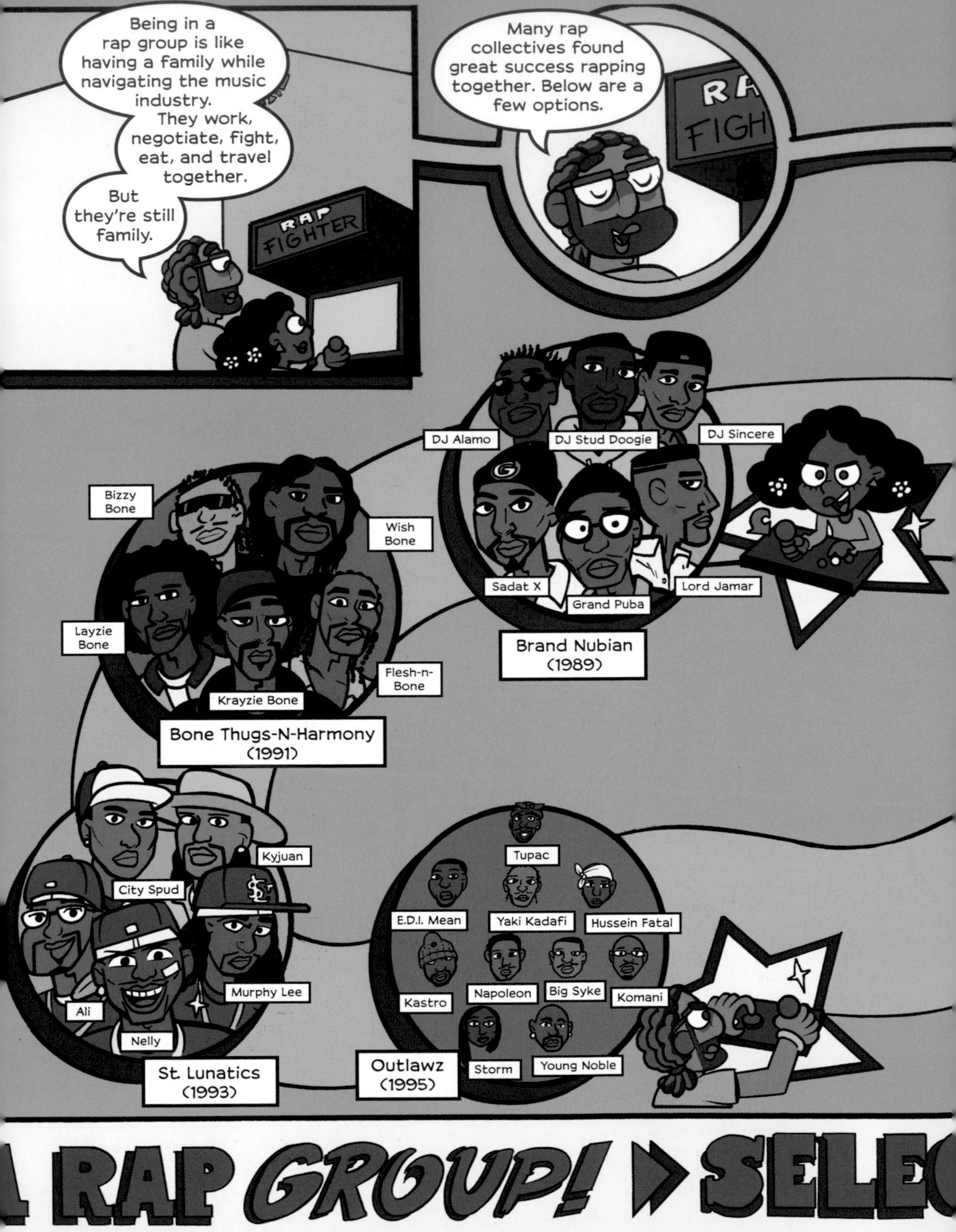
Being in a rap group is like having a family while navigating the music industry.
They work, negotiate, fight, eat, and travel together.
But they're still family.
RAP FIGHTER
Many rap collectives found great success rapping together. Below are a few options.
DJ Alamo
DJ Stud Doogie
DJ Sincere
Sadat X
Grand Puba
Lord Jamar
Brand Nubian (1989)
Bizzy Bone
Wish Bone
Layzie Bone
Krayzie Bone
Flesh-n-Bone
Bone Thugs-N-Harmony (1991)
Kyjuan
City Spud
Ali
Nelly
Murphy Lee
St. Lunatics (1993)
Tupac
E.D.I. Mean
Yaki Kadafi
Hussein Fatal
Kastro
Napoleon
Big Syke
Komani
Storm
Young Noble
Outlawz (1995)
A RAP GROUP! ▶ SELEC

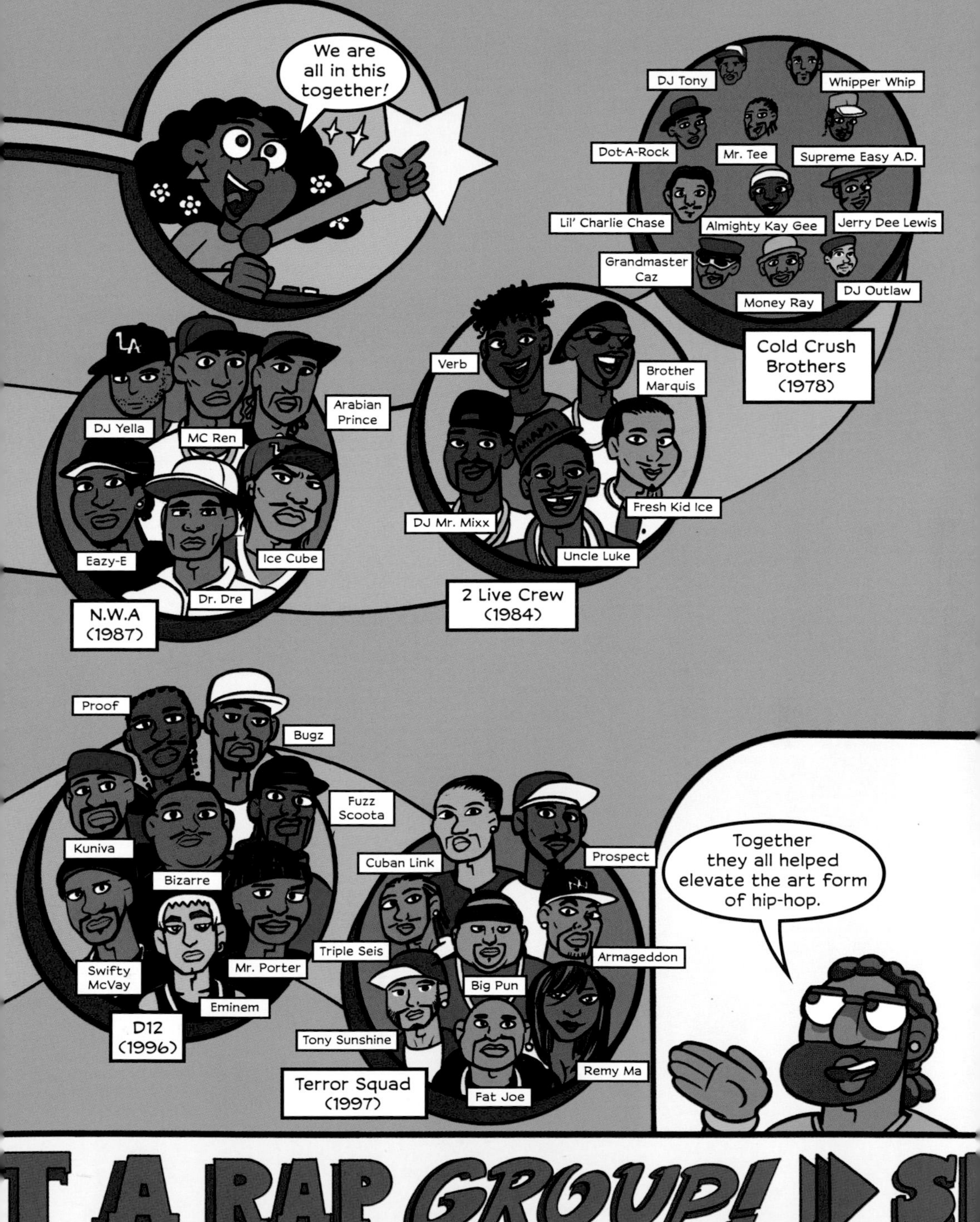

We are all in this together!
DJ Tony
Whipper Whip
Dot-A-Rock
Mr. Tee
Supreme Easy A.D.
Lil' Charlie Chase
Almighty Kay Gee
Jerry Dee Lewis
Grandmaster Caz
Money Ray
DJ Outlaw
Cold Crush Brothers (1978)
Verb
Brother Marquis
DJ Mr. Mixx
Fresh Kid Ice
Uncle Luke
2 Live Crew (1984)
DJ Yella
MC Ren
Arabian Prince
Eazy-E
Ice Cube
Dr. Dre
N.W.A (1987)
Proof
Bugz
Fuzz Scoota
Kuniva
Bizarre
Swifty McVay
Mr. Porter
Eminem
D12 (1996)
Cuban Link
Prospect
Triple Seis
Armageddon
Big Pun
Tony Sunshine
Remy Ma
Fat Joe
Terror Squad (1997)
Together they all helped elevate the art form of hip-hop.
T A RAP GROUP! SI

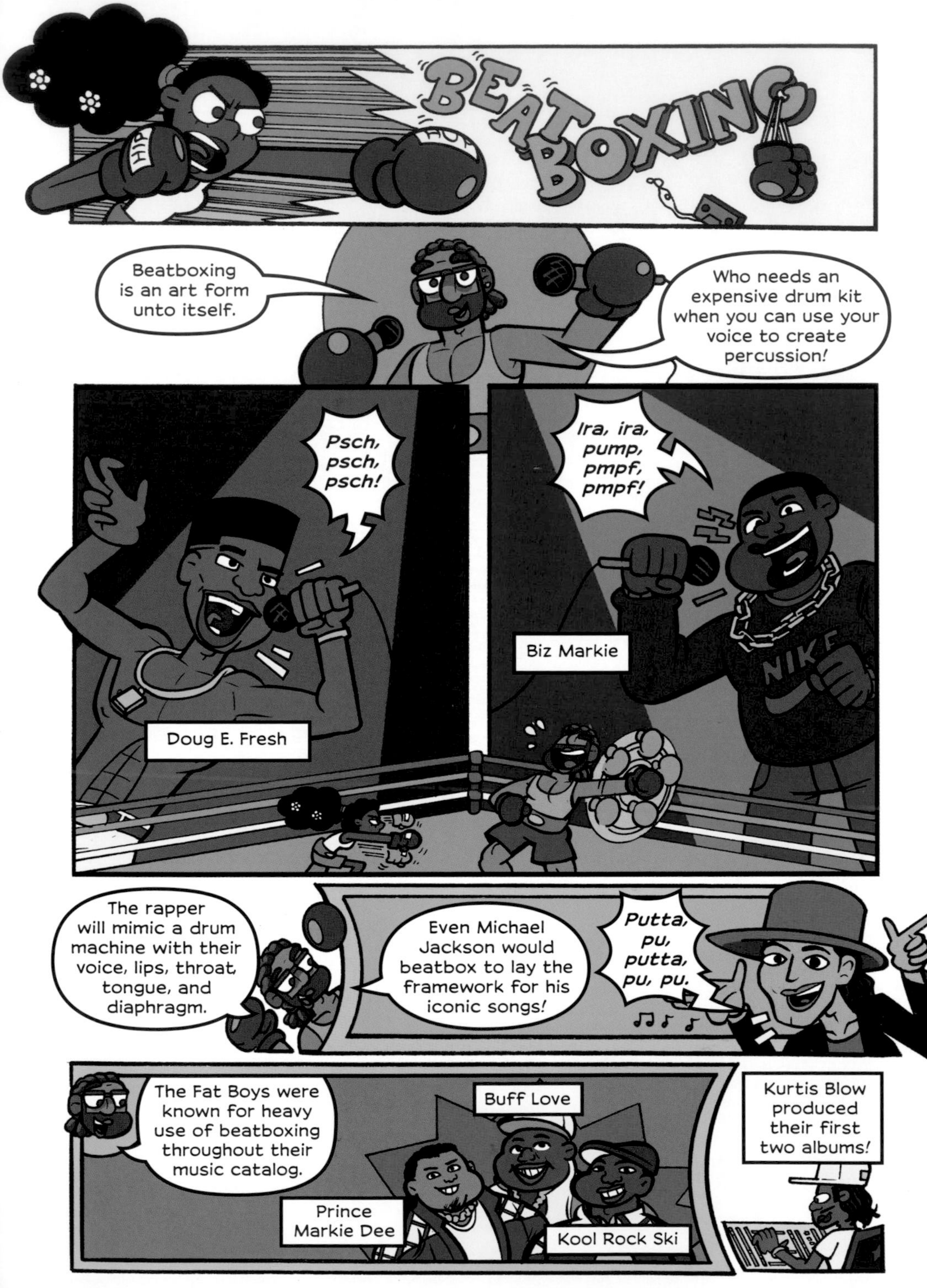

BEATBOXING
HIP
HOP
Beatboxing is an art form unto itself.
Who needs an expensive drum kit when you can use your voice to create percussion!
Psch, psch, psch!
Doug E. Fresh
Ira, ira, pump, pmpf, pmpf!
Biz Markie
NIKE
The rapper will mimic a drum machine with their voice, lips, throat, tongue, and diaphragm.
Even Michael Jackson would beatbox to lay the framework for his iconic songs!
Putta, pu, putta, pu, pu.
The Fat Boys were known for heavy use of beatboxing throughout their music catalog.
Buff Love
Prince Markie Dee
Kool Rock Ski
Kurtis Blow produced their first two albums!

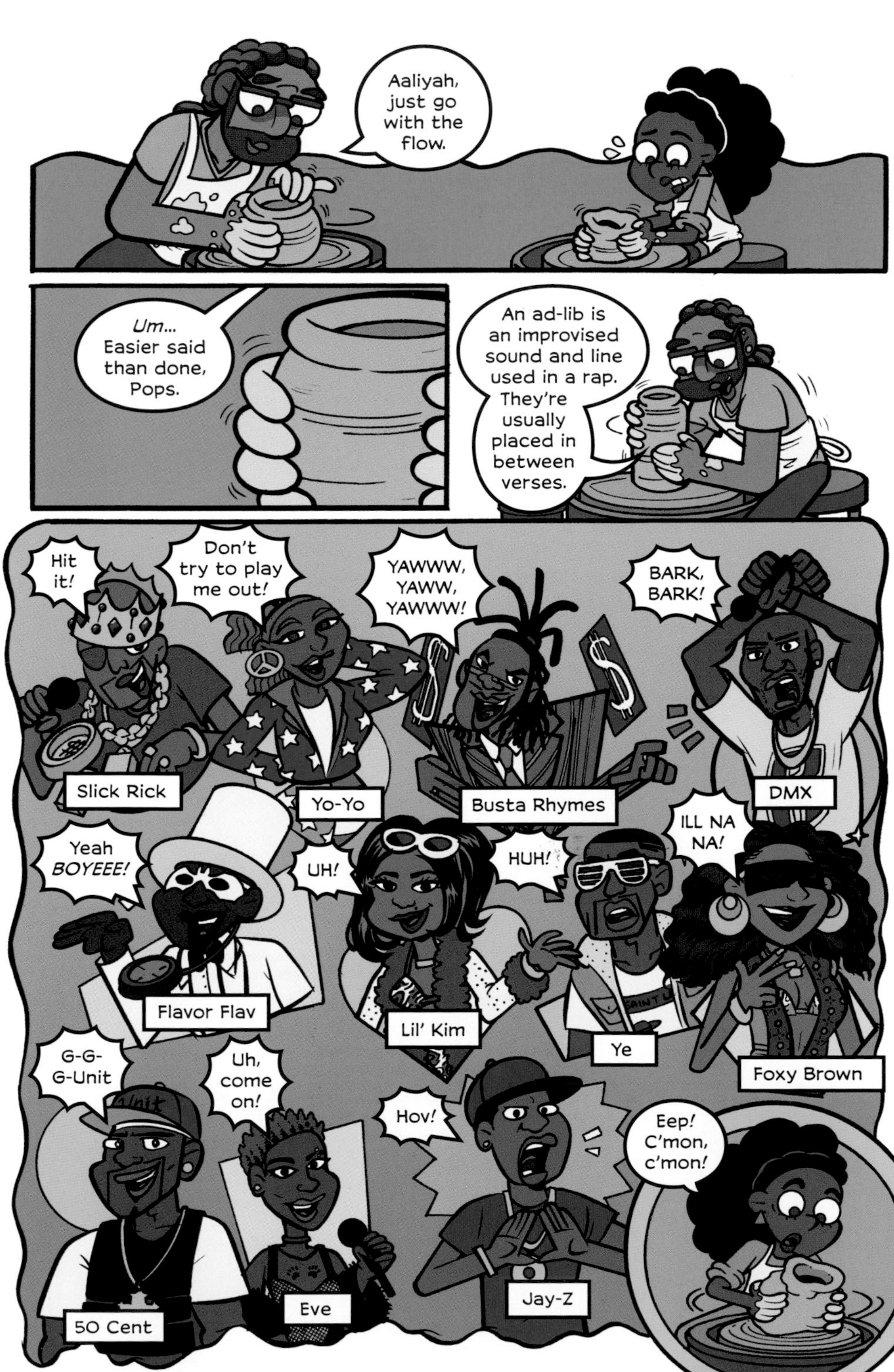
Aaliyah, just go with the flow.
Um... Easier said than done, Pops.
An ad-lib is an improvised sound and line used in a rap. They're usually placed in between verses.
Hit it!
Slick Rick
Don't try to play me out!
Yo-Yo
YAWWW, YAWW, YAWWW!
Busta Rhymes
BARK, BARK!
DMX
Yeah BOYEEE!
Flavor Flav
UH!
Lil' Kim
HUH!
Ye
ILL NA NA!
Foxy Brown
G-G-G-Unit
50 Cent
Uh, come on!
Eve
Hov!
Jay-Z
Eep! C'mon, c'mon!

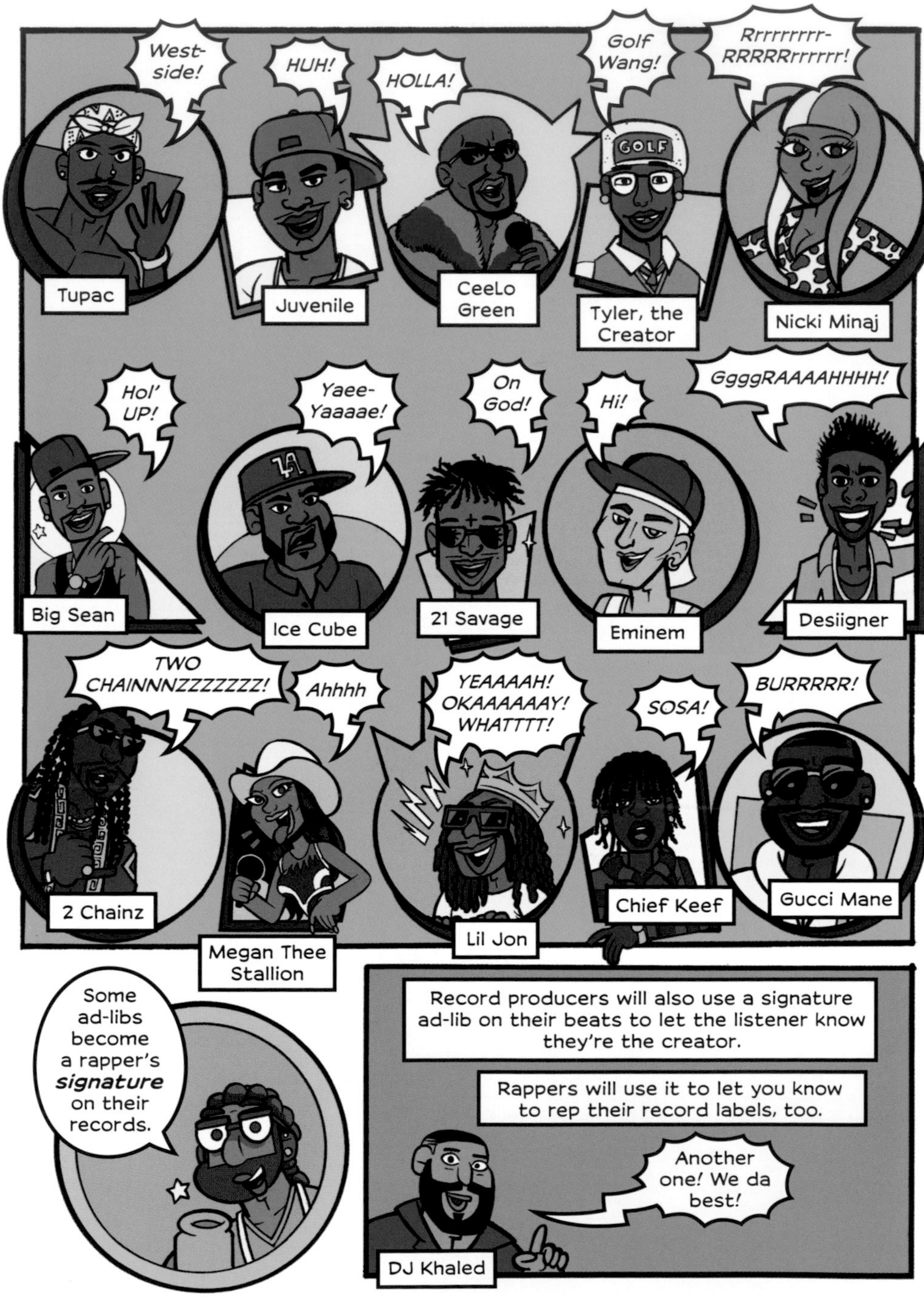
West-side!
Tupac
HUH!
Juvenile
HOLLA!
CeeLo Green
Golf Wang!
GOLF
Tyler, the Creator
Rrrrrrrrr-RRRRRrrrrrr!
Nicki Minaj
Hol' UP!
Big Sean
Yaee-Yaaaae!
LA
Ice Cube
On God!
21 Savage
Hi!
Eminem
GgggRAAAAHHHH!
Desiigner
TWO CHAINNNZZZZZZZ!
2 Chainz
Ahhhh
Megan Thee Stallion
YEAAAAH! OKAAAAAAY! WHATTTT!
Lil Jon
SOSA!
Chief Keef
BURRRRR!
Gucci Mane
Some ad-libs become a rapper's ***signature*** on their records.
Record producers will also use a signature ad-lib on their beats to let the listener know they're the creator.
Rappers will use it to let you know to rep their record labels, too.
Another one! We da best!
DJ Khaled

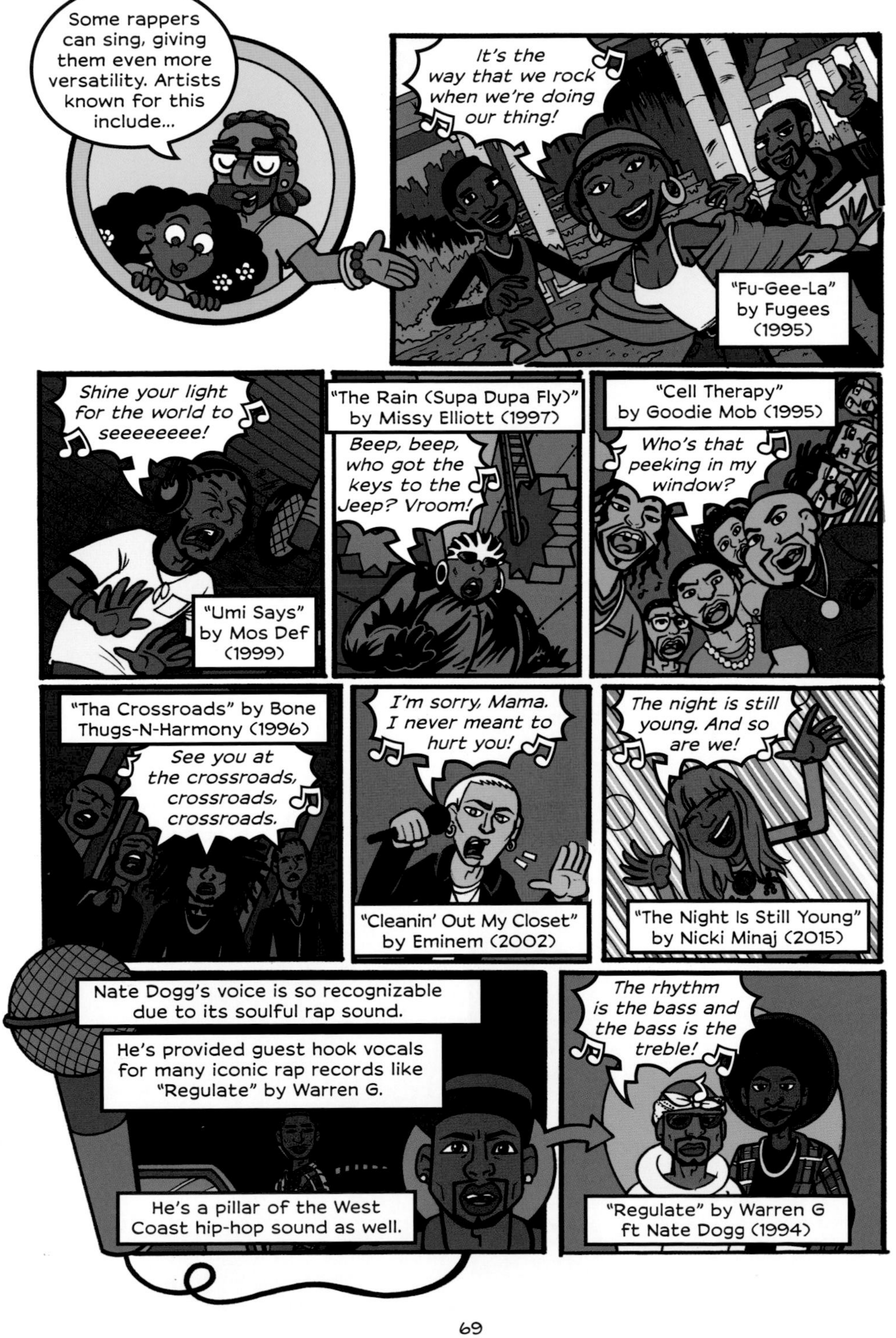
Some rappers can sing, giving them even more versatility. Artists known for this include...
It's the way that we rock when we're doing our thing!
"Fu-Gee-La" by Fugees (1995)
Shine your light for the world to seeeeeeee!
"Umi Says" by Mos Def (1999)
"The Rain (Supa Dupa Fly)" by Missy Elliott (1997)
Beep, beep, who got the keys to the Jeep? Vroom!
"Cell Therapy" by Goodie Mob (1995)
Who's that peeking in my window?
"Tha Crossroads" by Bone Thugs-N-Harmony (1996)
See you at the crossroads, crossroads, crossroads.
I'm sorry, Mama. I never meant to hurt you!
"Cleanin' Out My Closet" by Eminem (2002)
The night is still young. And so are we!
"The Night Is Still Young" by Nicki Minaj (2015)
Nate Dogg's voice is so recognizable due to its soulful rap sound.
He's provided guest hook vocals for many iconic rap records like "Regulate" by Warren G.
He's a pillar of the West Coast hip-hop sound as well.
The rhythm is the bass and the bass is the treble!
"Regulate" by Warren G ft Nate Dogg (1994)

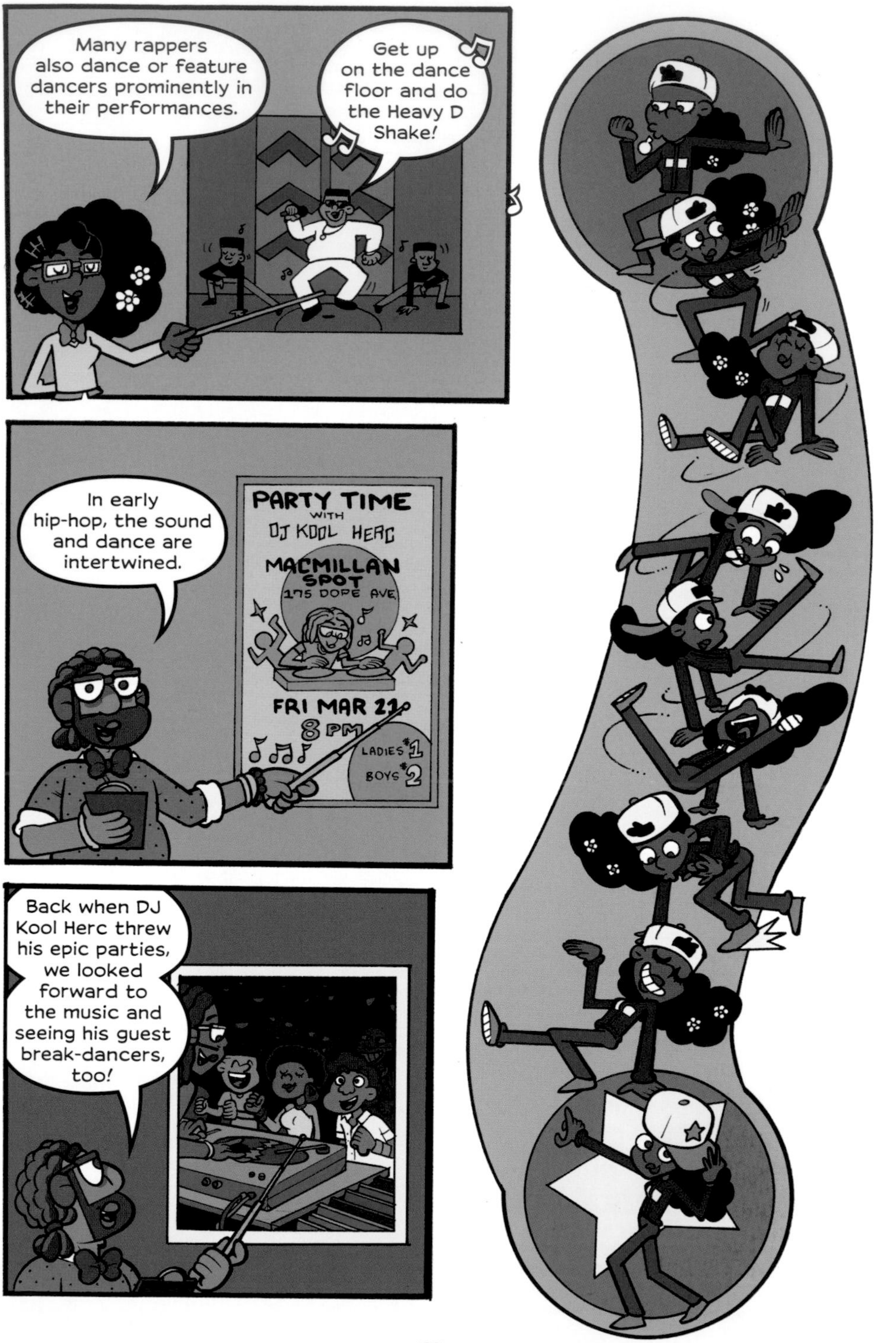

Many rappers also dance or feature dancers prominently in their performances.
Get up on the dance floor and do the Heavy D Shake!
In early hip-hop, the sound and dance are intertwined.
PARTY TIME WITH DJ KOOL HERC
MACMILLAN SPOT
175 DOPE AVE
FRI MAR 21
8 PM
LADIES $1
BOYS $2
Back when DJ Kool Herc threw his epic parties, we looked forward to the music and seeing his guest break-dancers, too!

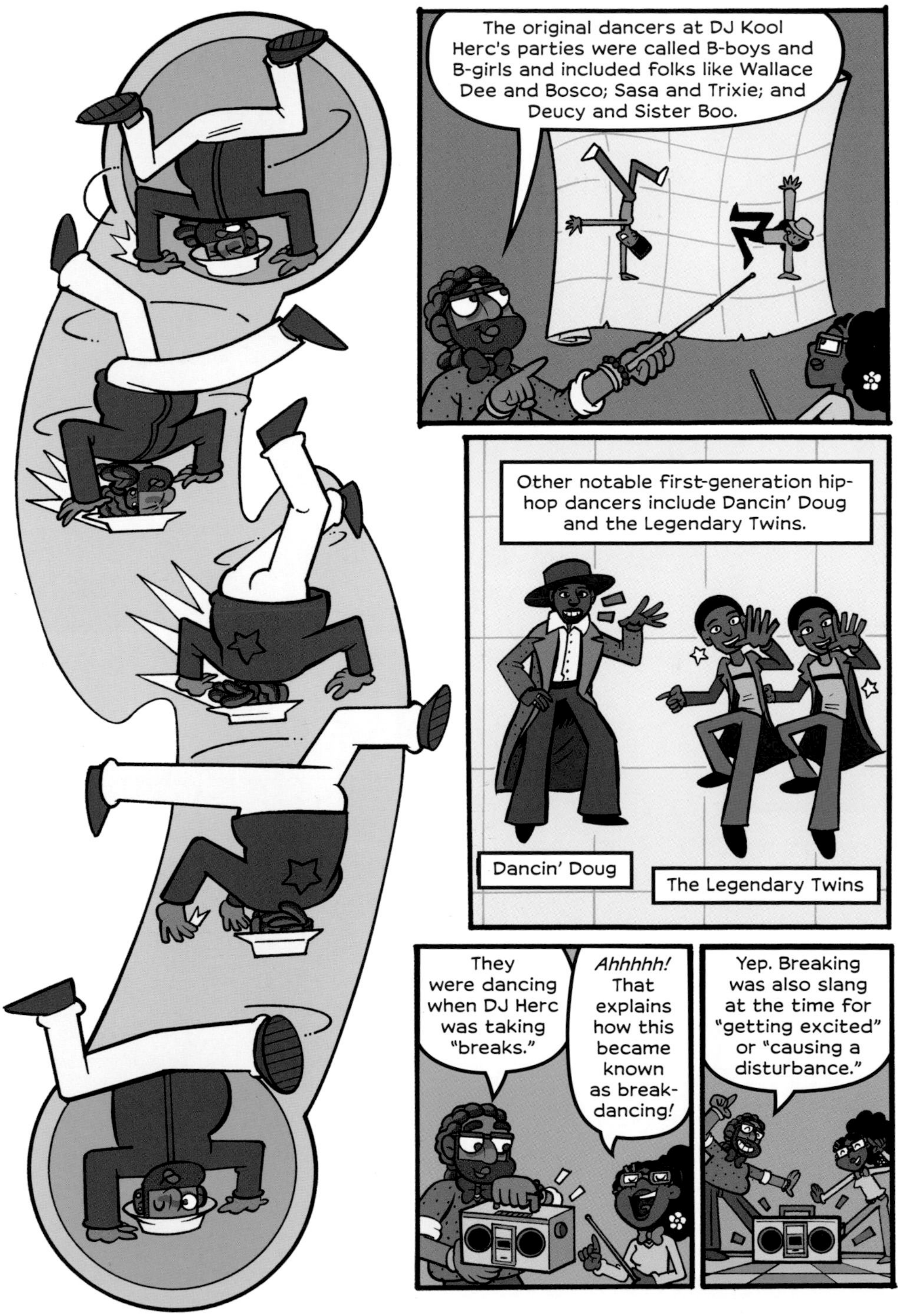

The original dancers at DJ Kool Herc's parties were called B-boys and B-girls and included folks like Wallace Dee and Bosco; Sasa and Trixie; and Deucy and Sister Boo.
Other notable first-generation hip-hop dancers include Dancin' Doug and the Legendary Twins.
Dancin' Doug
The Legendary Twins
They were dancing when DJ Herc was taking "breaks."
Ahhhhh! That explains how this became known as break-dancing!
Yep. Breaking was also slang at the time for "getting excited" or "causing a disturbance."

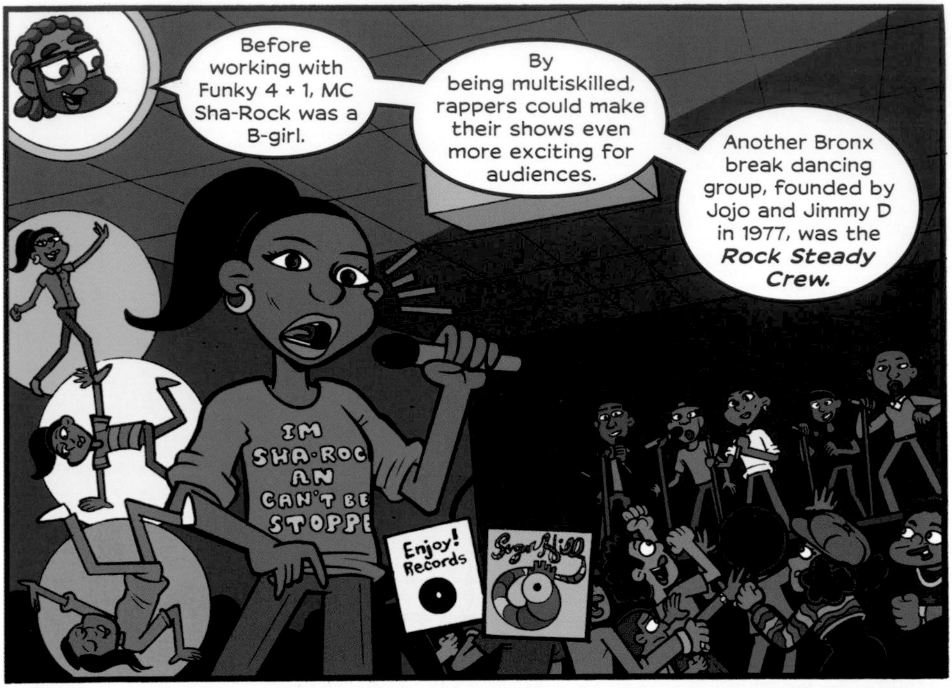
Before working with Funky 4 + 1, MC Sha-Rock was a B-girl.
By being multiskilled, rappers could make their shows even more exciting for audiences.
Another Bronx break dancing group, founded by Jojo and Jimmy D in 1977, was the ***Rock Steady Crew.***
IM SHA-ROC AN CAN'T BE STOPPE
Enjoy! Records

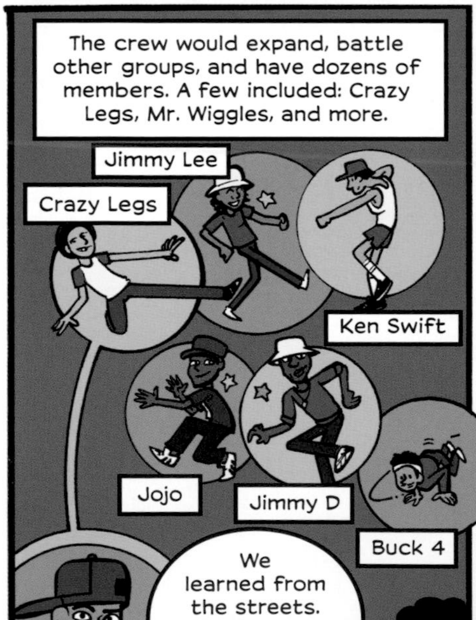
The crew would expand, battle other groups, and have dozens of members. A few included: Crazy Legs, Mr. Wiggles, and more.
Jimmy Lee
Crazy Legs
Ken Swift
Jojo
Jimmy D
Buck 4
We learned from the streets. And the streets learned from us.
PUERTO RICO

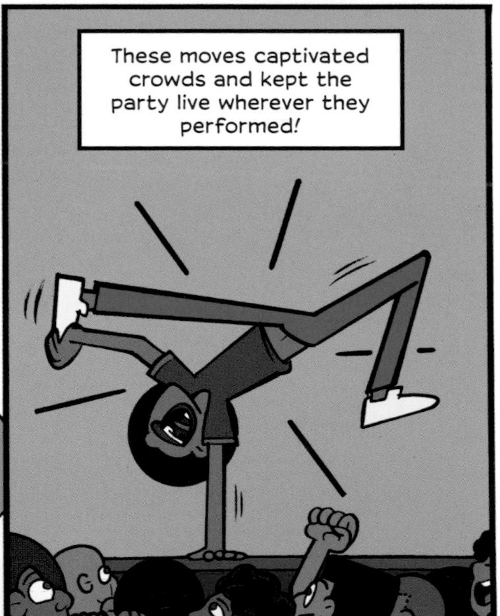
These moves captivated crowds and kept the party live wherever they performed!

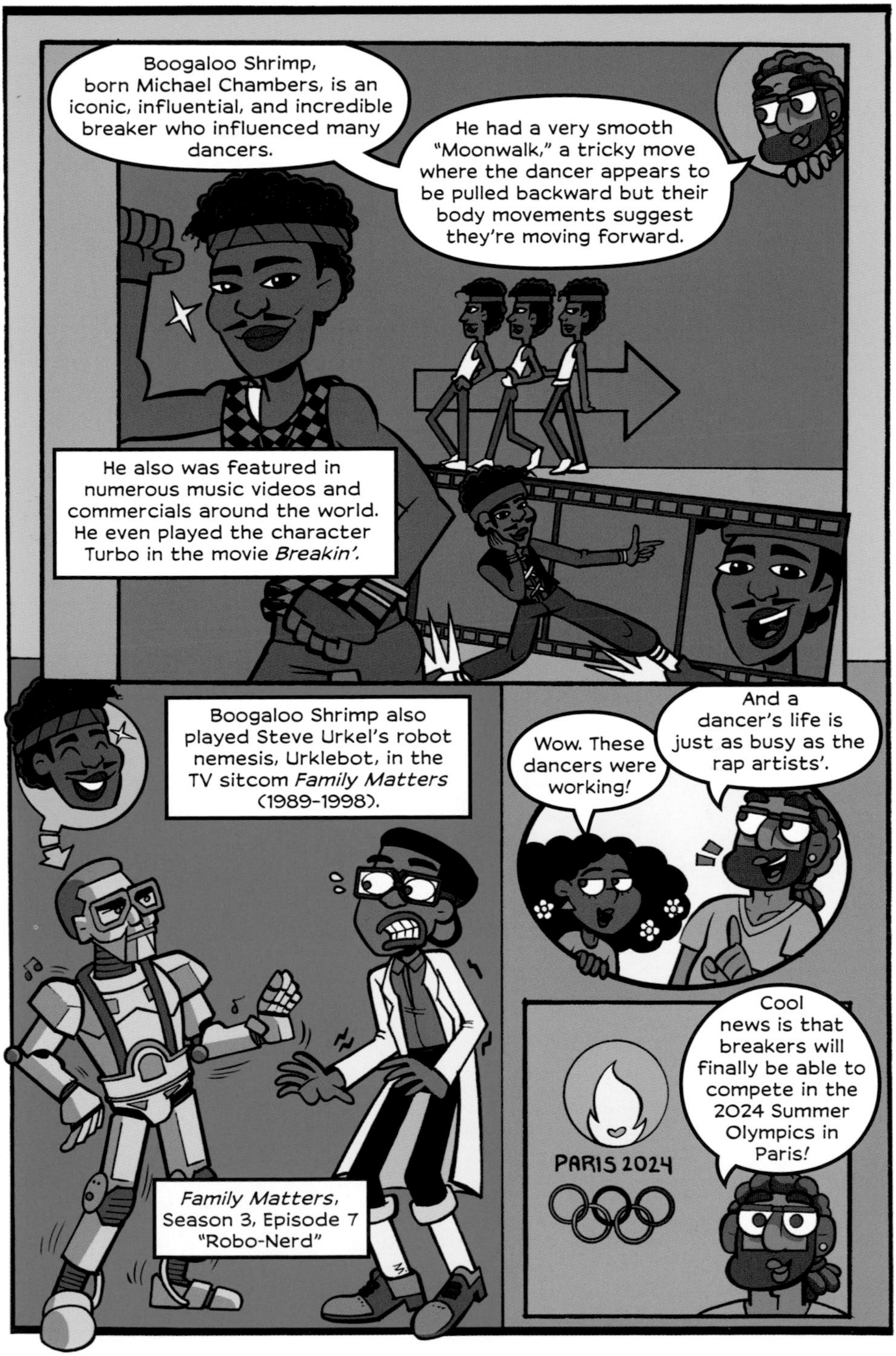
Boogaloo Shrimp, born Michael Chambers, is an iconic, influential, and incredible breaker who influenced many dancers.
He had a very smooth "Moonwalk," a tricky move where the dancer appears to be pulled backward but their body movements suggest they're moving forward.
He also was featured in numerous music videos and commercials around the world. He even played the character Turbo in the movie *Breakin'.*
Boogaloo Shrimp also played Steve Urkel's robot nemesis, Urklebot, in the TV sitcom *Family Matters* (1989–1998).
Family Matters, Season 3, Episode 7 "Robo-Nerd"
Wow. These dancers were *working!*
And a dancer's life is just as busy as the rap artists'.
PARIS 2024
Cool news is that breakers will finally be able to compete in the 2024 Summer Olympics in Paris!

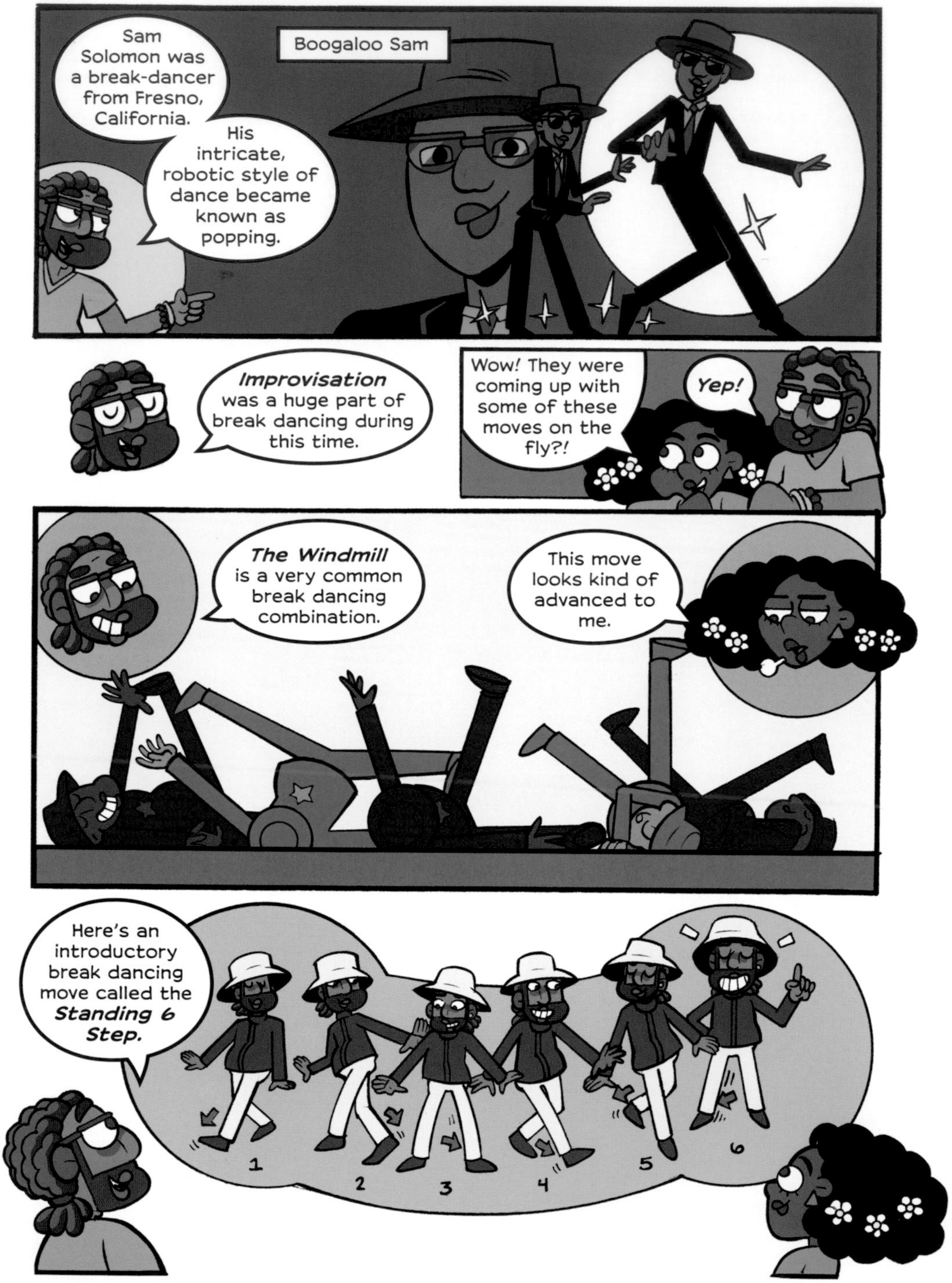
Sam Solomon was a break-dancer from Fresno, California.
Boogaloo Sam
His intricate, robotic style of dance became known as popping.
Improvisation was a huge part of break dancing during this time.
Wow! They were coming up with some of these moves on the fly?!
Yep!
The Windmill is a very common break dancing combination.
This move looks kind of advanced to me.
Here's an introductory break dancing move called the ***Standing 6 Step.***
1
2
3
4
5
6

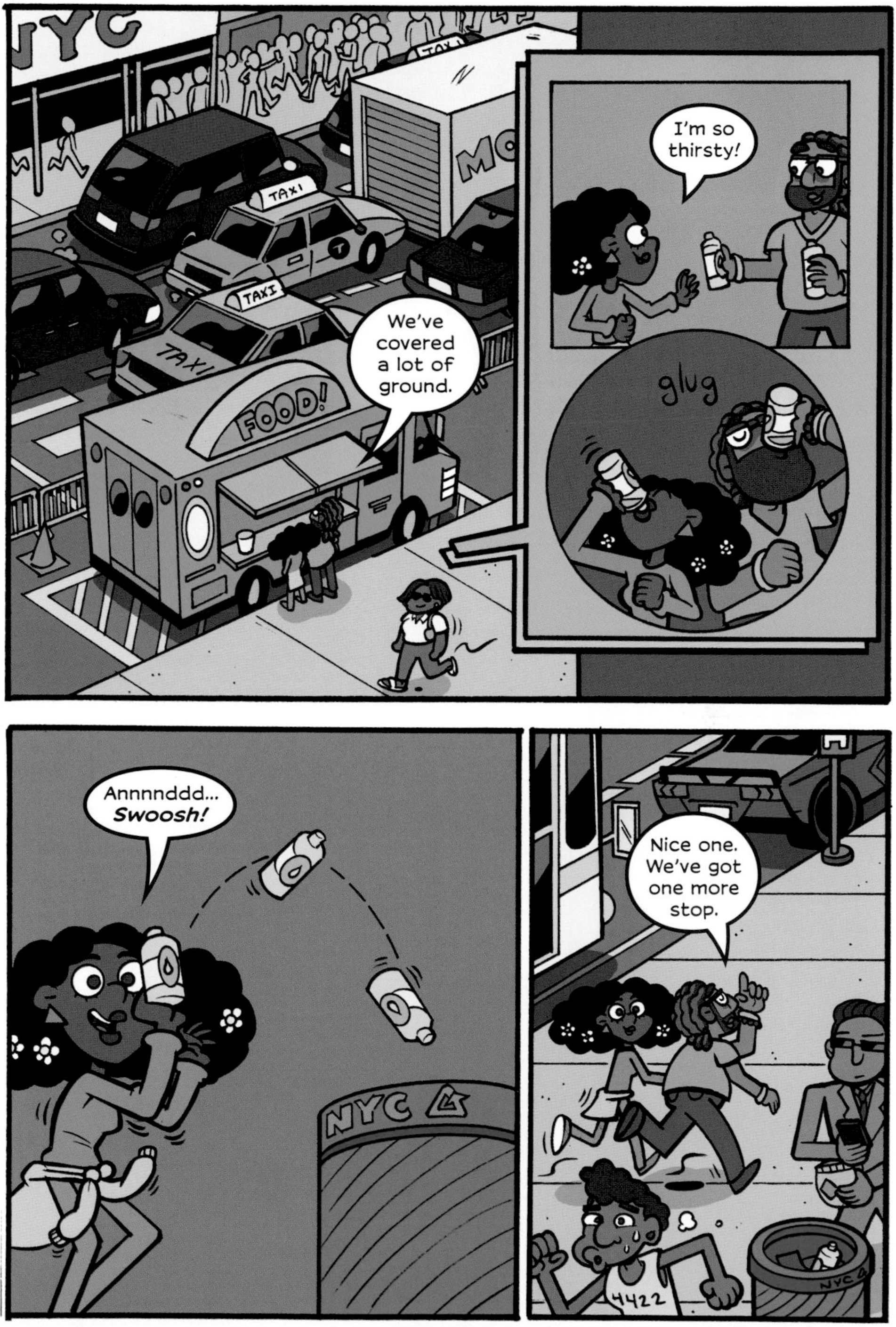
NYC
TAXI
MO
We've covered a lot of ground.
FOOD!
I'm so thirsty!
glug
Annnnddd... *Swoosh!*
NYC
Nice one. We've got one more stop.
4422
NYC

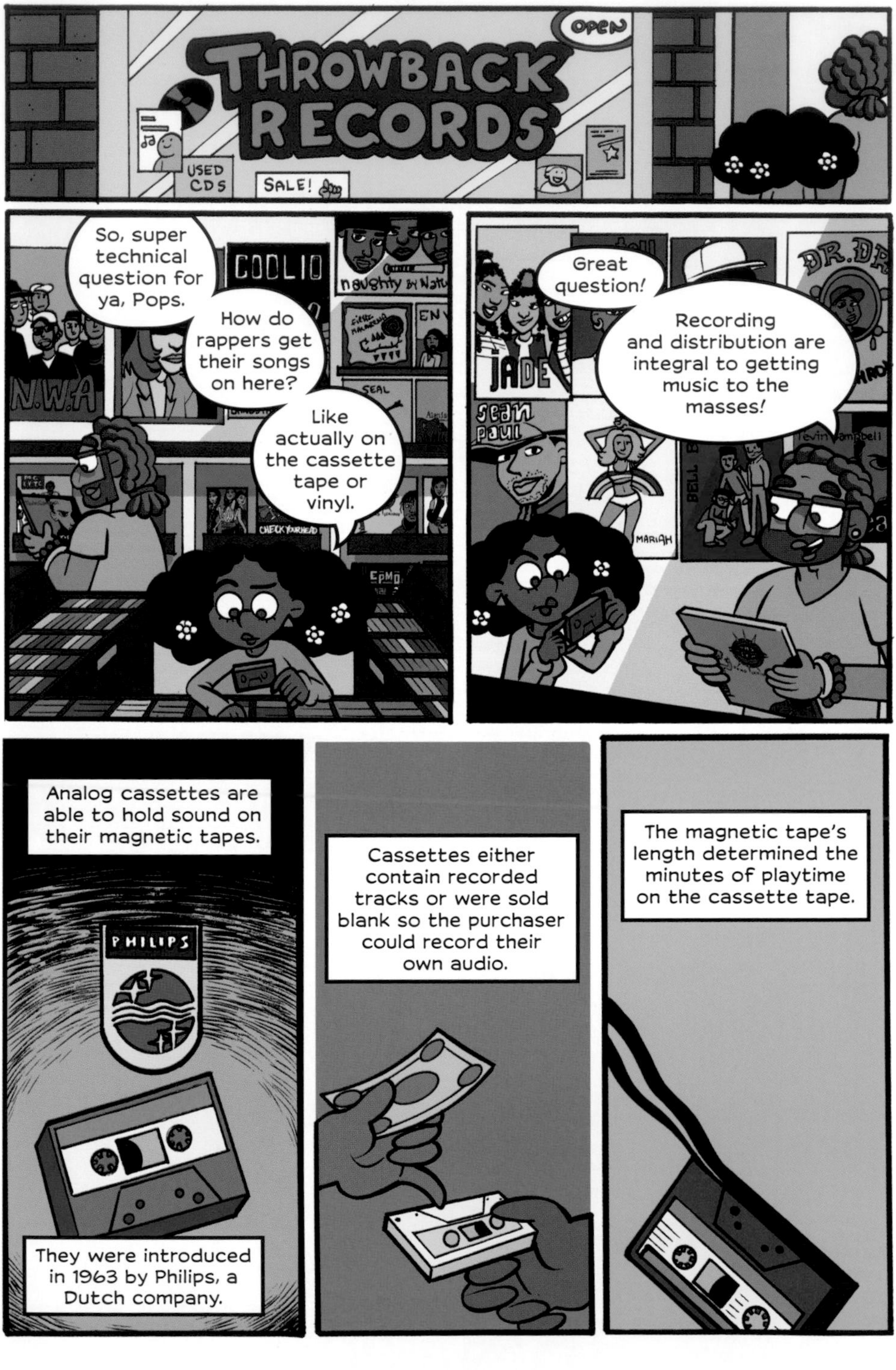
OPEN
THROWBACK RECORDS
USED CDS
SALE!
COOLIO
N.W.A
naughty by Nature
SEAL
CHECK YOUR HEAD
EPMD
So, super technical question for ya, Pops.
How do rappers get their songs on here?
Like actually on the cassette tape or vinyl.
JADE
Sean Paul
MARIAH
DR. DRE
Tevin Campbell
Great question!
Recording and distribution are integral to getting music to the masses!
Analog cassettes are able to hold sound on their magnetic tapes.
PHILIPS
They were introduced in 1963 by Philips, a Dutch company.
Cassettes either contain recorded tracks or were sold blank so the purchaser could record their own audio.
The magnetic tape's length determined the minutes of playtime on the cassette tape.

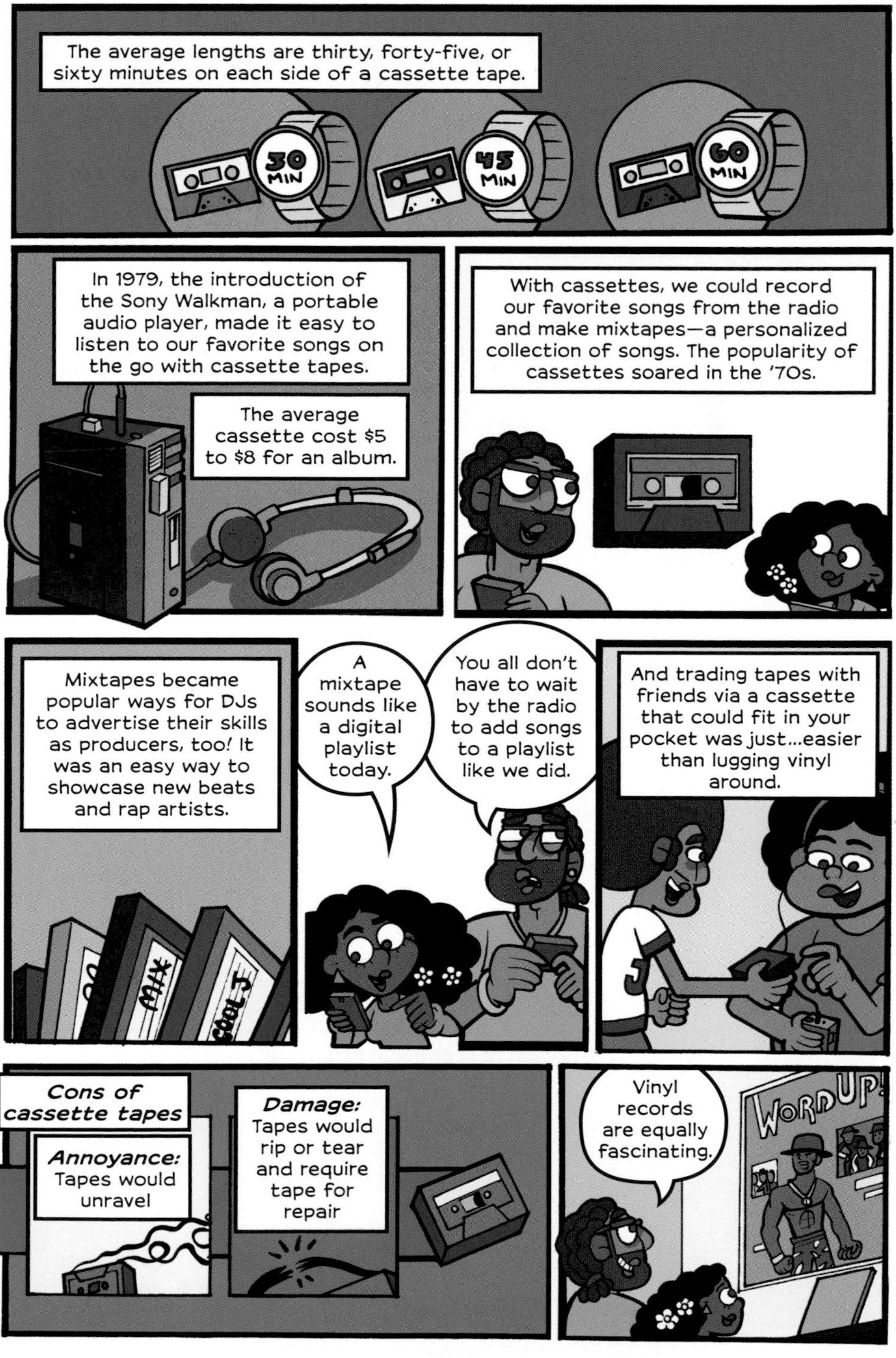
The average lengths are thirty, forty-five, or sixty minutes on each side of a cassette tape.
30 MIN
45 MIN
60 MIN
In 1979, the introduction of the Sony Walkman, a portable audio player, made it easy to listen to our favorite songs on the go with cassette tapes.
The average cassette cost $5 to $8 for an album.
With cassettes, we could record our favorite songs from the radio and make mixtapes—a personalized collection of songs. The popularity of cassettes soared in the '70s.
Mixtapes became popular ways for DJs to advertise their skills as producers, too! It was an easy way to showcase new beats and rap artists.
MIX
COOL J
A mixtape sounds like a digital playlist today.
You all don't have to wait by the radio to add songs to a playlist like we did.
And trading tapes with friends via a cassette that could fit in your pocket was just...easier than lugging vinyl around.
Cons of cassette tapes
Annoyance: Tapes would unravel
Damage: Tapes would rip or tear and require tape for repair
Vinyl records are equally fascinating.
WORD UP!

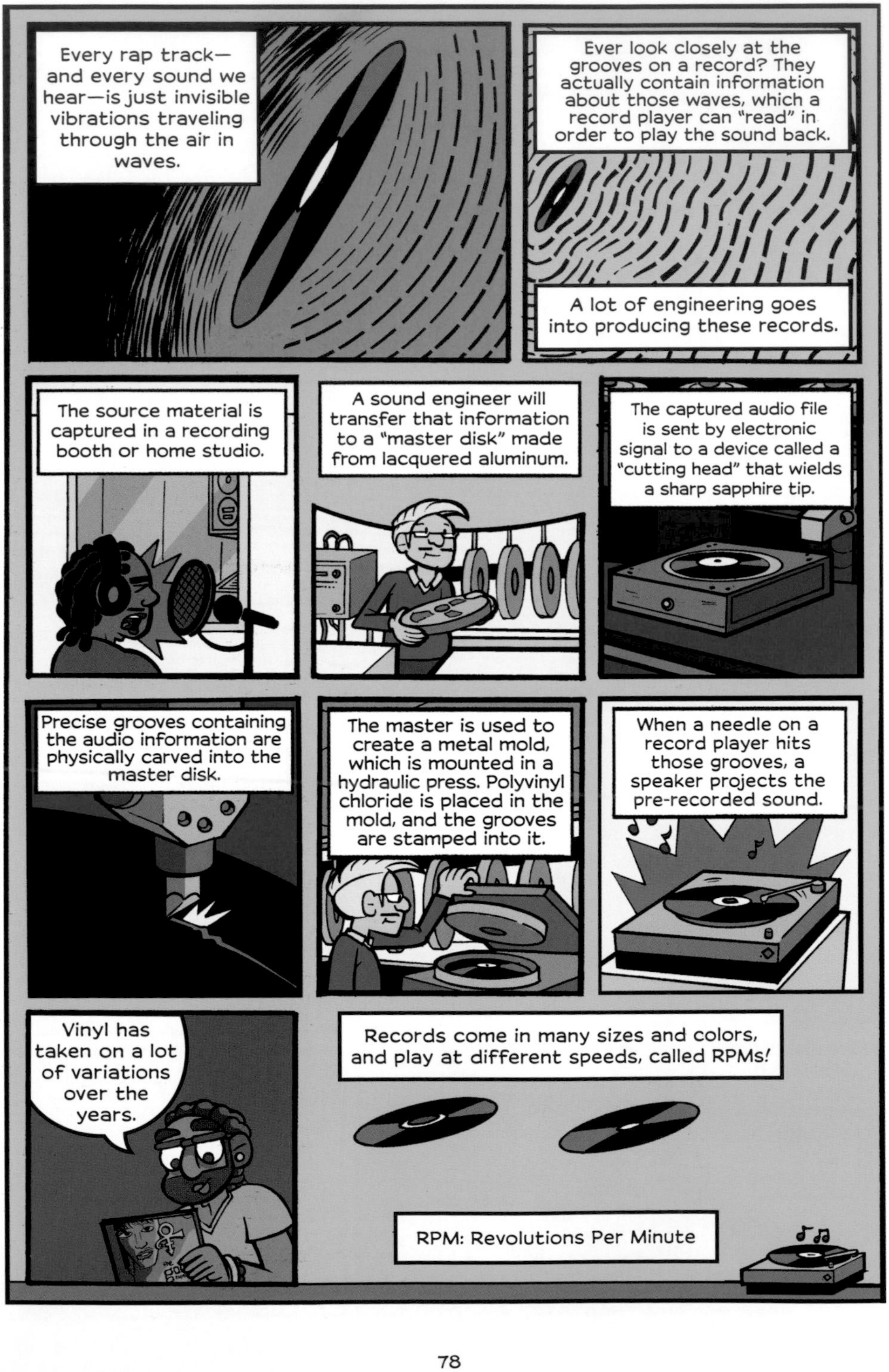

Every rap track—and every sound we hear—is just invisible vibrations traveling through the air in waves.
Ever look closely at the grooves on a record? They actually contain information about those waves, which a record player can "read" in order to play the sound back.
A lot of engineering goes into producing these records.
The source material is captured in a recording booth or home studio.
A sound engineer will transfer that information to a "master disk" made from lacquered aluminum.
The captured audio file is sent by electronic signal to a device called a "cutting head" that wields a sharp sapphire tip.
Precise grooves containing the audio information are physically carved into the master disk.
The master is used to create a metal mold, which is mounted in a hydraulic press. Polyvinyl chloride is placed in the mold, and the grooves are stamped into it.
When a needle on a record player hits those grooves, a speaker projects the pre-recorded sound.
Vinyl has taken on a lot of variations over the years.
Records come in many sizes and colors, and play at different speeds, called RPMs!
RPM: Revolutions Per Minute

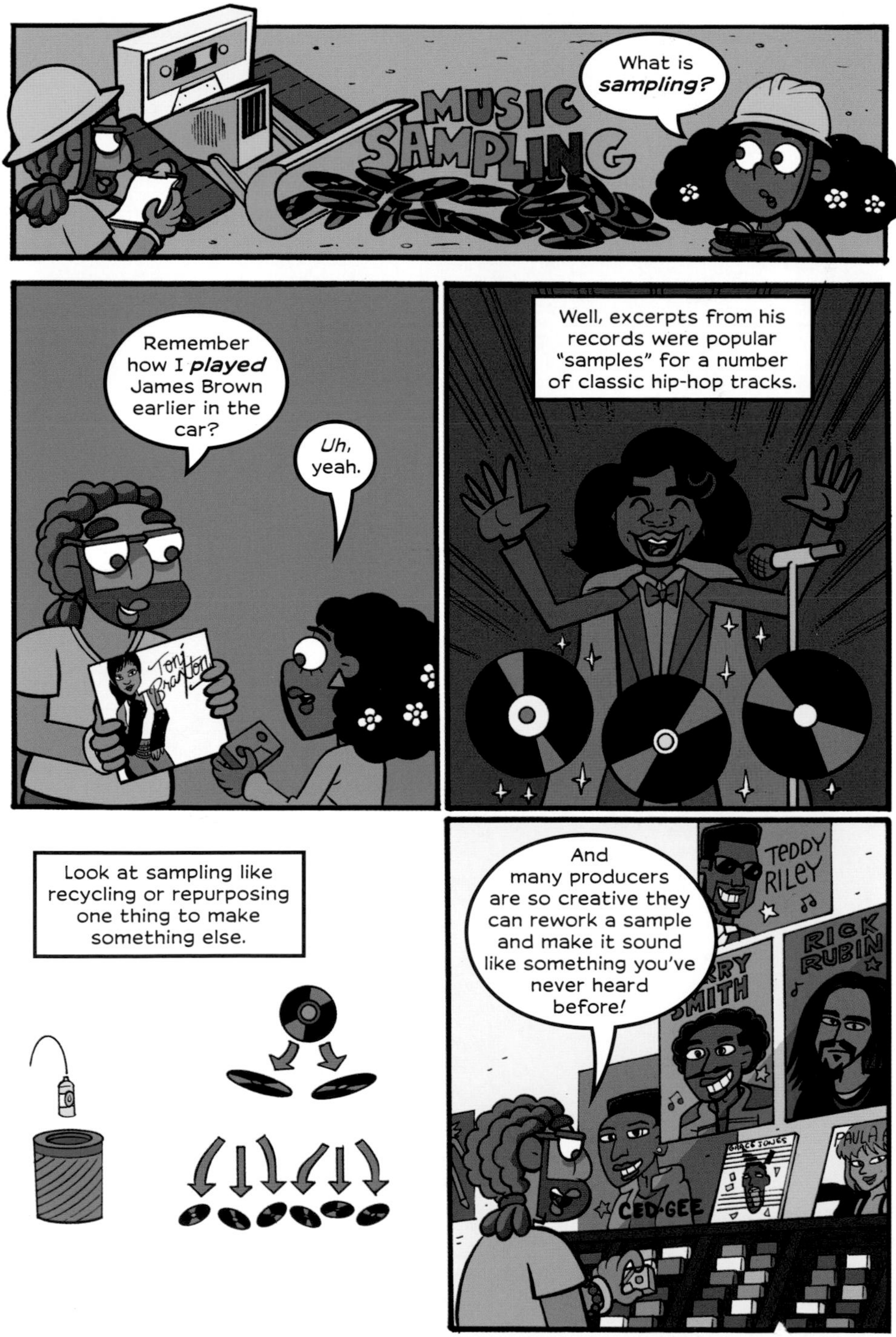
MUSIC SAMPLING
What is *sampling?*
Remember how I *played* James Brown earlier in the car?
Uh, yeah.
Toni Braxton
Well, excerpts from his records were popular "samples" for a number of classic hip-hop tracks.
Look at sampling like recycling or repurposing one thing to make something else.
And many producers are so creative they can rework a sample and make it sound like something you've never heard before!
TEDDY RILEY
RICK RUBIN
CED-GEE

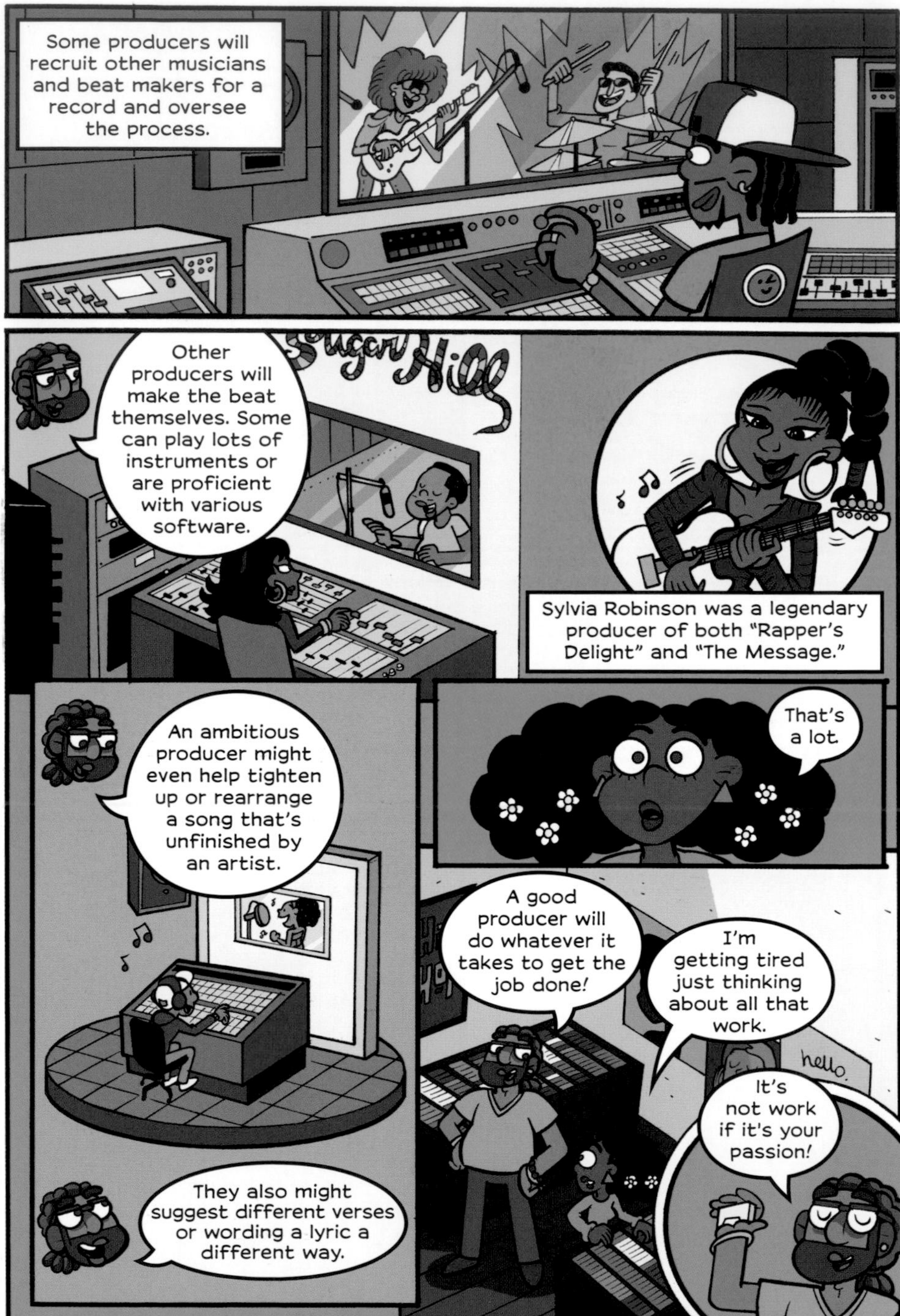
Some producers will recruit other musicians and beat makers for a record and oversee the process.
Other producers will make the beat themselves. Some can play lots of instruments or are proficient with various software.
Sugar Hill
Sylvia Robinson was a legendary producer of both "Rapper's Delight" and "The Message."
An ambitious producer might even help tighten up or rearrange a song that's unfinished by an artist.
They also might suggest different verses or wording a lyric a different way.
That's a lot.
A good producer will do whatever it takes to get the job done!
I'm getting tired just thinking about all that work.
hello.
It's not work if it's your passion!

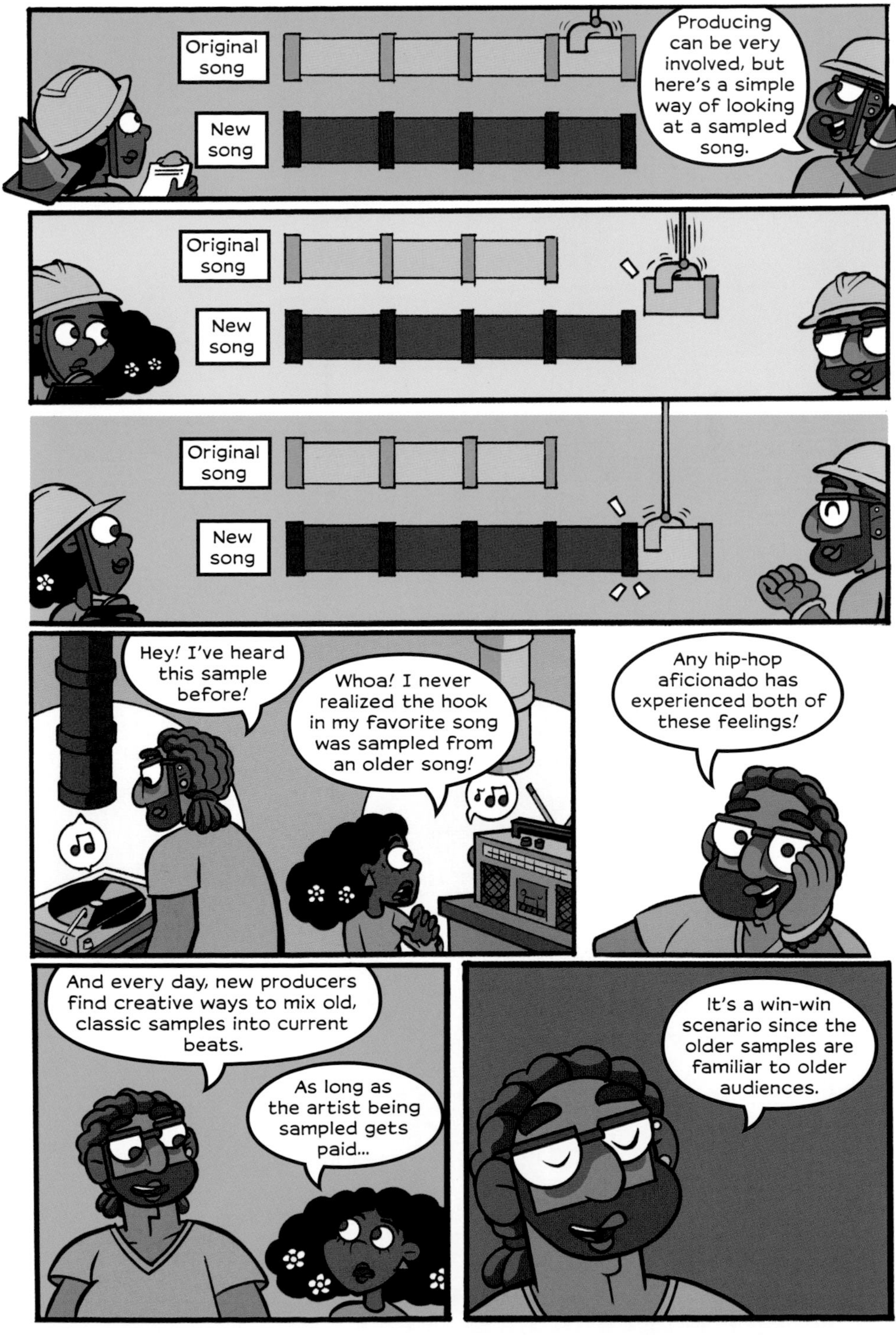
Original song
New song
Producing can be very involved, but here's a simple way of looking at a sampled song.
Original song
New song
Original song
New song
Hey! I've heard this sample before!
Whoa! I never realized the hook in my favorite song was sampled from an older song!
Any hip-hop aficionado has experienced both of these feelings!
And every day, new producers find creative ways to mix old, classic samples into current beats.
As long as the artist being sampled gets paid...
It's a win-win scenario since the older samples are familiar to older audiences.

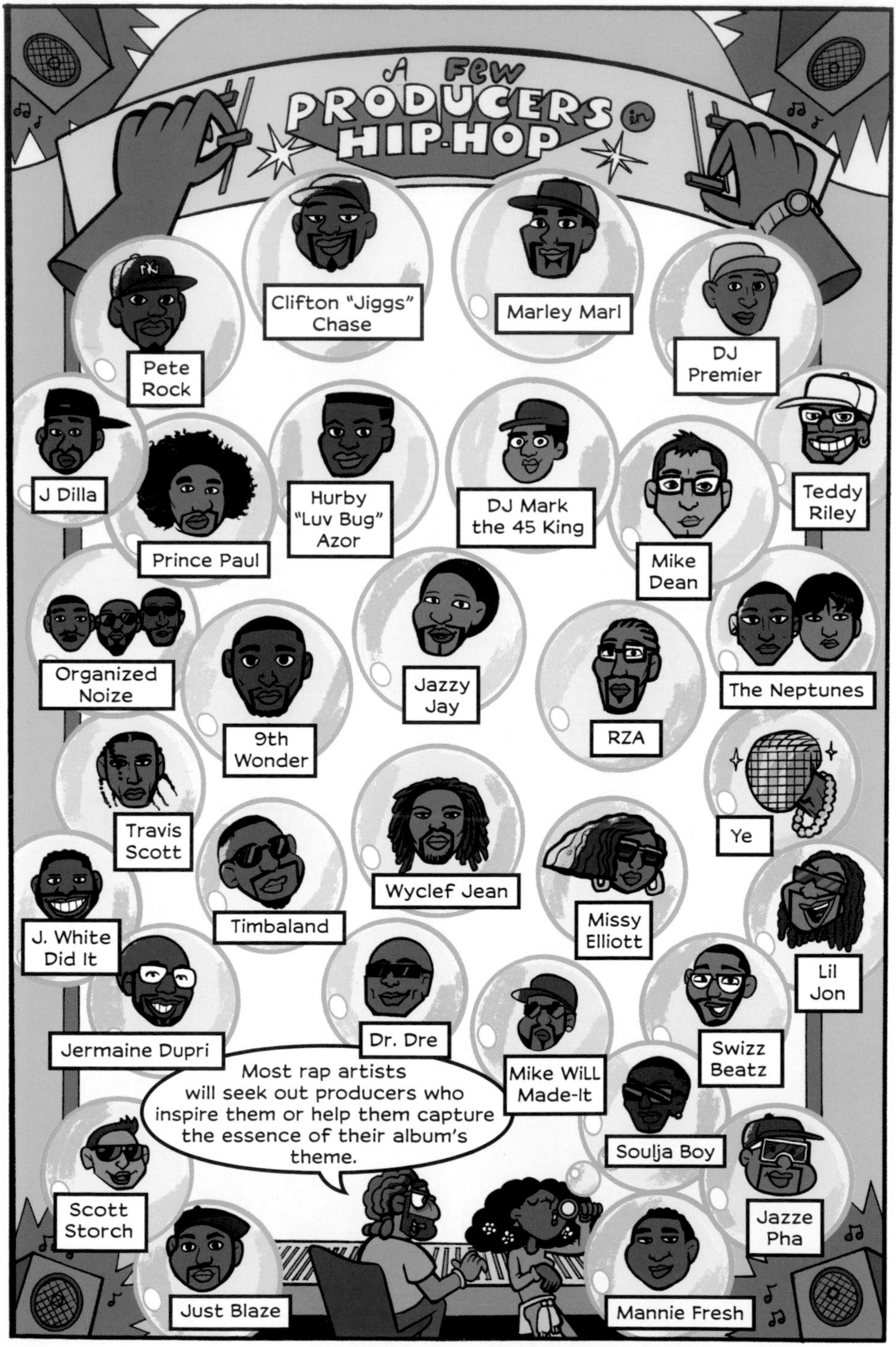
A Few PRODUCERS in HIP-HOP
Clifton "Jiggs" Chase
Marley Marl
Pete Rock
DJ Premier
J Dilla
Teddy Riley
Hurby "Luv Bug" Azor
DJ Mark the 45 King
Prince Paul
Mike Dean
Organized Noize
Jazzy Jay
The Neptunes
9th Wonder
RZA
Travis Scott
Ye
Wyclef Jean
Timbaland
Missy Elliott
J. White Did It
Lil Jon
Jermaine Dupri
Dr. Dre
Swizz Beatz
Mike WiLL Made-It
Most rap artists will seek out producers who inspire them or help them capture the essence of their album's theme.
Soulja Boy
Scott Storch
Jazze Pha
Just Blaze
Mannie Fresh

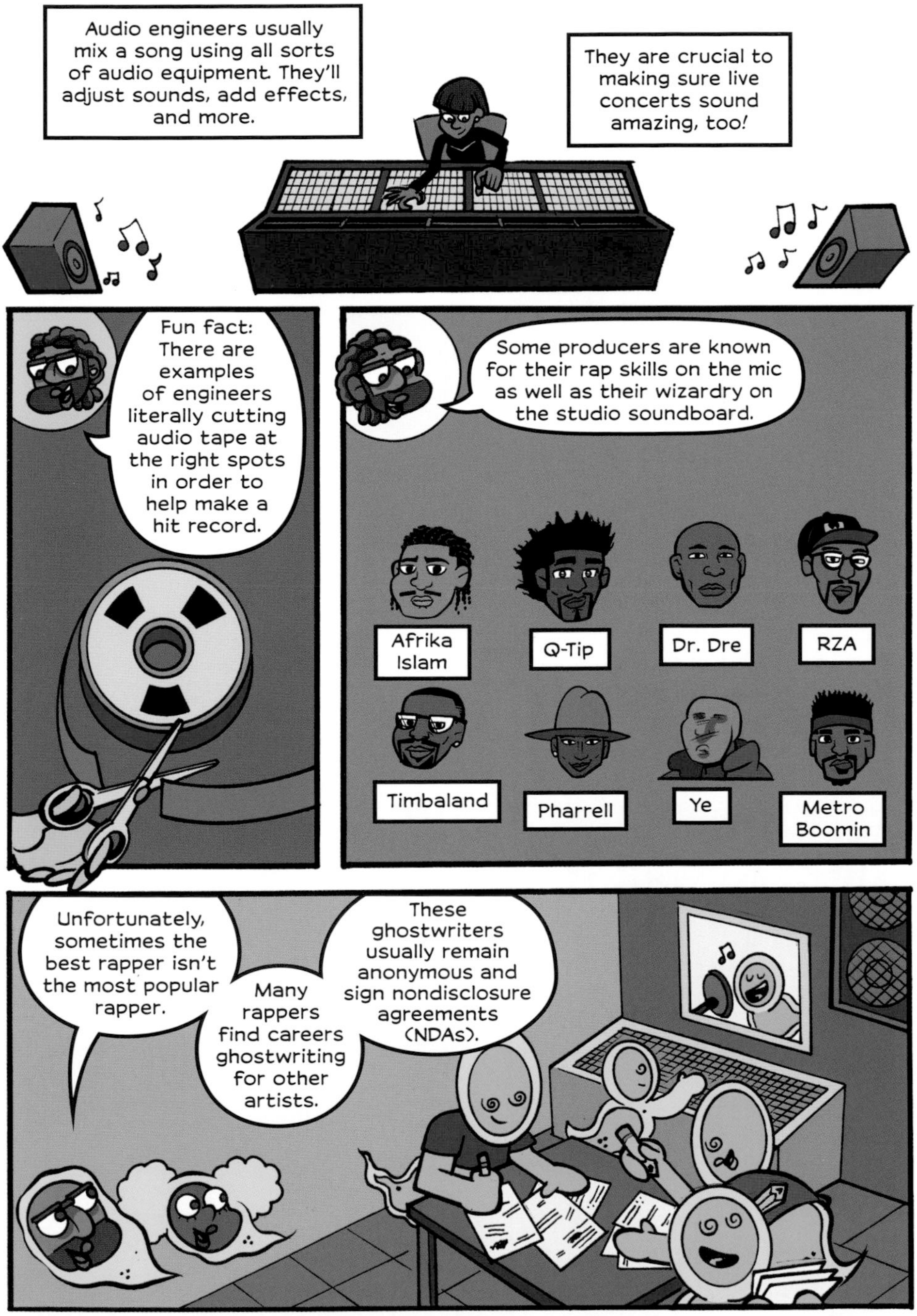
Audio engineers usually mix a song using all sorts of audio equipment. They'll adjust sounds, add effects, and more.
They are crucial to making sure live concerts sound amazing, too!
Fun fact: There are examples of engineers literally cutting audio tape at the right spots in order to help make a hit record.
Some producers are known for their rap skills on the mic as well as their wizardry on the studio soundboard.
Afrika Islam
Q-Tip
Dr. Dre
RZA
Timbaland
Pharrell
Ye
Metro Boomin
Unfortunately, sometimes the best rapper isn't the most popular rapper.
Many rappers find careers ghostwriting for other artists.
These ghostwriters usually remain anonymous and sign nondisclosure agreements (NDAs).

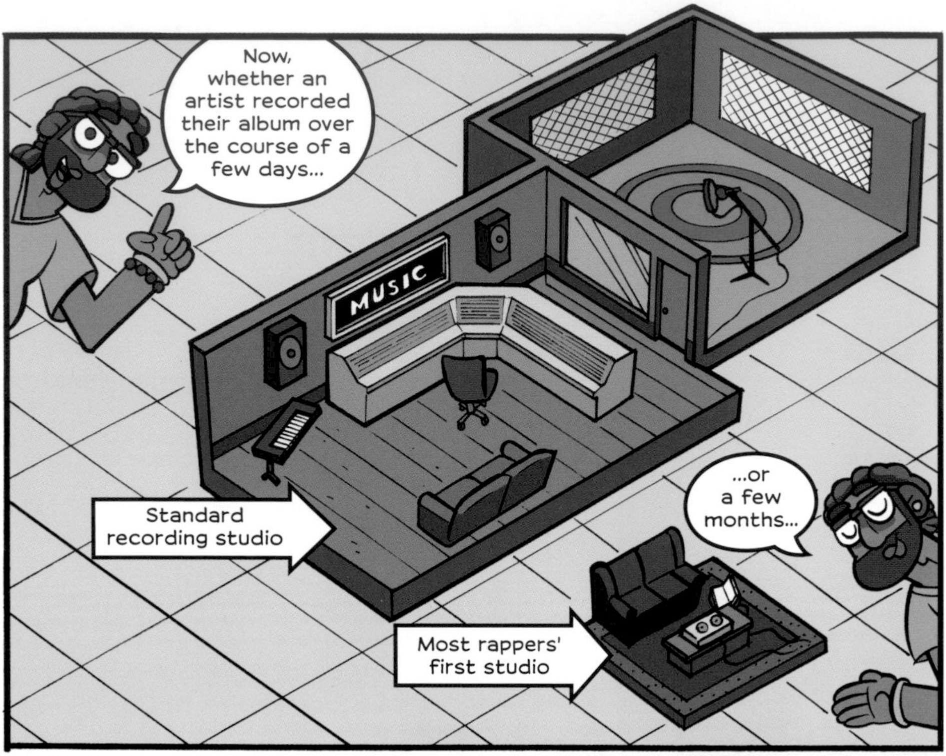
Now, whether an artist recorded their album over the course of a few days...
MUSIC
Standard recording studio
...or a few months...
Most rappers' first studio

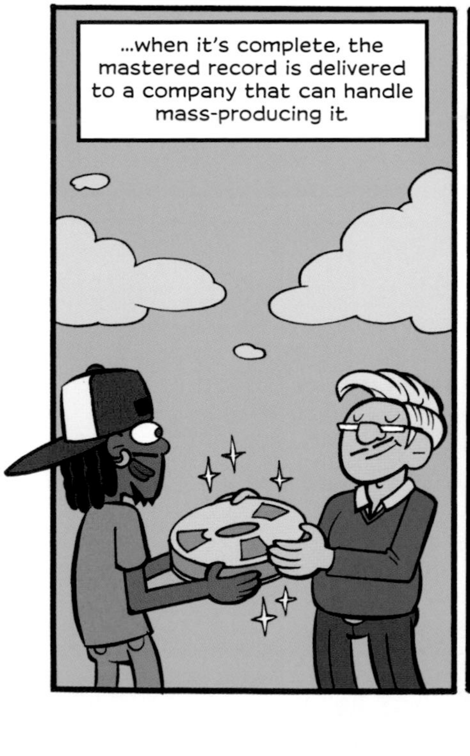
...when it's complete, the mastered record is delivered to a company that can handle mass-producing it.

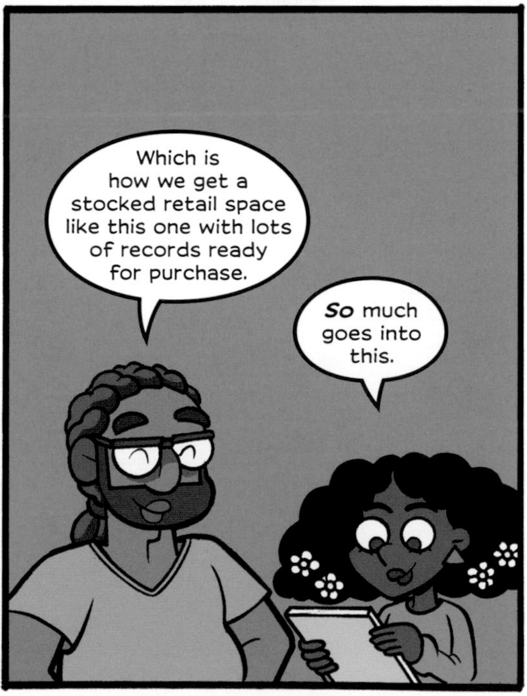
Which is how we get a stocked retail space like this one with lots of records ready for purchase.
So much goes into this.

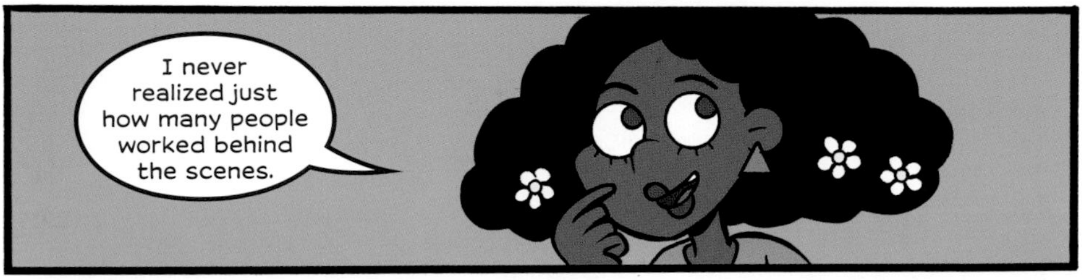
I never realized just how many people worked behind the scenes.

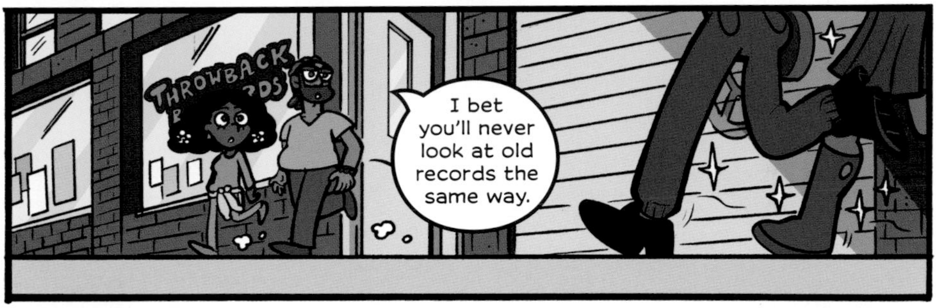
THROWBACK
I bet you'll never look at old records the same way.

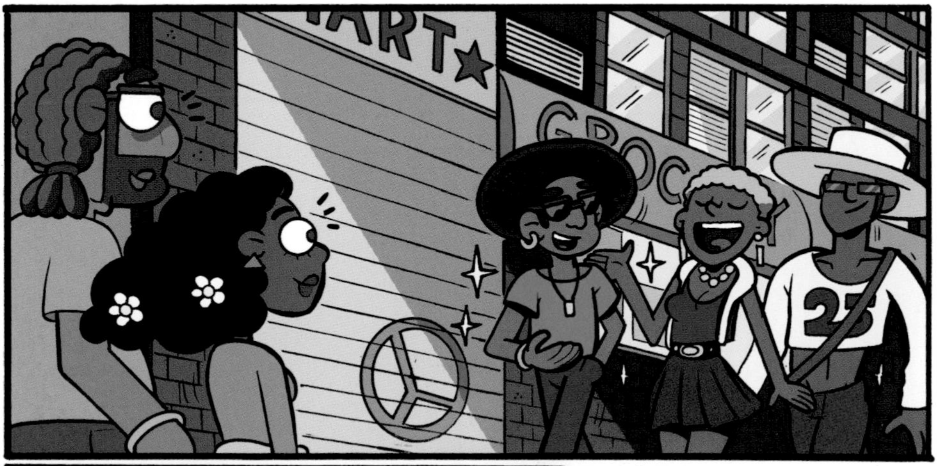
ART
GROC

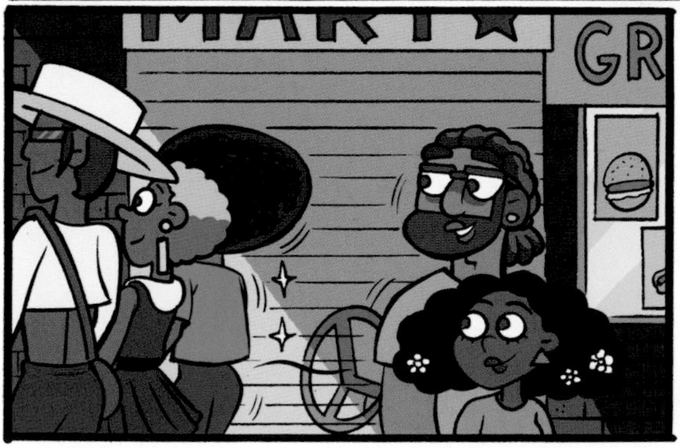
MART
GR

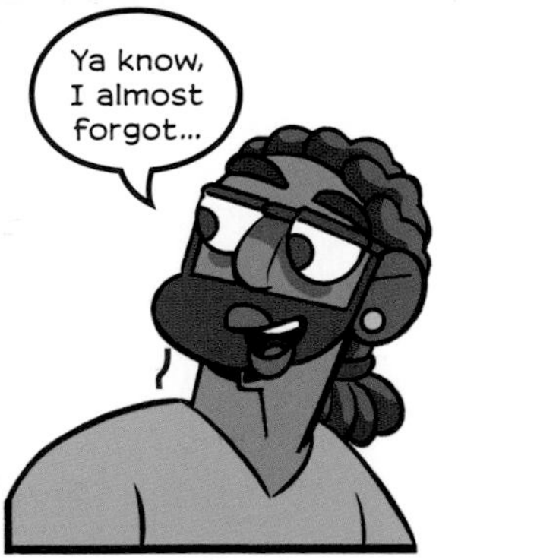
Ya know, I almost forgot...

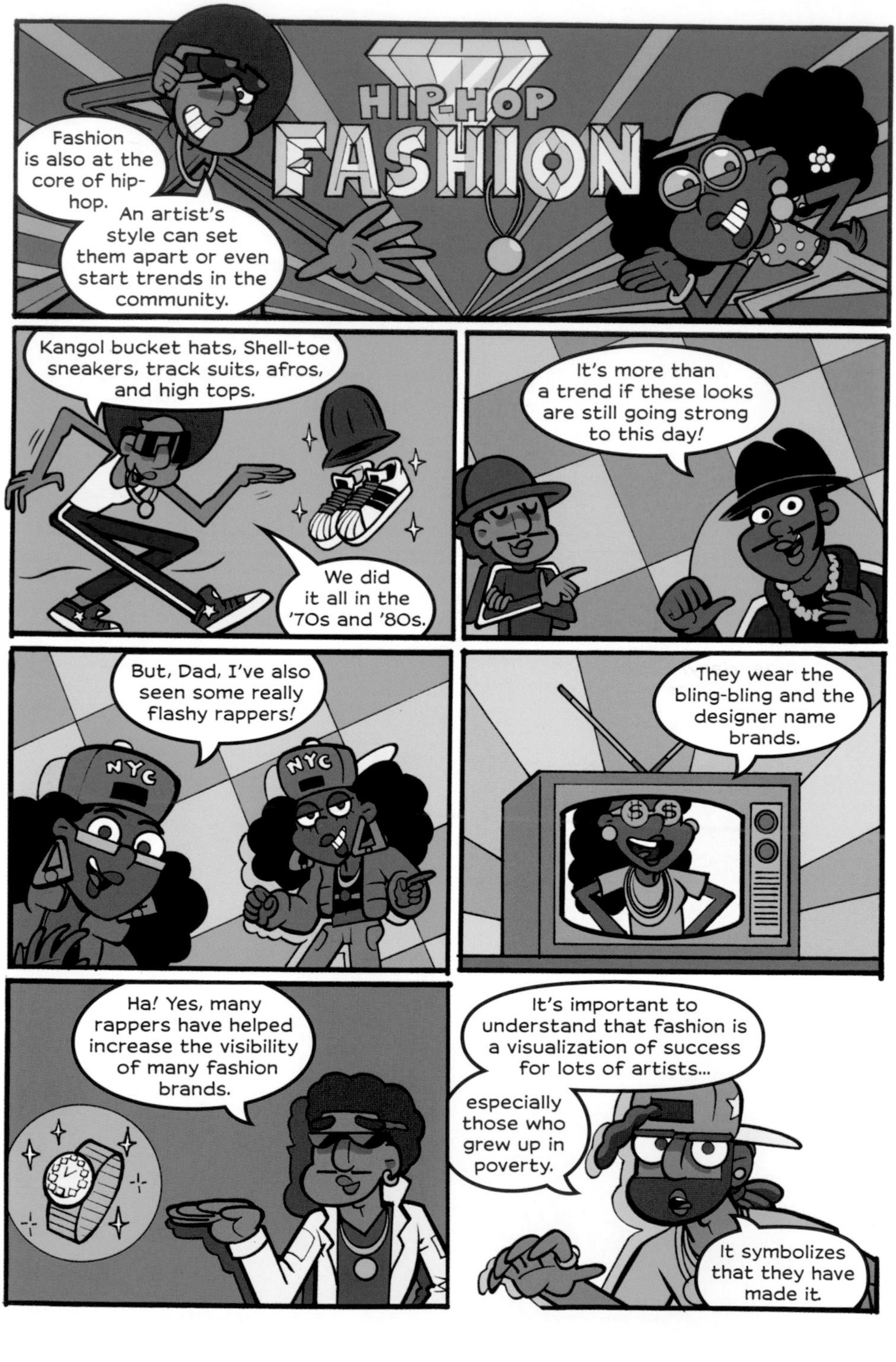
HIP-HOP FASHION
Fashion is also at the core of hip-hop.
An artist's style can set them apart or even start trends in the community.
Kangol bucket hats, Shell-toe sneakers, track suits, afros, and high tops.
We did it all in the '70s and '80s.
It's more than a trend if these looks are still going strong to this day!
But, Dad, I've also seen some really flashy rappers!
NYC
NYC
They wear the bling-bling and the designer name brands.
Ha! Yes, many rappers have helped increase the visibility of many fashion brands.
It's important to understand that fashion is a visualization of success for lots of artists...
especially those who grew up in poverty.
It symbolizes that they have made it.

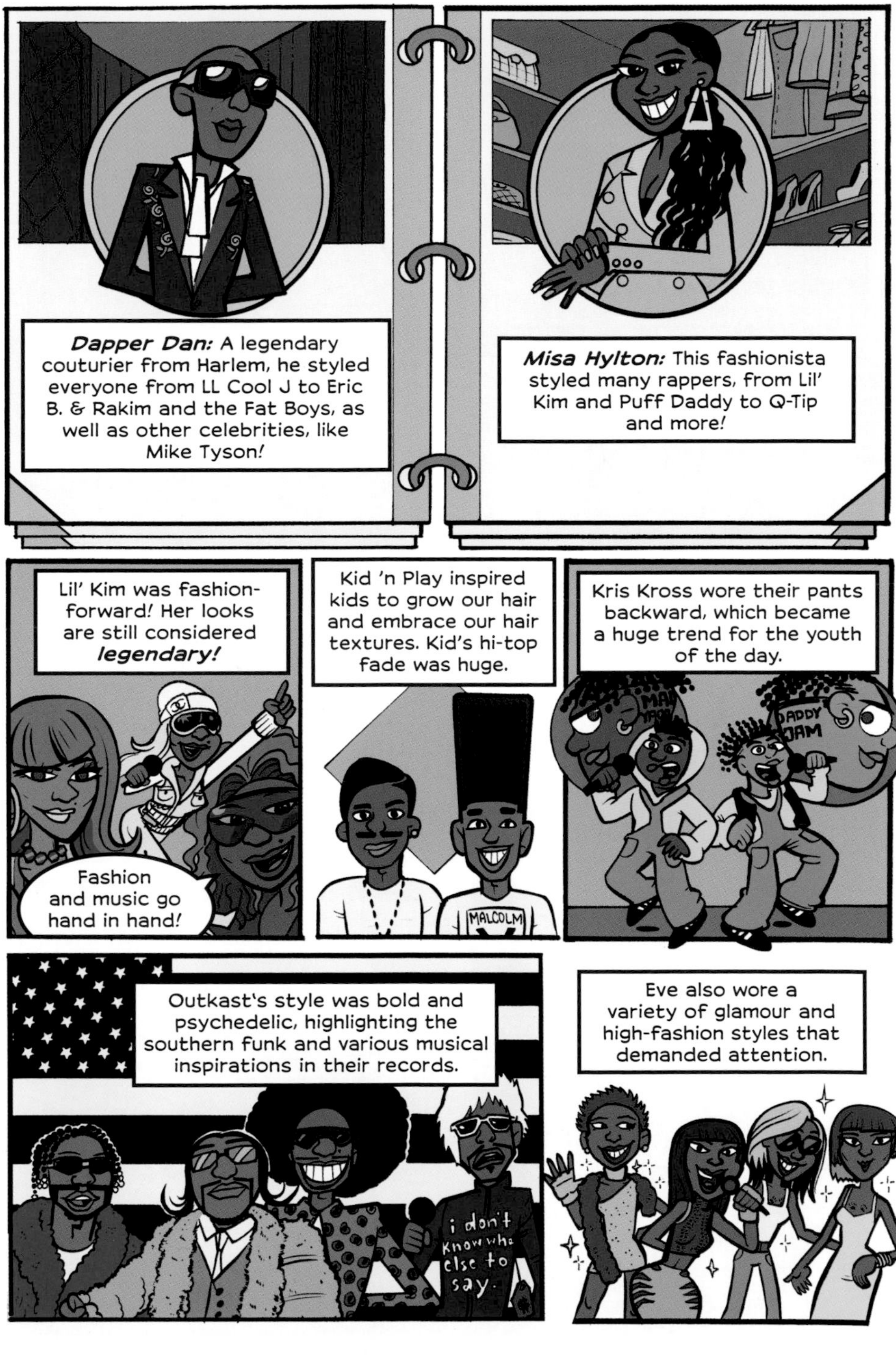

Dapper Dan: A legendary couturier from Harlem, he styled everyone from LL Cool J to Eric B. & Rakim and the Fat Boys, as well as other celebrities, like Mike Tyson!
Misa Hylton: This fashionista styled many rappers, from Lil' Kim and Puff Daddy to Q-Tip and more!
Lil' Kim was fashion-forward! Her looks are still considered *legendary!*
Fashion and music go hand in hand!
Kid 'n Play inspired kids to grow our hair and embrace our hair textures. Kid's hi-top fade was huge.
MALCOLM
Kris Kross wore their pants backward, which became a huge trend for the youth of the day.
Outkast's style was bold and psychedelic, highlighting the southern funk and various musical inspirations in their records.
i don't Know wha else to say.
Eve also wore a variety of glamour and high-fashion styles that demanded attention.

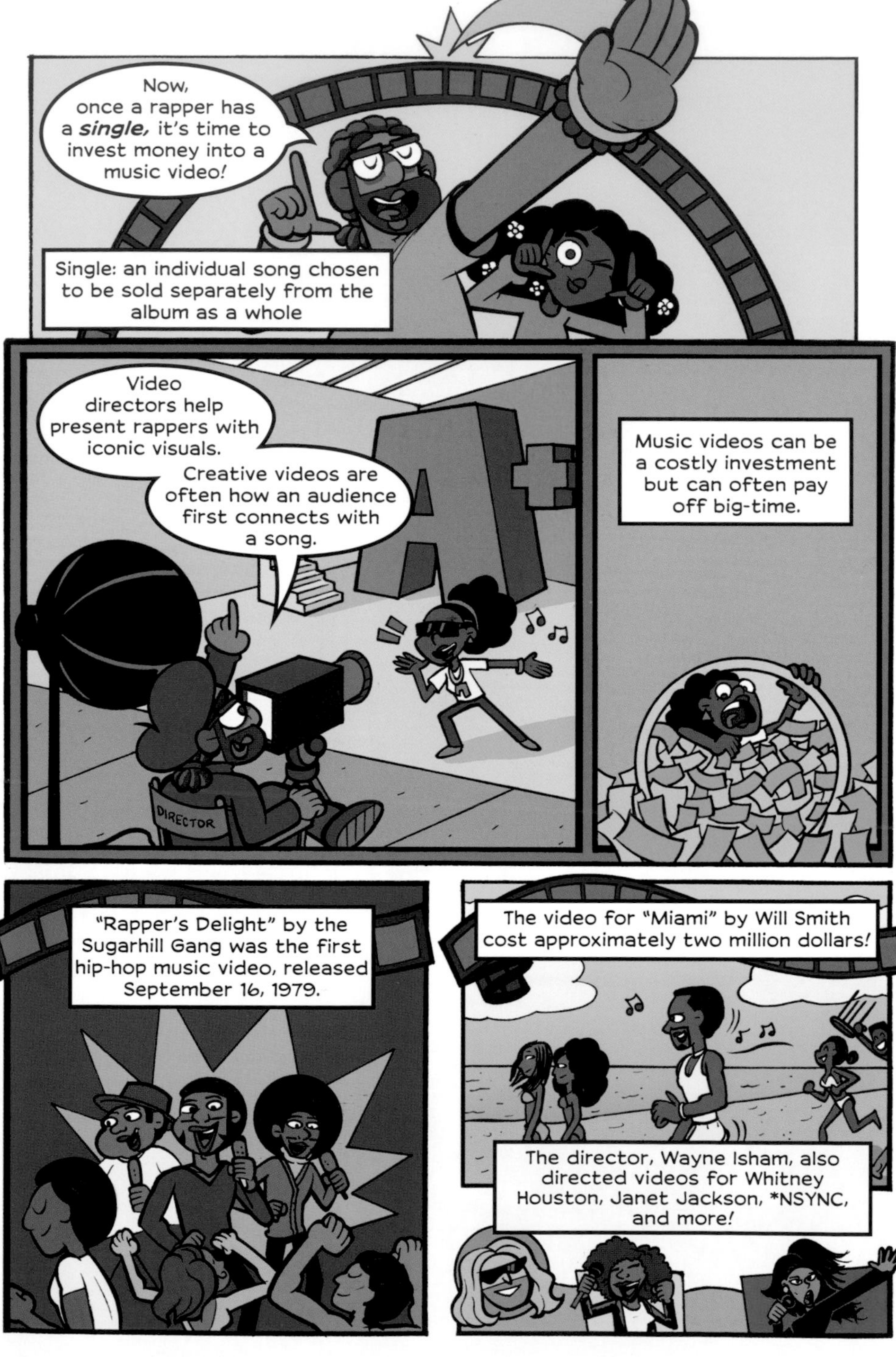
Now, once a rapper has a ***single,*** it's time to invest money into a music video!
Single: an individual song chosen to be sold separately from the album as a whole
Video directors help present rappers with iconic visuals.
Creative videos are often how an audience first connects with a song.
DIRECTOR
Music videos can be a costly investment but can often pay off big-time.
"Rapper's Delight" by the Sugarhill Gang was the first hip-hop music video, released September 16, 1979.
The video for "Miami" by Will Smith cost approximately two million dollars!
The director, Wayne Isham, also directed videos for Whitney Houston, Janet Jackson, *NSYNC, and more!

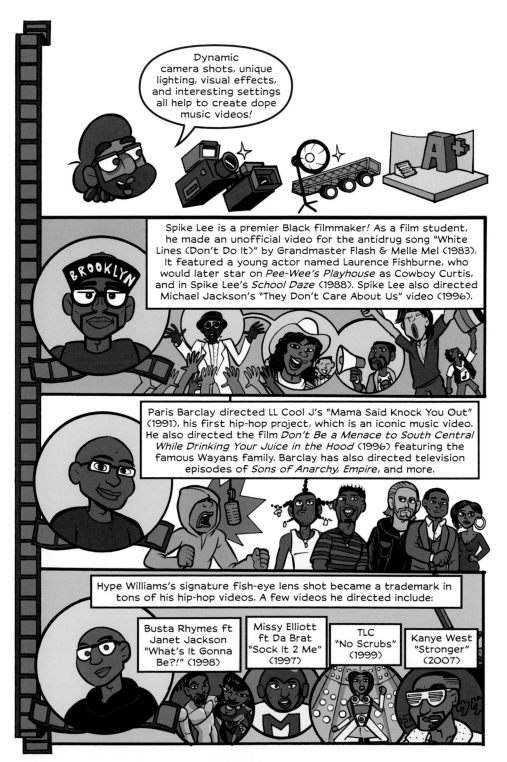

Dynamic camera shots, unique lighting, visual effects, and interesting settings all help to create dope music videos!

Spike Lee is a premier Black filmmaker! As a film student, he made an unofficial video for the antidrug song "White Lines (Don't Do It)" by Grandmaster Flash & Melle Mel (1983). It featured a young actor named Laurence Fishburne, who would later star on *Pee-Wee's Playhouse* as Cowboy Curtis, and in Spike Lee's *School Daze* (1988). Spike Lee also directed Michael Jackson's "They Don't Care About Us" video (1996).

Paris Barclay directed LL Cool J's "Mama Said Knock You Out" (1991), his first hip-hop project, which is an iconic music video. He also directed the film *Don't Be a Menace to South Central While Drinking Your Juice in the Hood* (1996) featuring the famous Wayans family. Barclay has also directed television episodes of *Sons of Anarchy*, *Empire*, and more.

Hype Williams's signature fish-eye lens shot became a trademark in tons of his hip-hop videos. A few videos he directed include:

Busta Rhymes ft Janet Jackson "What's It Gonna Be?!" (1998)

Missy Elliott ft Da Brat "Sock It 2 Me" (1997)

TLC "No Scrubs" (1999)

Kanye West "Stronger" (2007)

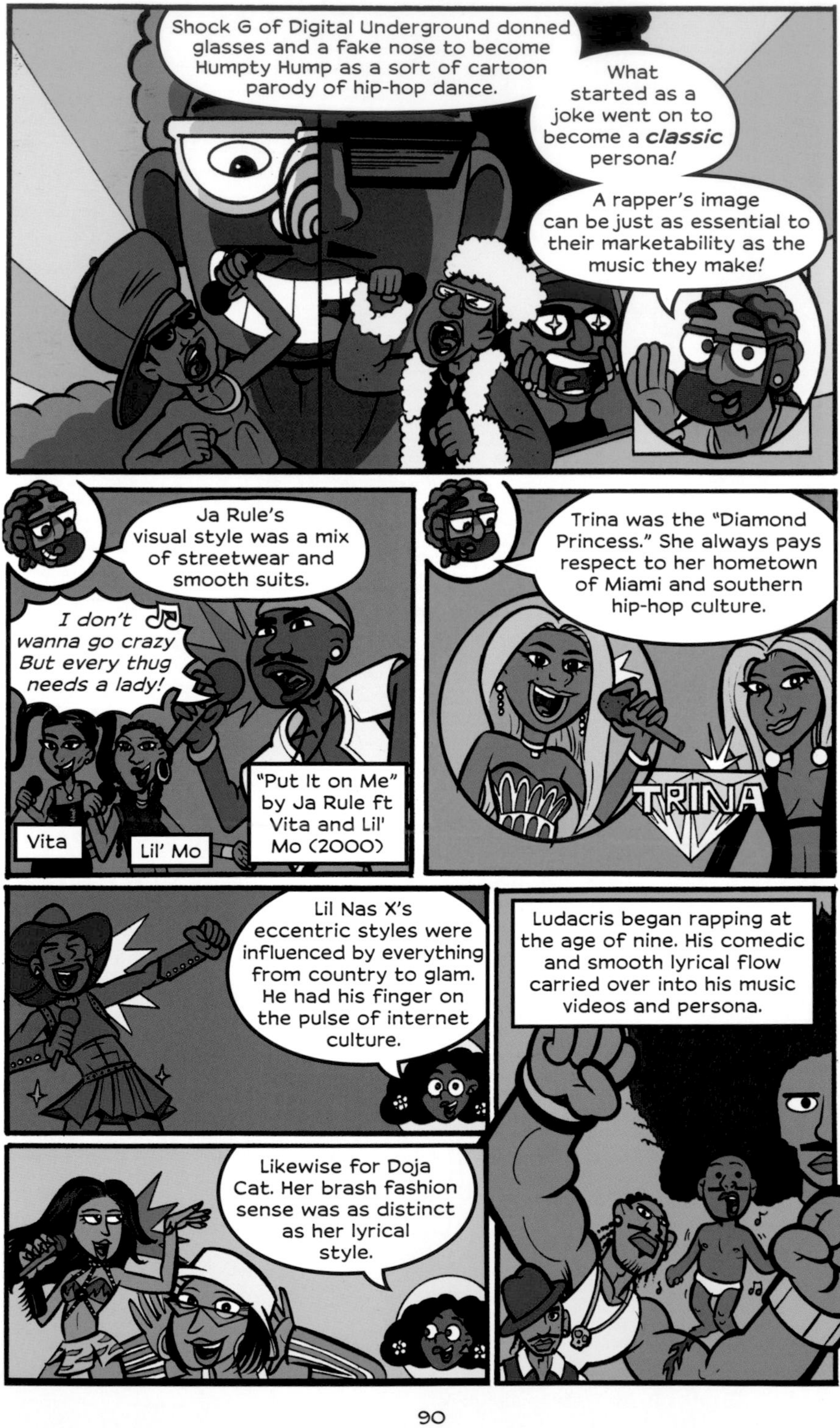
Shock G of Digital Underground donned glasses and a fake nose to become Humpty Hump as a sort of cartoon parody of hip-hop dance.
What started as a joke went on to become a *classic* persona!
A rapper's image can be just as essential to their marketability as the music they make!
Ja Rule's visual style was a mix of streetwear and smooth suits.
I don't wanna go crazy But every thug needs a lady!
Vita
Lil' Mo
"Put It on Me" by Ja Rule ft Vita and Lil' Mo (2000)
Trina was the "Diamond Princess." She always pays respect to her hometown of Miami and southern hip-hop culture.
TRINA
Lil Nas X's eccentric styles were influenced by everything from country to glam. He had his finger on the pulse of internet culture.
Ludacris began rapping at the age of nine. His comedic and smooth lyrical flow carried over into his music videos and persona.
Likewise for Doja Cat. Her brash fashion sense was as distinct as her lyrical style.

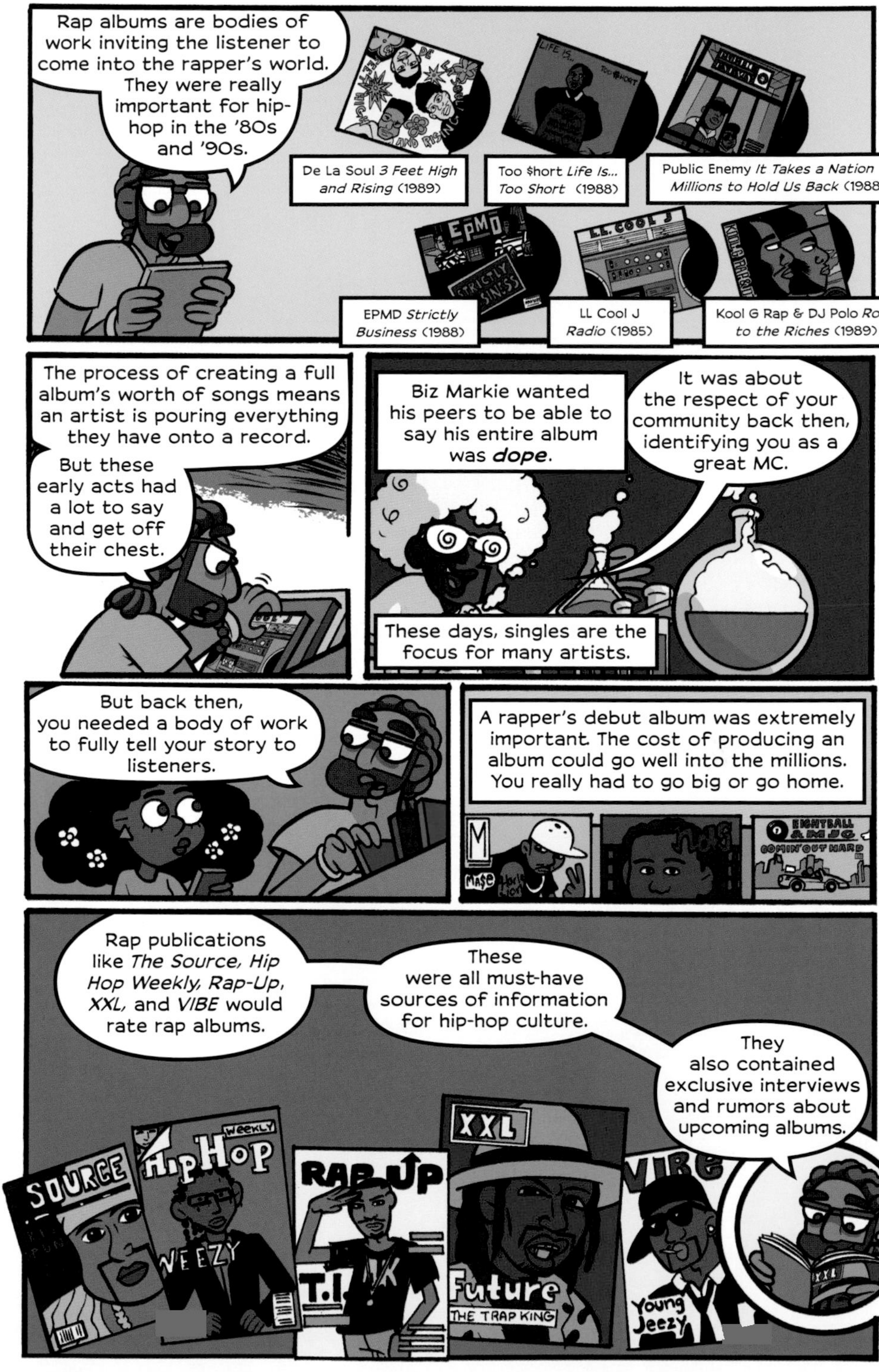
Rap albums are bodies of work inviting the listener to come into the rapper's world.
They were really important for hip-hop in the '80s and '90s.
De La Soul *3 Feet High and Rising* (1989)
Too $hort *Life Is… Too Short* (1988)
Public Enemy *It Takes a Nation of Millions to Hold Us Back* (1988)
EPMD *Strictly Business* (1988)
LL Cool J *Radio* (1985)
Kool G Rap & DJ Polo *Road to the Riches* (1989)
The process of creating a full album's worth of songs means an artist is pouring everything they have onto a record.
But these early acts had a lot to say and get off their chest.
Biz Markie wanted his peers to be able to say his entire album was ***dope***.
It was about the respect of your community back then, identifying you as a great MC.
These days, singles are the focus for many artists.
But back then, you needed a body of work to fully tell your story to listeners.
A rapper's debut album was extremely important. The cost of producing an album could go well into the millions. You really had to go big or go home.
Rap publications like *The Source, Hip Hop Weekly, Rap-Up, XXL,* and *VIBE* would rate rap albums.
These were all must-have sources of information for hip-hop culture.
They also contained exclusive interviews and rumors about upcoming albums.
SOURCE
HipHop WEEKLY
WEEZY
RAP UP
T.I.
XXL
Future
THE TRAP KING
VIBE
Young Jeezy

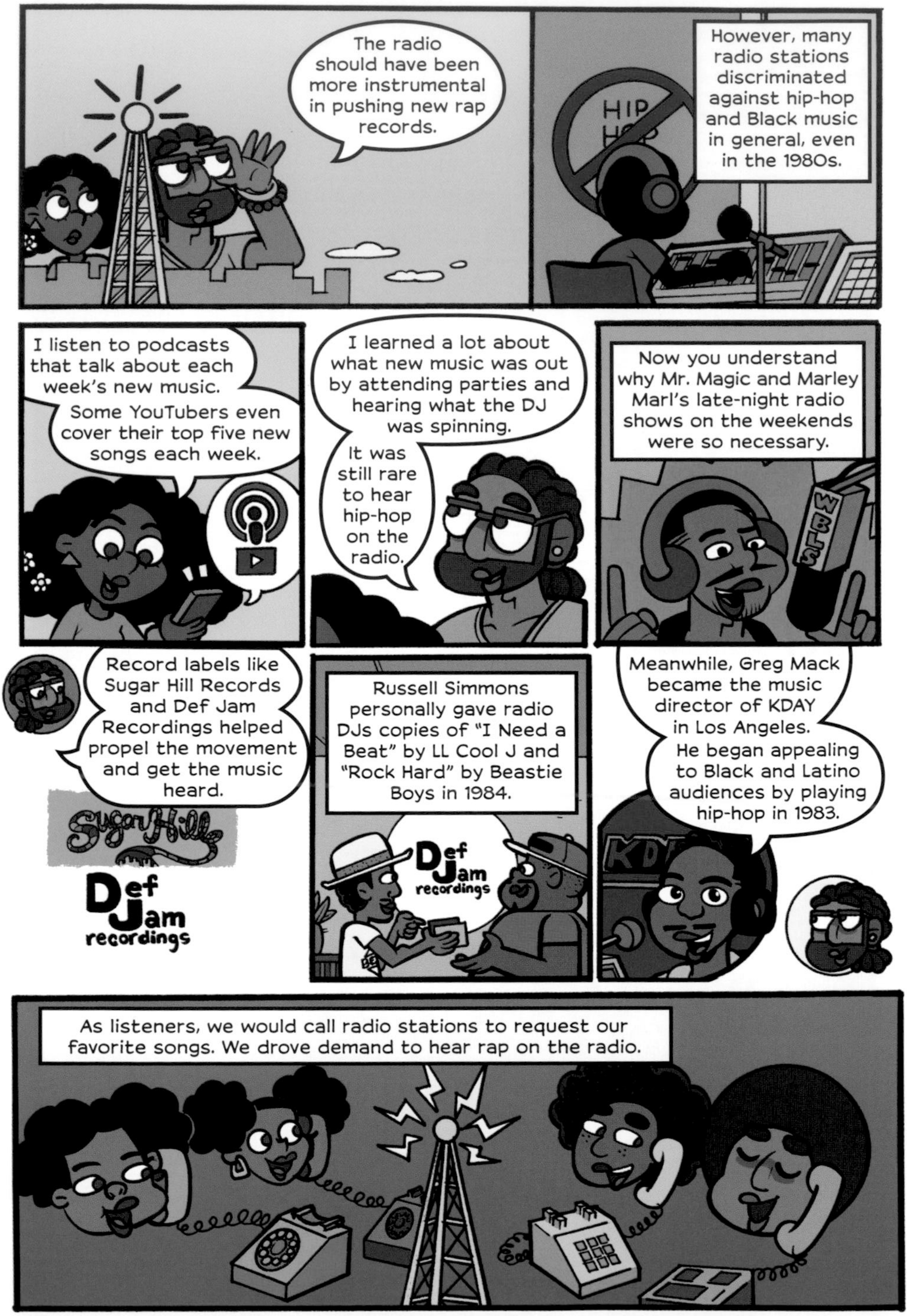

The radio should have been more instrumental in pushing new rap records.
HIP HOP
However, many radio stations discriminated against hip-hop and Black music in general, even in the 1980s.
I listen to podcasts that talk about each week's new music.
Some YouTubers even cover their top five new songs each week.
I learned a lot about what new music was out by attending parties and hearing what the DJ was spinning.
It was still rare to hear hip-hop on the radio.
Now you understand why Mr. Magic and Marley Marl's late-night radio shows on the weekends were so necessary.
WBLS
Record labels like Sugar Hill Records and Def Jam Recordings helped propel the movement and get the music heard.
Sugar Hill
Def Jam recordings
Russell Simmons personally gave radio DJs copies of "I Need a Beat" by LL Cool J and "Rock Hard" by Beastie Boys in 1984.
Def Jam recordings
Meanwhile, Greg Mack became the music director of KDAY in Los Angeles.
He began appealing to Black and Latino audiences by playing hip-hop in 1983.
As listeners, we would call radio stations to request our favorite songs. We drove demand to hear rap on the radio.

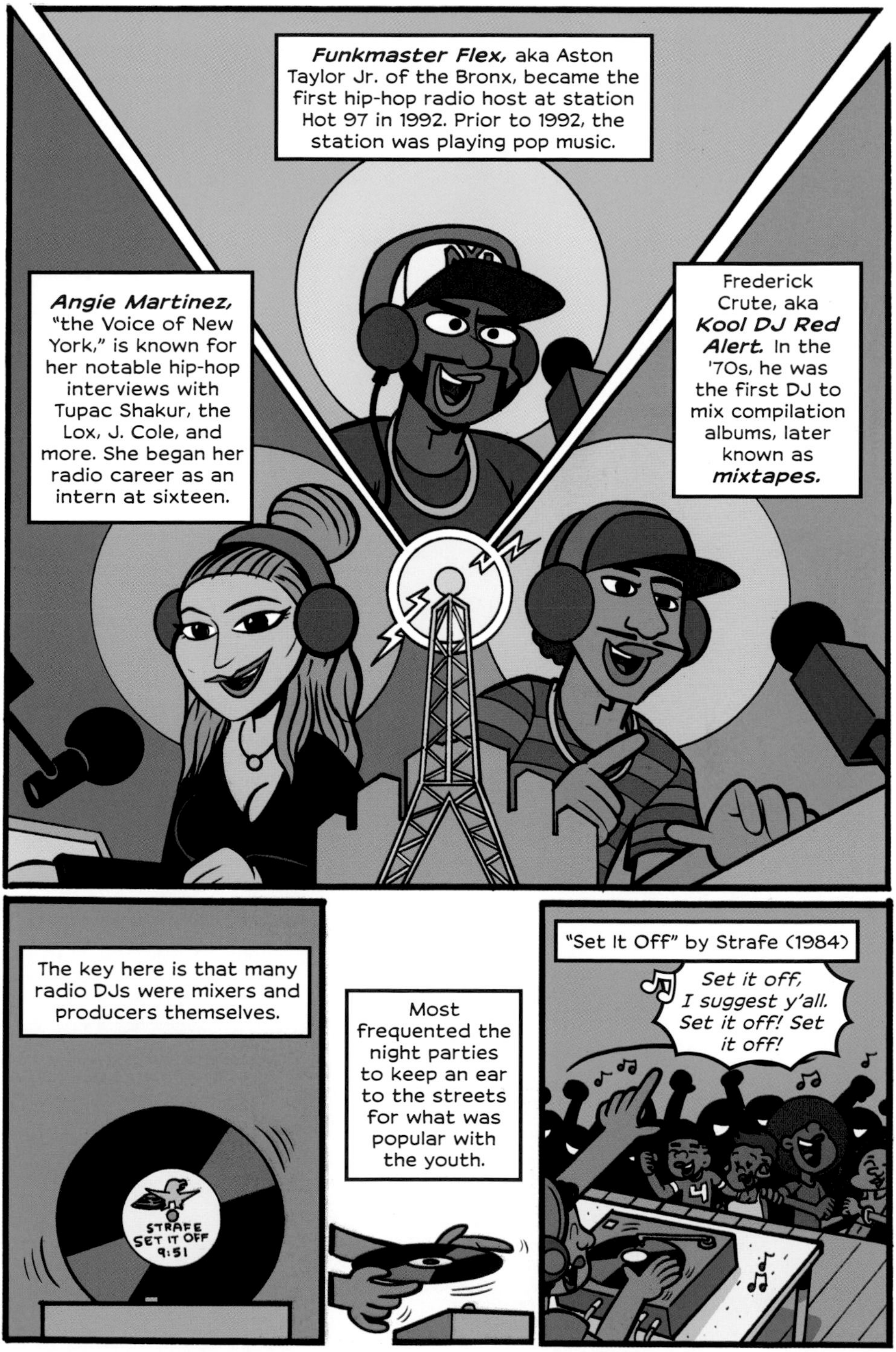
Funkmaster Flex, aka Aston Taylor Jr. of the Bronx, became the first hip-hop radio host at station Hot 97 in 1992. Prior to 1992, the station was playing pop music.
Angie Martinez, "the Voice of New York," is known for her notable hip-hop interviews with Tupac Shakur, the Lox, J. Cole, and more. She began her radio career as an intern at sixteen.
Frederick Crute, aka *Kool DJ Red Alert.* In the '70s, he was the first DJ to mix compilation albums, later known as *mixtapes.*
The key here is that many radio DJs were mixers and producers themselves.
STRAFE
SET IT OFF
9:51
Most frequented the night parties to keep an ear to the streets for what was popular with the youth.
"Set It Off" by Strafe (1984)
Set it off, I suggest y'all. Set it off! Set it off!

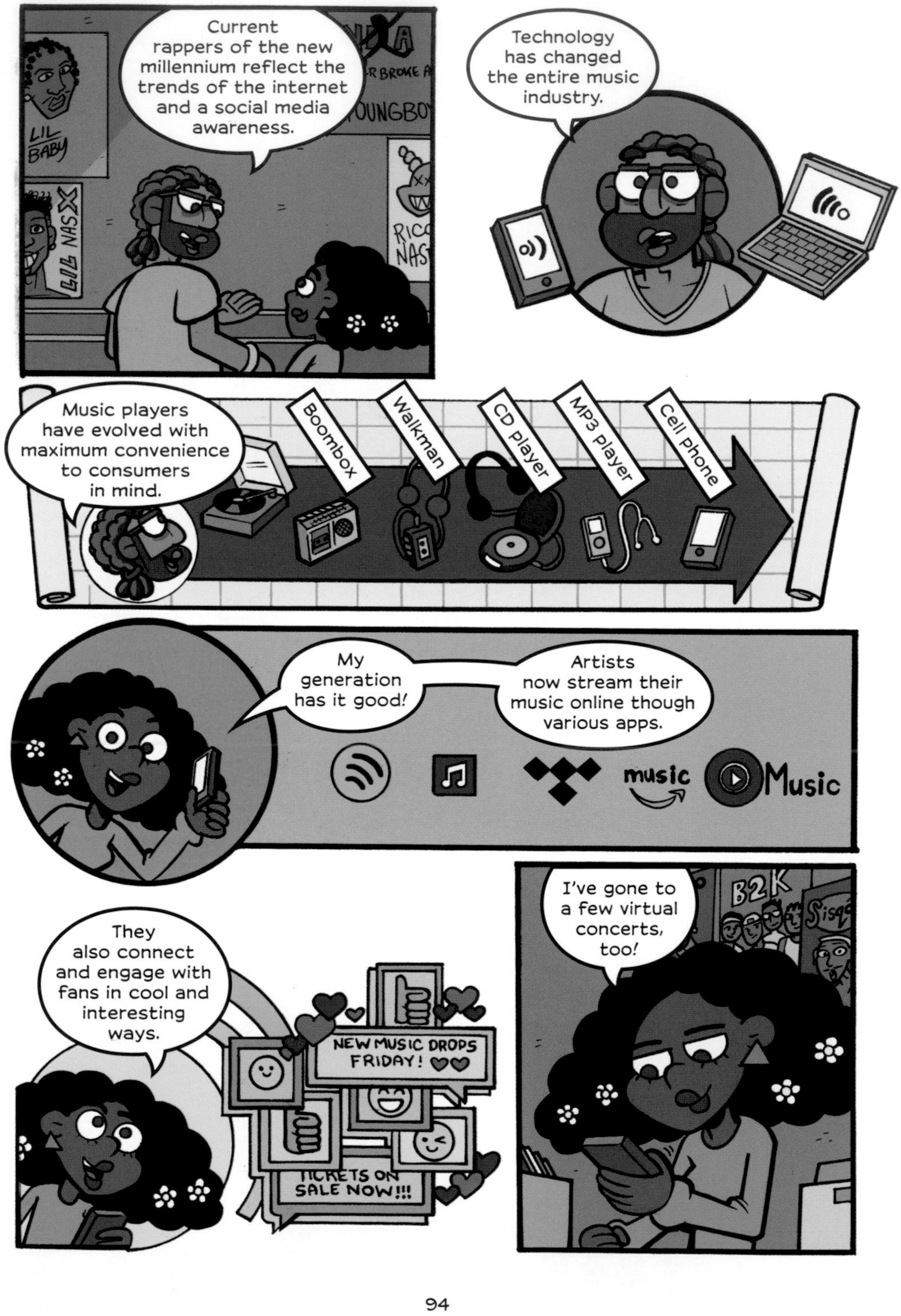
Current rappers of the new millennium reflect the trends of the internet and a social media awareness.
LIL BABY
LIL NAS X
Technology has changed the entire music industry.
Music players have evolved with maximum convenience to consumers in mind.
Boombox
Walkman
CD player
MP3 player
Cell phone
My generation has it good!
Artists now stream their music online though various apps.
music
Music
They also connect and engage with fans in cool and interesting ways.
NEW MUSIC DROPS FRIDAY!
SALE NOW!!!
I've gone to a few virtual concerts, too!
B2K

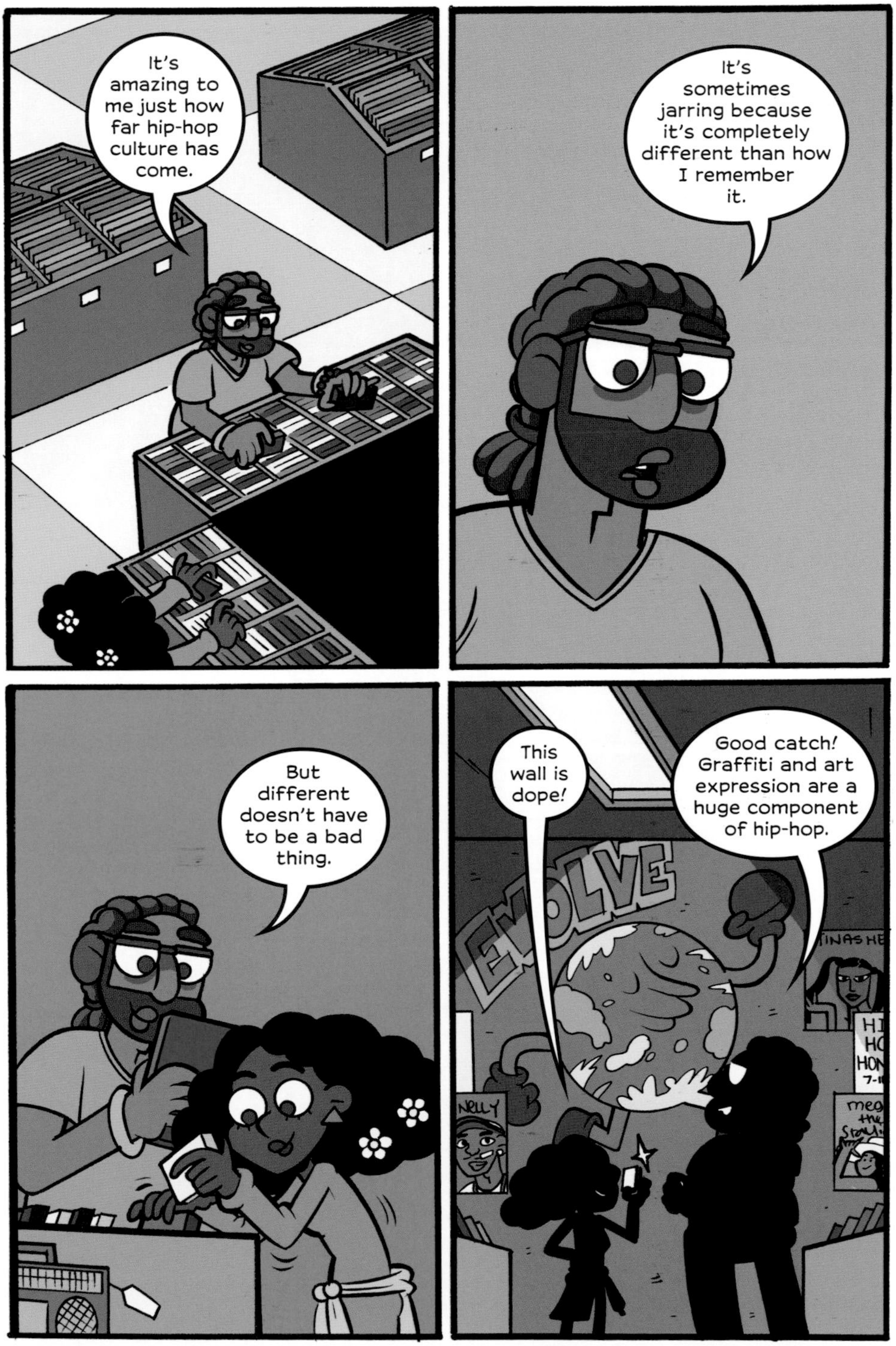
It's amazing to me just how far hip-hop culture has come.
It's sometimes jarring because it's completely different than how I remember it.
But different doesn't have to be a bad thing.
This wall is dope!
Good catch! Graffiti and art expression are a huge component of hip-hop.
EVOLVE
NELLY

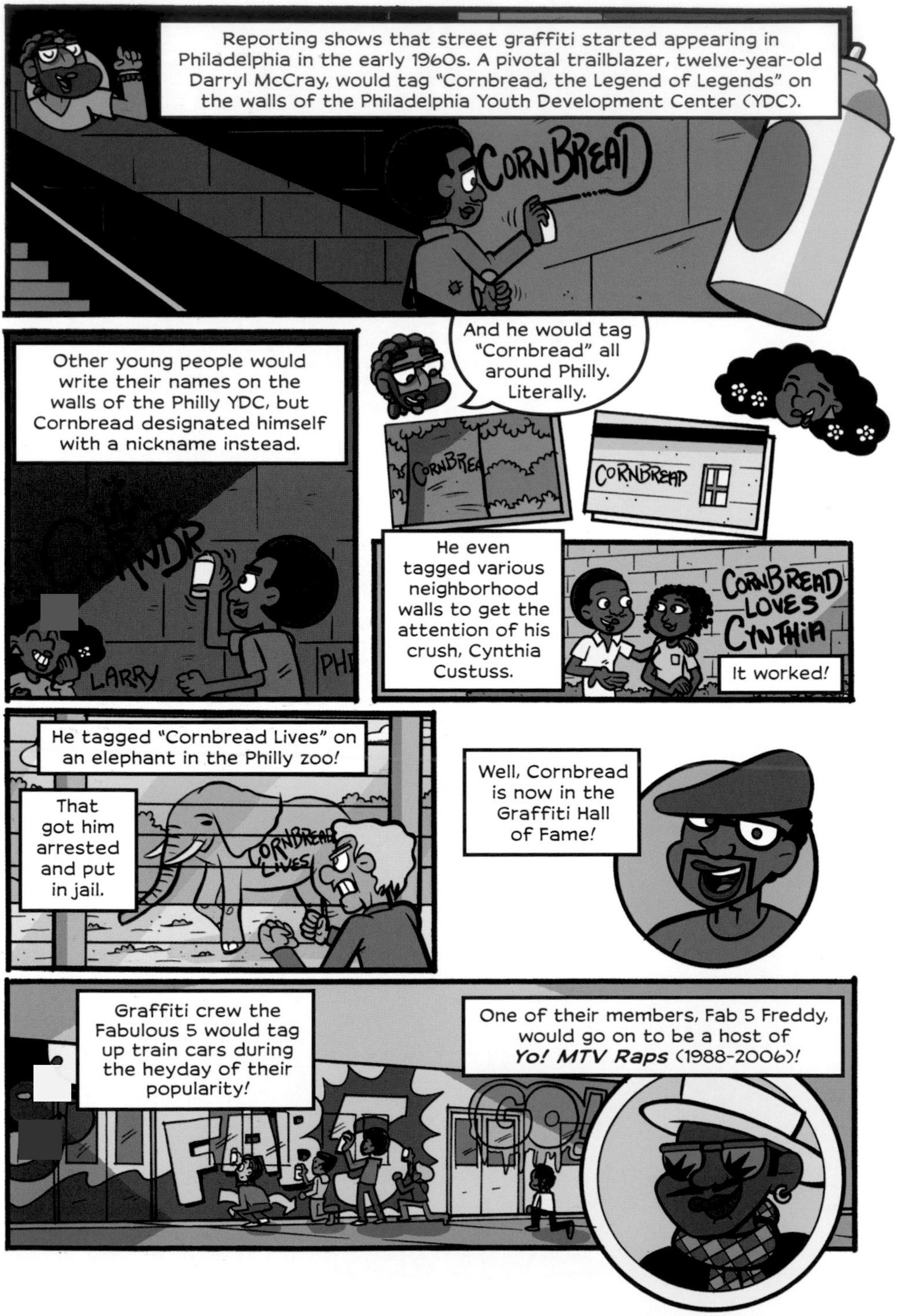
Reporting shows that street graffiti started appearing in Philadelphia in the early 1960s. A pivotal trailblazer, twelve-year-old Darryl McCray, would tag "Cornbread, the Legend of Legends" on the walls of the Philadelphia Youth Development Center (YDC).
CORNBREAD
Other young people would write their names on the walls of the Philly YDC, but Cornbread designated himself with a nickname instead.
LARRY
And he would tag "Cornbread" all around Philly. Literally.
CORNBREAD
He even tagged various neighborhood walls to get the attention of his crush, Cynthia Custuss.
CORNBREAD LOVES CYNTHIA
It worked!
He tagged "Cornbread Lives" on an elephant in the Philly zoo!
That got him arrested and put in jail.
CORNBREAD LIVES
Well, Cornbread is now in the Graffiti Hall of Fame!
Graffiti crew the Fabulous 5 would tag up train cars during the heyday of their popularity!
One of their members, Fab 5 Freddy, would go on to be a host of *Yo! MTV Raps* (1988–2006)!

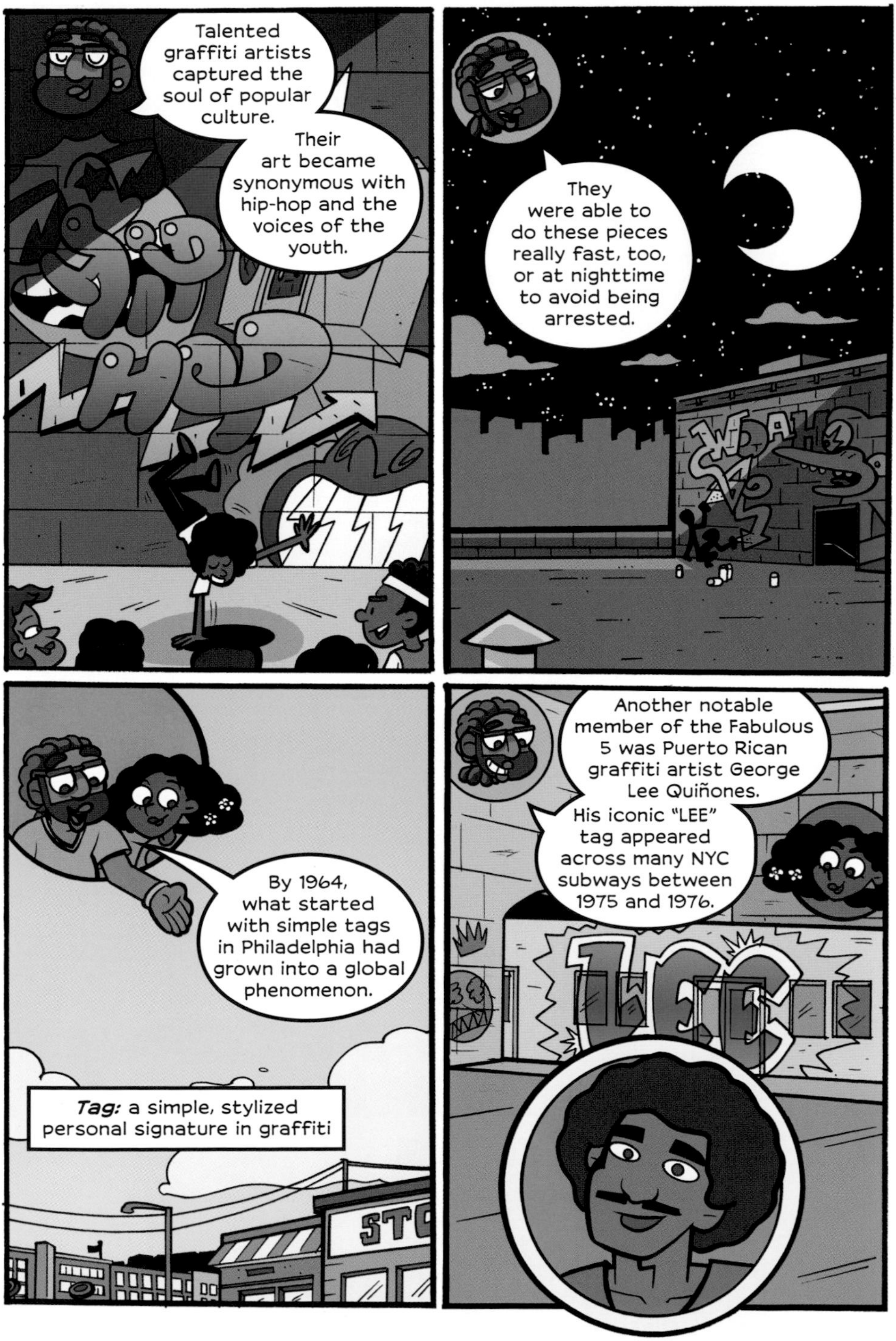
Talented graffiti artists captured the soul of popular culture.
Their art became synonymous with hip-hop and the voices of the youth.
They were able to do these pieces really fast, too, or at nighttime to avoid being arrested.
By 1964, what started with simple tags in Philadelphia had grown into a global phenomenon.
Tag: a simple, stylized personal signature in graffiti
Another notable member of the Fabulous 5 was Puerto Rican graffiti artist George Lee Quiñones.
His iconic "LEE" tag appeared across many NYC subways between 1975 and 1976.

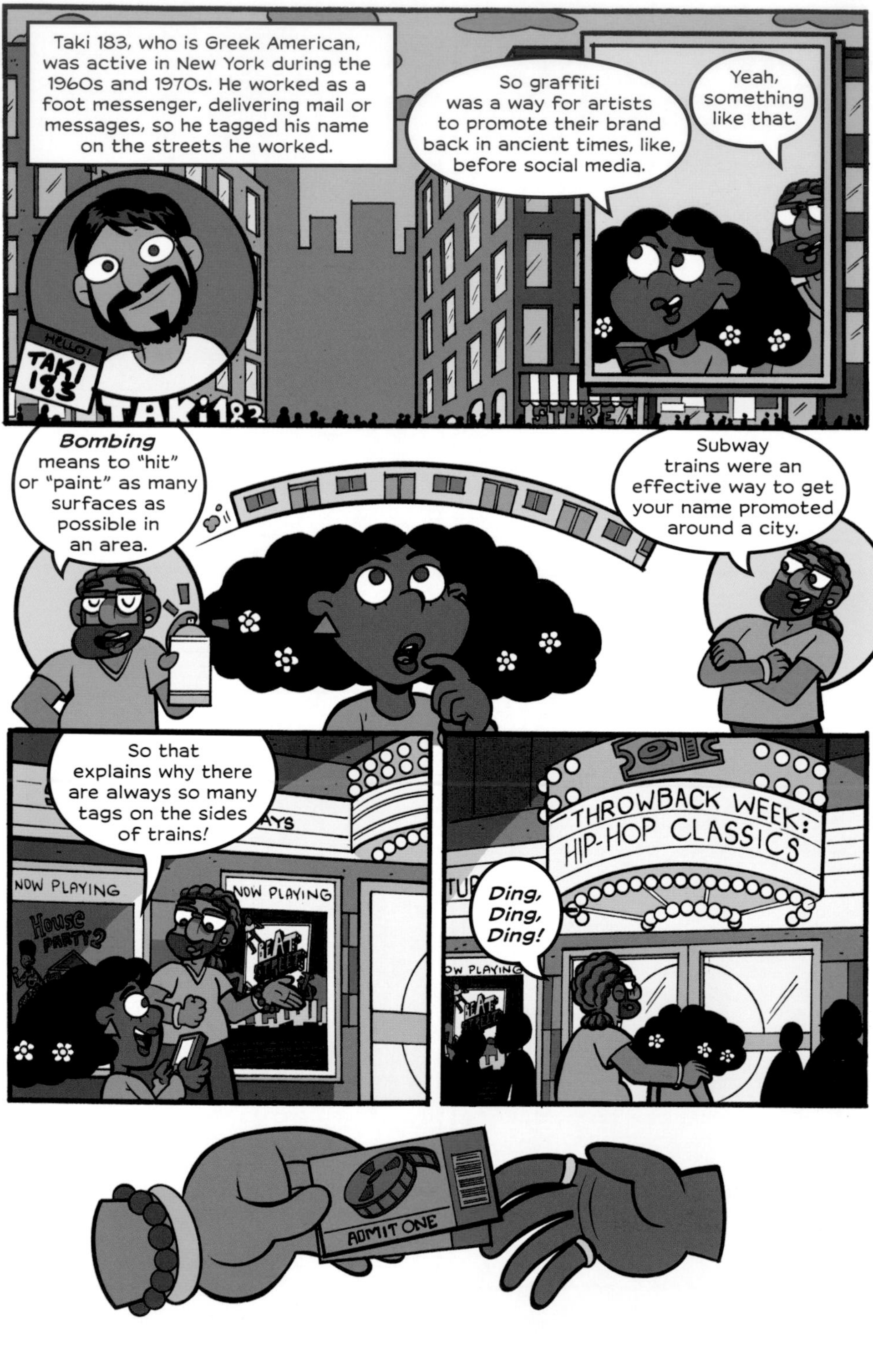
Taki 183, who is Greek American, was active in New York during the 1960s and 1970s. He worked as a foot messenger, delivering mail or messages, so he tagged his name on the streets he worked.
HELLO! TAKI 183
TAKI 183
So graffiti was a way for artists to promote their brand back in ancient times, like, before social media.
Yeah, something like that.
Bombing means to "hit" or "paint" as many surfaces as possible in an area.
Subway trains were an effective way to get your name promoted around a city.
So that explains why there are always so many tags on the sides of trains!
NOW PLAYING
House PARTY 2
NOW PLAYING
THROWBACK WEEK: HIP-HOP CLASSICS
Ding, Ding, Ding!
ADMIT ONE

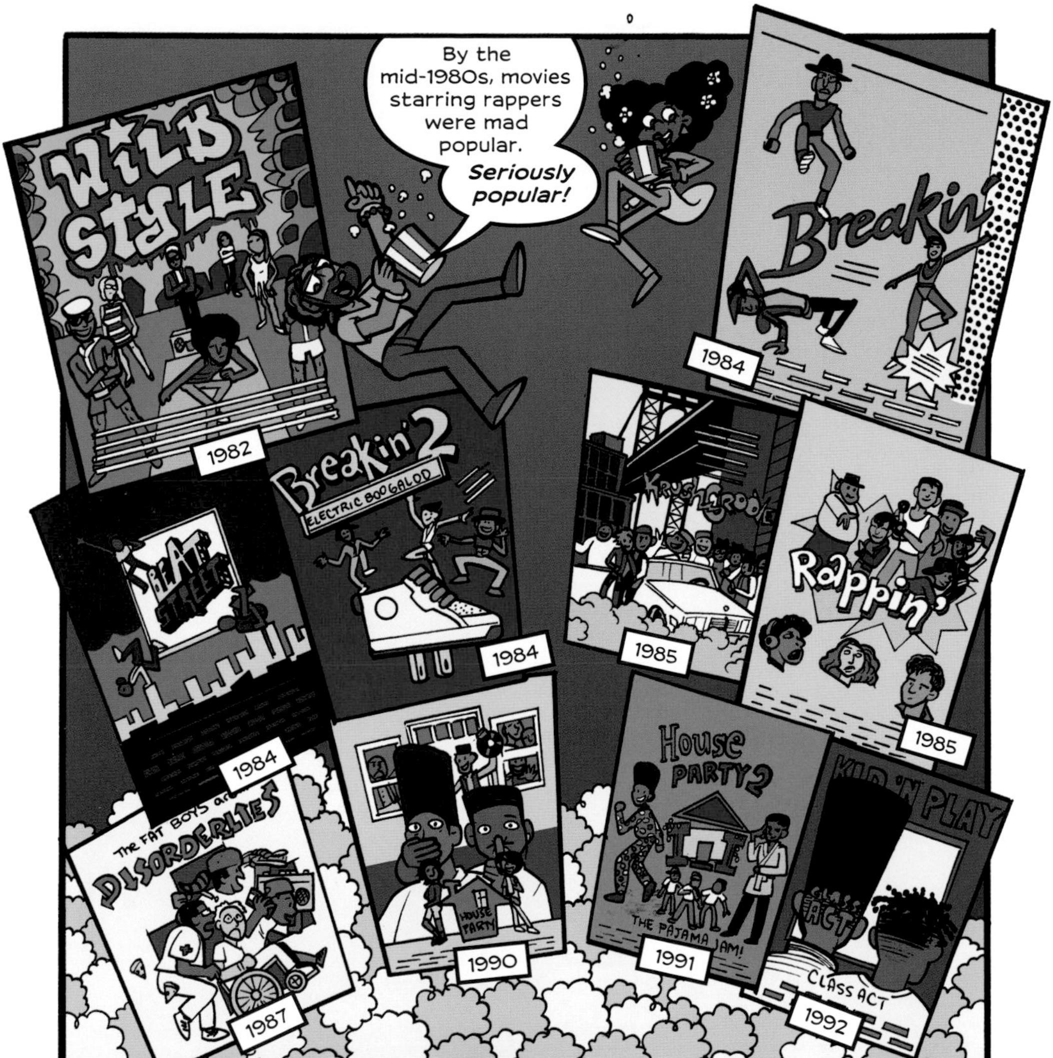
By the mid-1980s, movies starring rappers were mad popular.
Seriously popular!
WILD STYLE
1982
Breakin'
1984
Breakin' 2
ELECTRIC BOOGALOO
1984
BEAT STREET
1984
1985
Rappin'
1985
DISORDERLIES
1987
HOUSE PARTY
1990
House PARTY 2
THE PAJAMA JAM!
1991
KID 'N PLAY
CLASS ACT
1992

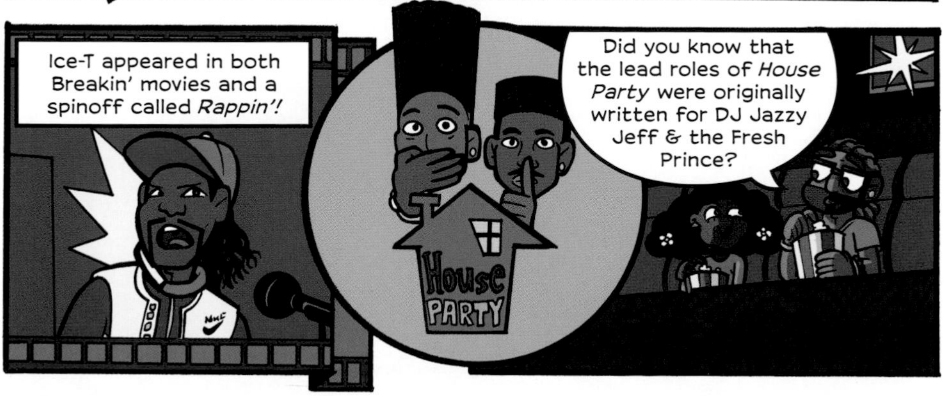
Ice-T appeared in both Breakin' movies and a spinoff called *Rappin'*!
House PARTY
Did you know that the lead roles of *House Party* were originally written for DJ Jazzy Jeff & the Fresh Prince?

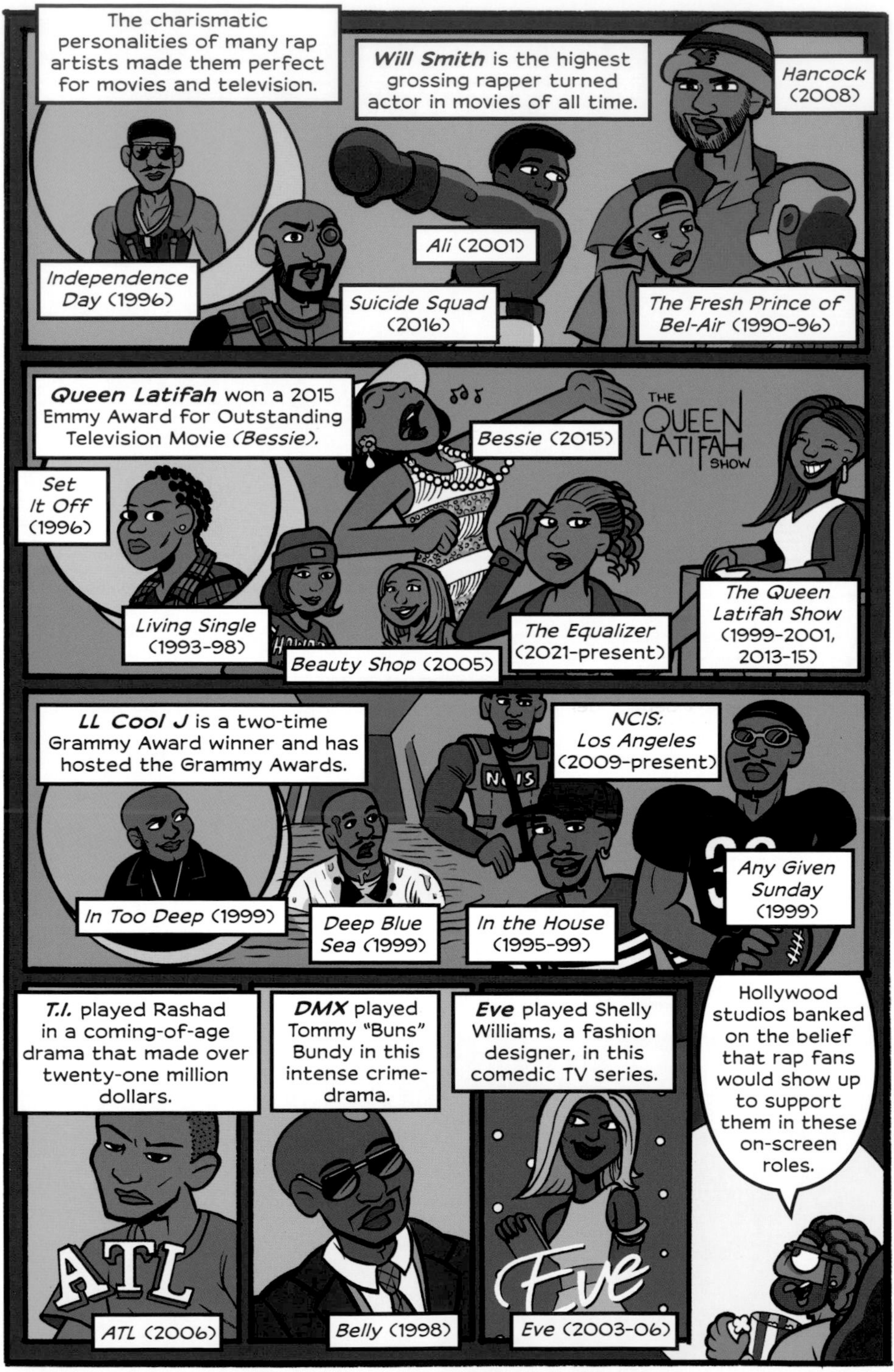
The charismatic personalities of many rap artists made them perfect for movies and television.
Will Smith is the highest grossing rapper turned actor in movies of all time.
Hancock (2008)
Ali (2001)
Independence Day (1996)
Suicide Squad (2016)
The Fresh Prince of Bel-Air (1990-96)
Queen Latifah won a 2015 Emmy Award for Outstanding Television Movie *(Bessie)*.
Bessie (2015)
THE QUEEN LATIFAH SHOW
Set It Off (1996)
Living Single (1993-98)
Beauty Shop (2005)
The Equalizer (2021-present)
The Queen Latifah Show (1999-2001, 2013-15)
LL Cool J is a two-time Grammy Award winner and has hosted the Grammy Awards.
NCIS: Los Angeles (2009-present)
NCIS
In Too Deep (1999)
Deep Blue Sea (1999)
In the House (1995-99)
Any Given Sunday (1999)
T.I. played Rashad in a coming-of-age drama that made over twenty-one million dollars.
ATL
ATL (2006)
DMX played Tommy "Buns" Bundy in this intense crime-drama.
Belly (1998)
Eve played Shelly Williams, a fashion designer, in this comedic TV series.
Eve
Eve (2003-06)
Hollywood studios banked on the belief that rap fans would show up to support them in these on-screen roles.

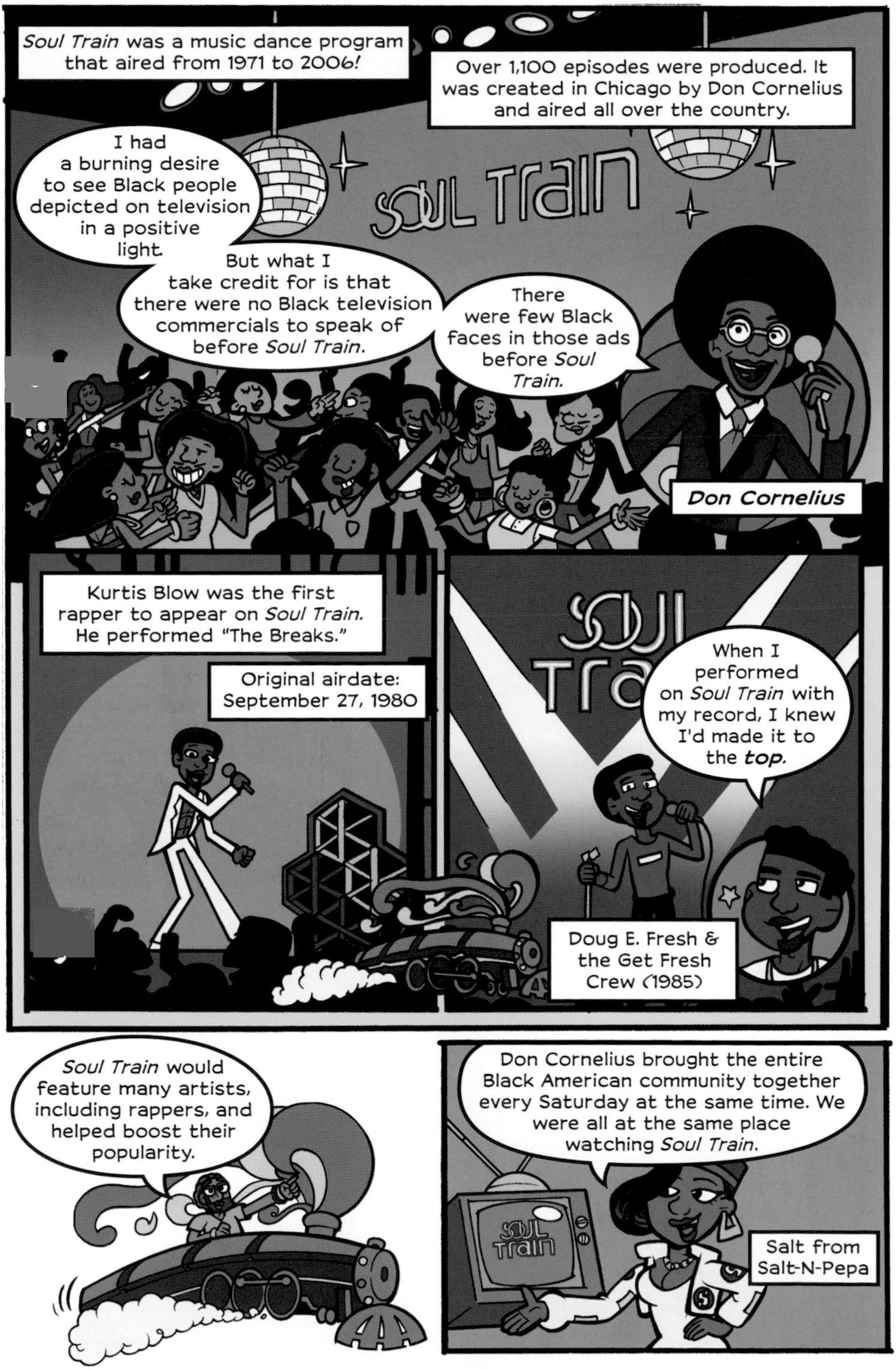
Soul Train was a music dance program that aired from 1971 to 2006!
Over 1,100 episodes were produced. It was created in Chicago by Don Cornelius and aired all over the country.
SOUL TRAIN
I had a burning desire to see Black people depicted on television in a positive light.
But what I take credit for is that there were no Black television commercials to speak of before *Soul Train*.
There were few Black faces in those ads before *Soul Train*.
Don Cornelius
Kurtis Blow was the first rapper to appear on *Soul Train*. He performed "The Breaks."
Original airdate: September 27, 1980
When I performed on *Soul Train* with my record, I knew I'd made it to the ***top***.
Doug E. Fresh & the Get Fresh Crew (1985)
Soul Train would feature many artists, including rappers, and helped boost their popularity.
Don Cornelius brought the entire Black American community together every Saturday at the same time. We were all at the same place watching *Soul Train*.
Salt from Salt-N-Pepa

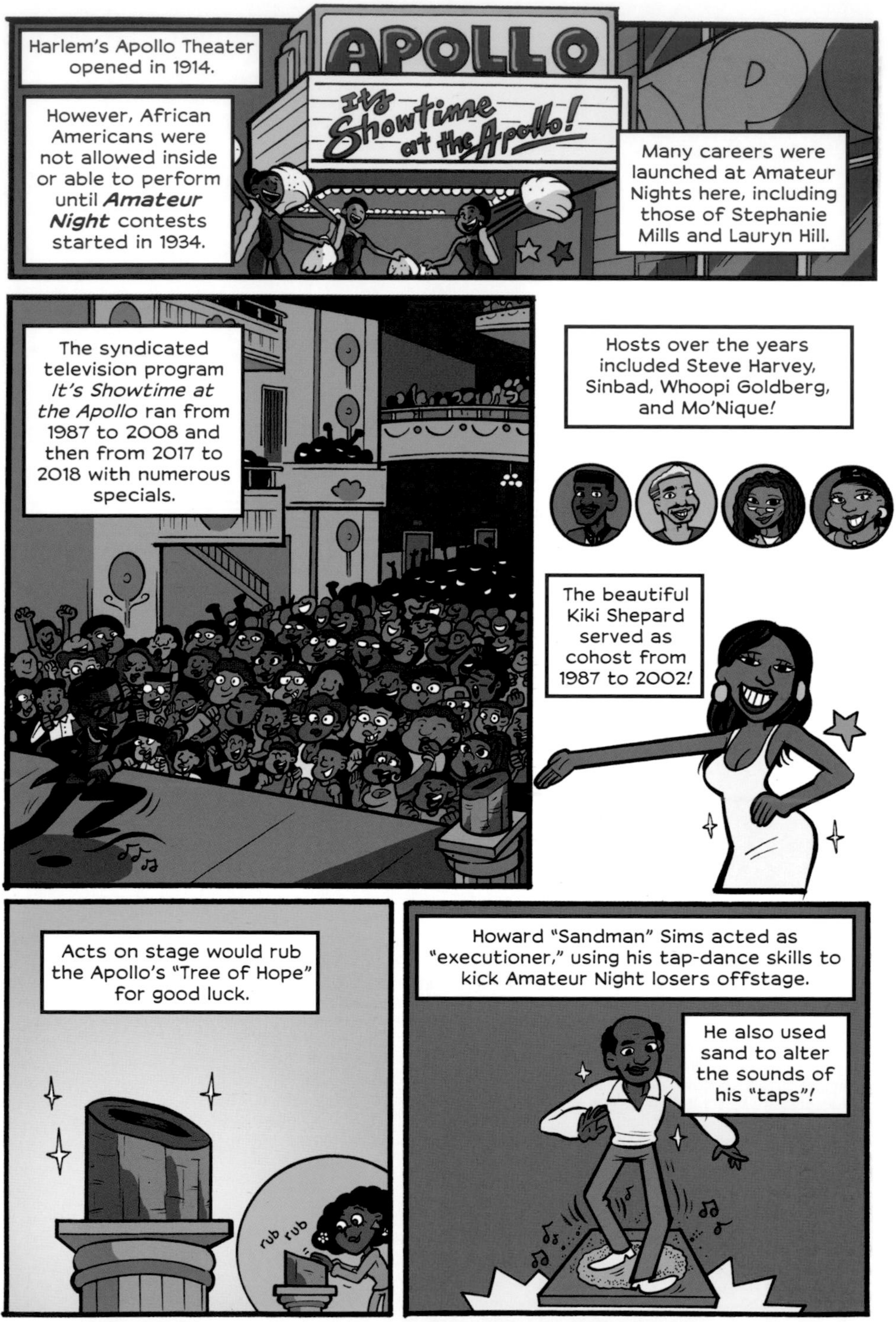
Harlem's Apollo Theater opened in 1914.
However, African Americans were not allowed inside or able to perform until ***Amateur Night*** contests started in 1934.
APOLLO
It's Showtime at the Apollo!
Many careers were launched at Amateur Nights here, including those of Stephanie Mills and Lauryn Hill.
The syndicated television program *It's Showtime at the Apollo* ran from 1987 to 2008 and then from 2017 to 2018 with numerous specials.
Hosts over the years included Steve Harvey, Sinbad, Whoopi Goldberg, and Mo'Nique!
The beautiful Kiki Shepard served as cohost from 1987 to 2002!
Acts on stage would rub the Apollo's "Tree of Hope" for good luck.
rub rub
Howard "Sandman" Sims acted as "executioner," using his tap-dance skills to kick Amateur Night losers offstage.
He also used sand to alter the sounds of his "taps"!

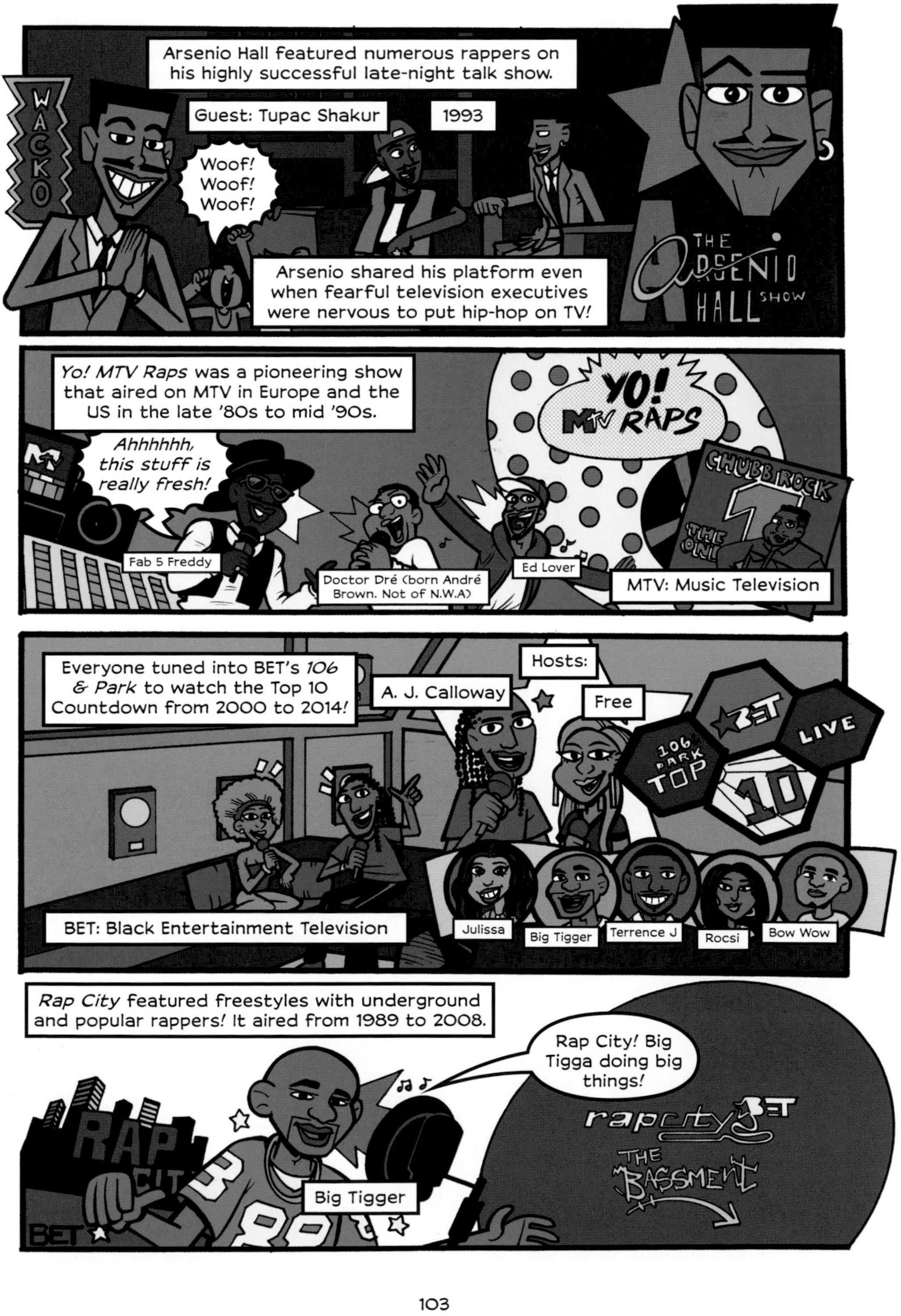

Arsenio Hall featured numerous rappers on his highly successful late-night talk show.
Guest: Tupac Shakur
1993
WACKO
Woof! Woof! Woof!
Arsenio shared his platform even when fearful television executives were nervous to put hip-hop on TV!
THE ARSENIO HALL SHOW
Yo! MTV Raps was a pioneering show that aired on MTV in Europe and the US in the late '80s to mid '90s.
YO! MTV RAPS
Ahhhhhh, this stuff is really fresh!
CHUBB ROCK
Fab 5 Freddy
Doctor Dré (born André Brown. Not of N.W.A)
Ed Lover
MTV: Music Television
Everyone tuned into BET's *106 & Park* to watch the Top 10 Countdown from 2000 to 2014!
Hosts:
A. J. Calloway
Free
BET
LIVE
106 & PARK TOP
10
BET: Black Entertainment Television
Julissa
Big Tigger
Terrence J
Rocsi
Bow Wow
Rap City featured freestyles with underground and popular rappers! It aired from 1989 to 2008.
Rap City! Big Tigga doing big things!
RAP CITY
rap city BET
THE BASSMENT
Big Tigger
BET

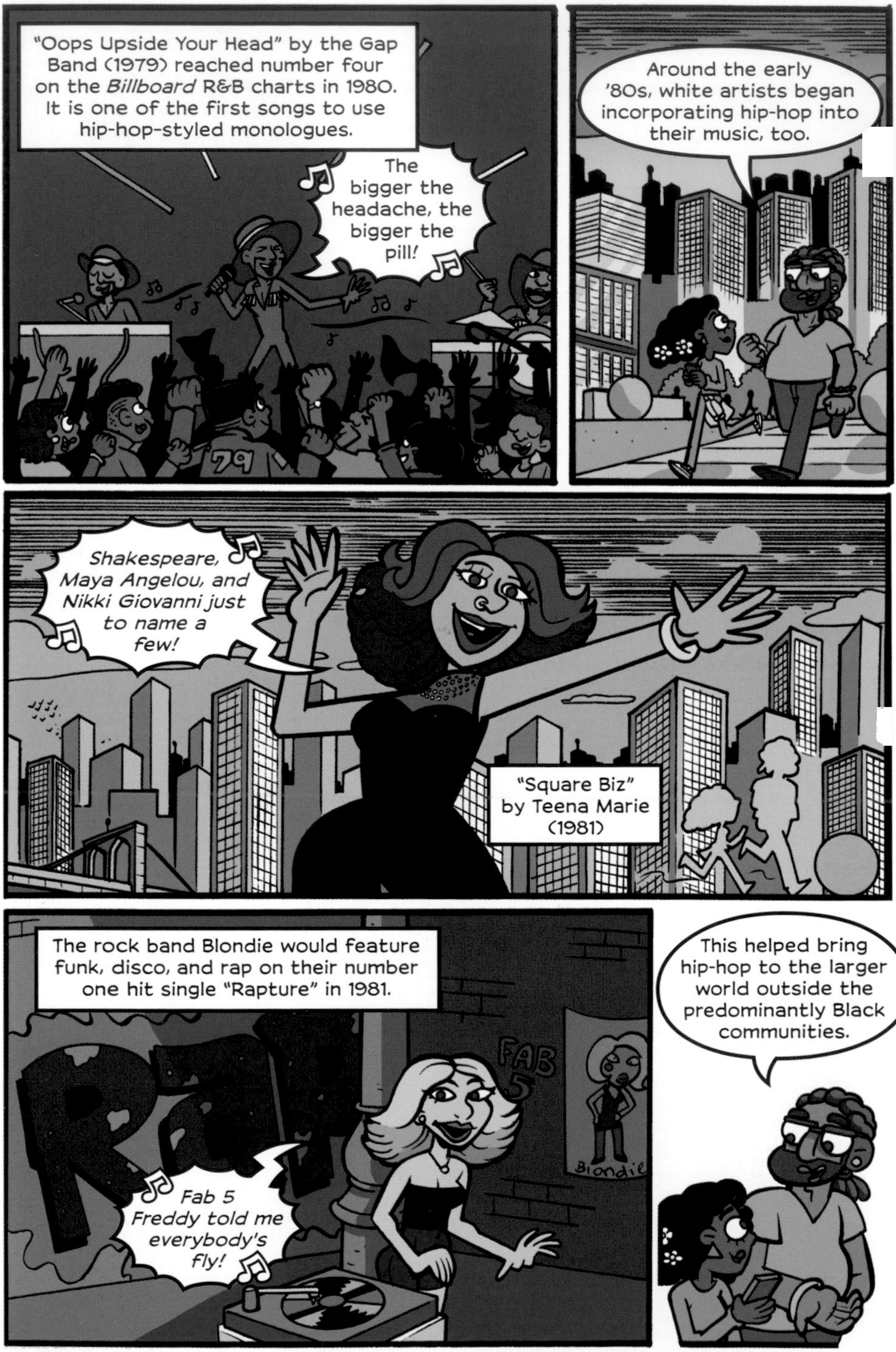

"Oops Upside Your Head" by the Gap Band (1979) reached number four on the *Billboard* R&B charts in 1980. It is one of the first songs to use hip-hop-styled monologues.
The bigger the headache, the bigger the pill!
79
Around the early '80s, white artists began incorporating hip-hop into their music, too.
Shakespeare, Maya Angelou, and Nikki Giovanni just to name a few!
"Square Biz" by Teena Marie (1981)
The rock band Blondie would feature funk, disco, and rap on their number one hit single "Rapture" in 1981.
FAB 5
Blondie
Fab 5 Freddy told me everybody's fly!
This helped bring hip-hop to the larger world outside the predominantly Black communities.

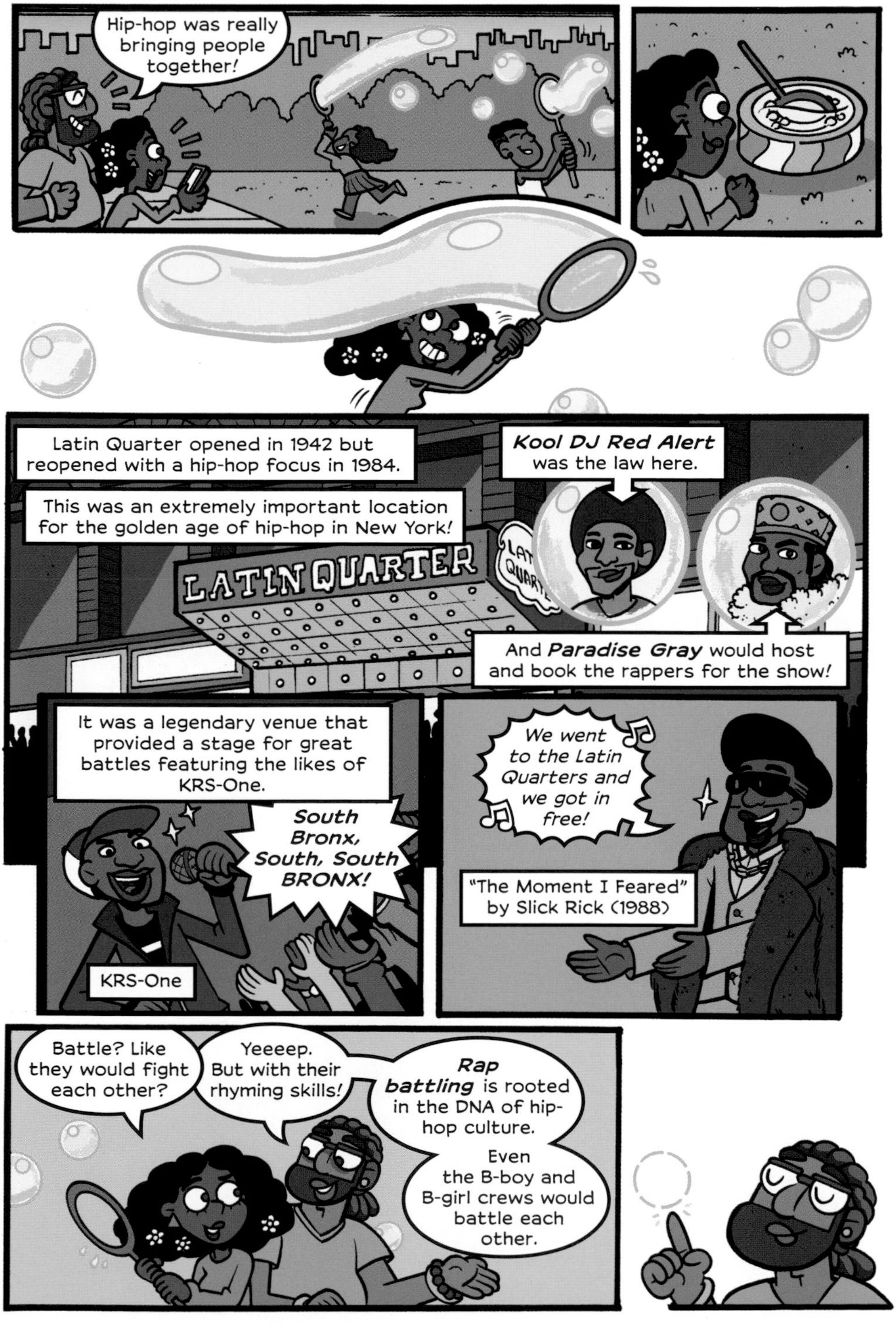
Hip-hop was really bringing people together!
Latin Quarter opened in 1942 but reopened with a hip-hop focus in 1984.
This was an extremely important location for the golden age of hip-hop in New York!
LATIN QUARTER
Kool DJ Red Alert was the law here.
And *Paradise Gray* would host and book the rappers for the show!
It was a legendary venue that provided a stage for great battles featuring the likes of KRS-One.
South Bronx, South, South BRONX!
KRS-One
We went to the Latin Quarters and we got in free!
"The Moment I Feared" by Slick Rick (1988)
Battle? Like they would fight each other?
Yeeeep. But with their rhyming skills!
Rap battling is rooted in the DNA of hip-hop culture.
Even the B-boy and B-girl crews would battle each other.

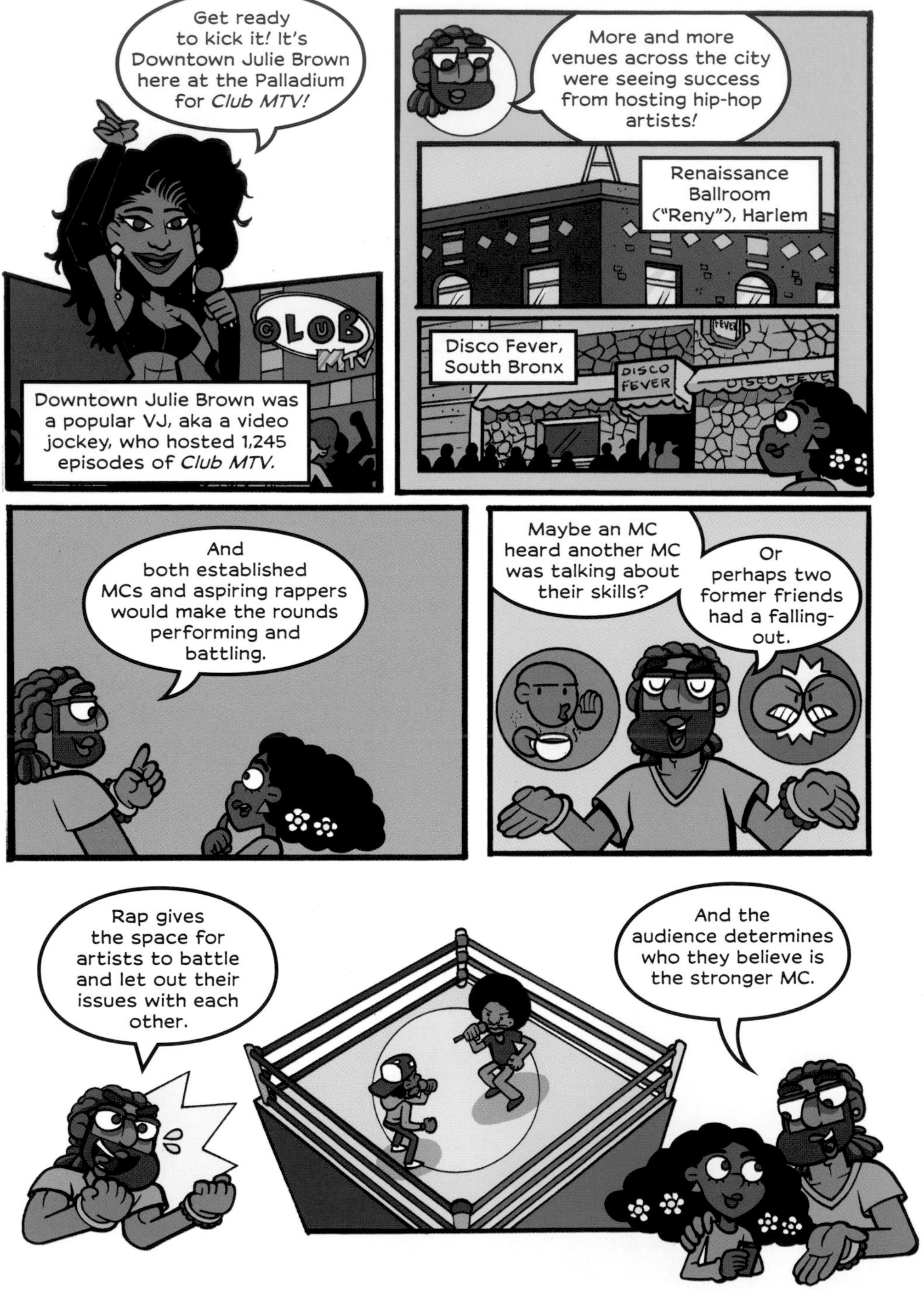

Get ready to kick it! It's Downtown Julie Brown here at the Palladium for *Club MTV!*
CLUB MTV
Downtown Julie Brown was a popular VJ, aka a video jockey, who hosted 1,245 episodes of *Club MTV.*
More and more venues across the city were seeing success from hosting hip-hop artists!
Renaissance Ballroom ("Reny"), Harlem
Disco Fever, South Bronx
DISCO FEVER
And both established MCs and aspiring rappers would make the rounds performing and battling.
Maybe an MC heard another MC was talking about their skills?
Or perhaps two former friends had a falling-out.
Rap gives the space for artists to battle and let out their issues with each other.
And the audience determines who they believe is the stronger MC.

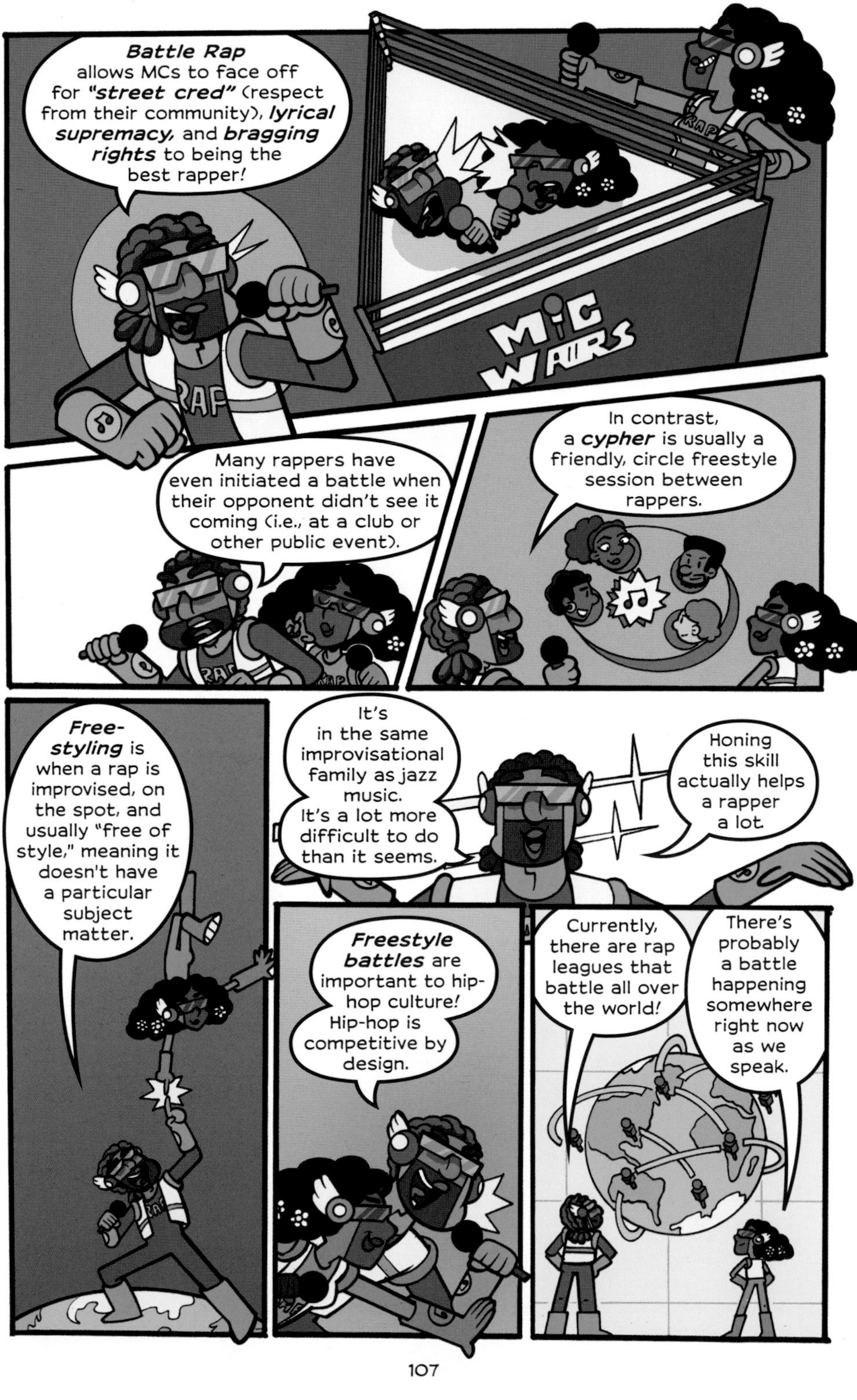
Battle Rap allows MCs to face off for *"street cred"* (respect from their community), *lyrical supremacy,* and *bragging rights* to being the best rapper!
MIC WARS
RAP
Many rappers have even initiated a battle when their opponent didn't see it coming (i.e., at a club or other public event).
In contrast, a *cypher* is usually a friendly, circle freestyle session between rappers.
Free-styling is when a rap is improvised, on the spot, and usually "free of style," meaning it doesn't have a particular subject matter.
It's in the same improvisational family as jazz music. It's a lot more difficult to do than it seems.
Honing this skill actually helps a rapper a lot.
Freestyle battles are important to hip-hop culture! Hip-hop is competitive by design.
Currently, there are rap leagues that battle all over the world!
There's probably a battle happening somewhere right now as we speak.

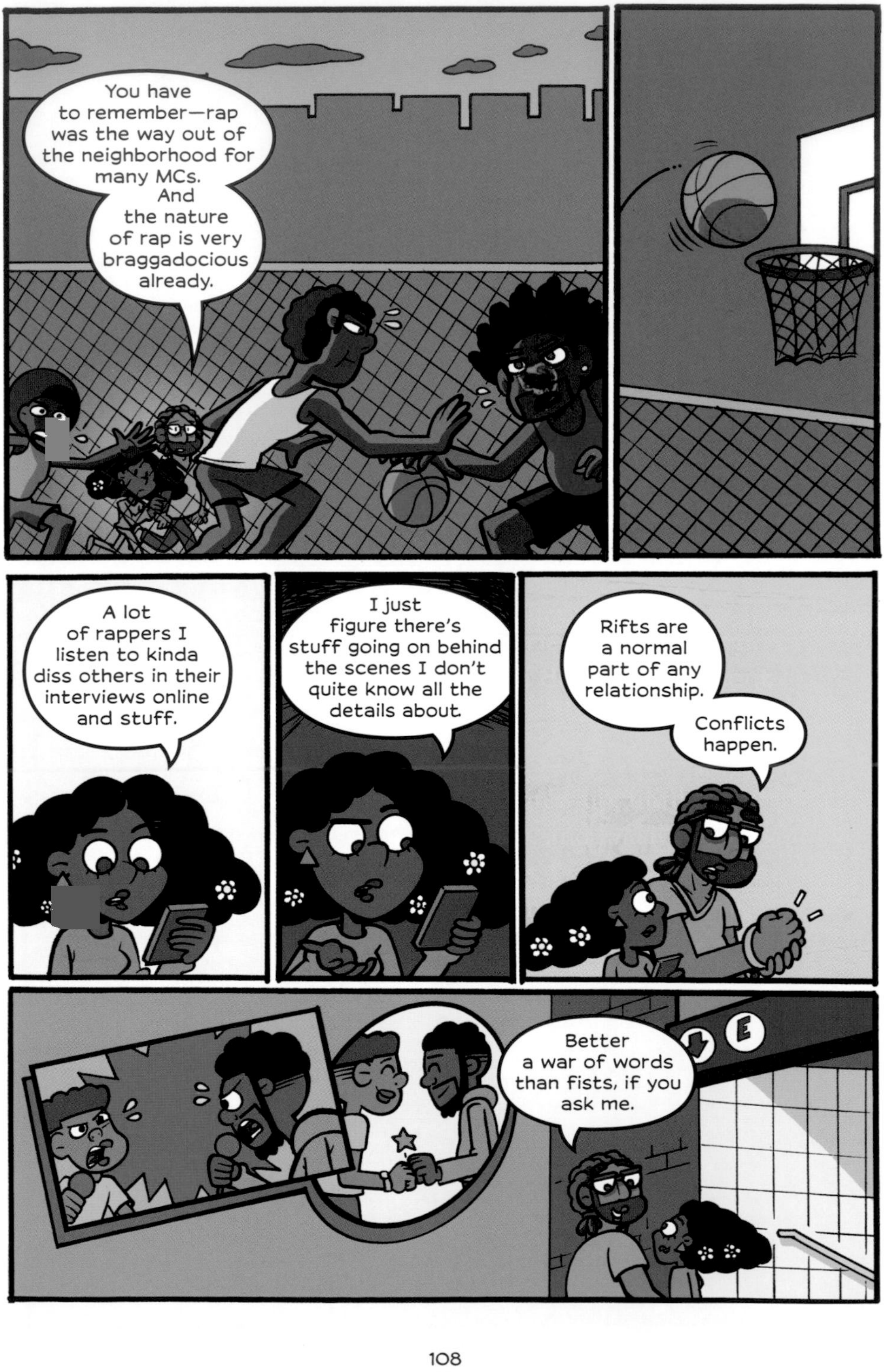
You have to remember—rap was the way out of the neighborhood for many MCs.
And the nature of rap is very braggadocious already.
A lot of rappers I listen to kinda diss others in their interviews online and stuff.
I just figure there's stuff going on behind the scenes I don't quite know all the details about.
Rifts are a normal part of any relationship.
Conflicts happen.
Better a war of words than fists, if you ask me.
E

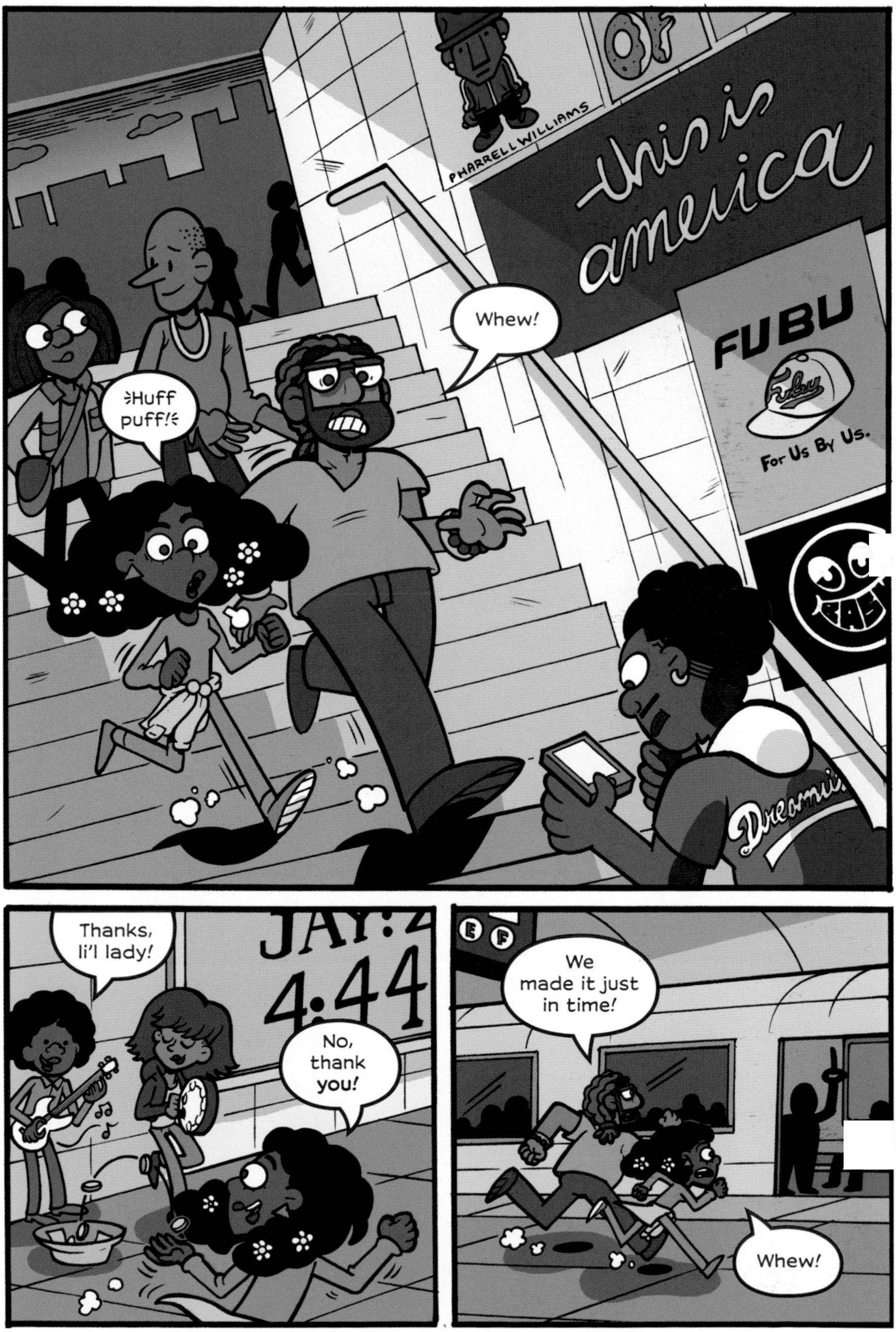
PHARRELL WILLIAMS
this is america
FUBU
For Us By Us.
Whew!
Huff puff!
Thanks, li'l lady!
4:44
No, thank you!
We made it just in time!
Whew!

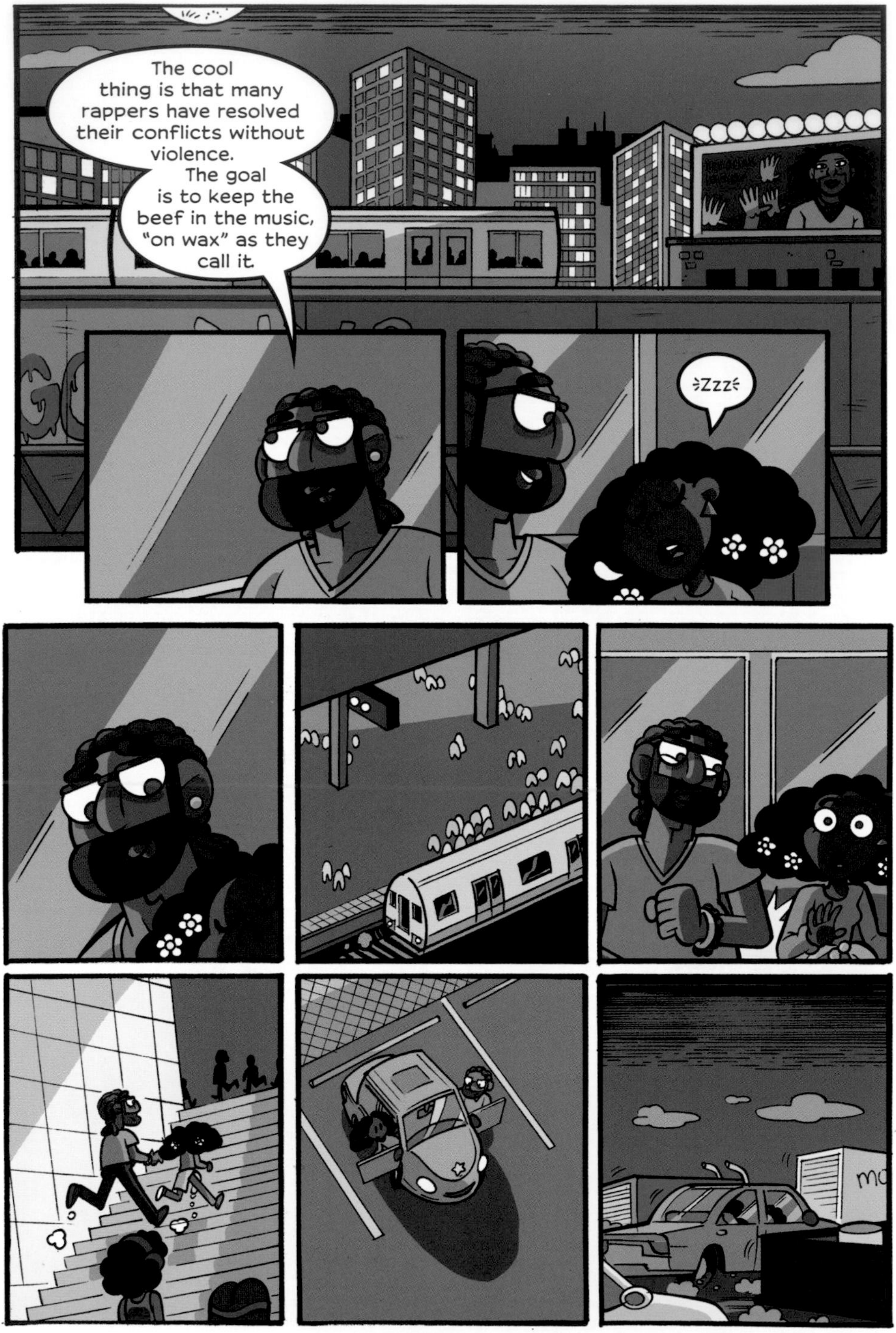
The cool thing is that many rappers have resolved their conflicts without violence.
The goal is to keep the beef in the music, "on wax" as they call it.
Zzz

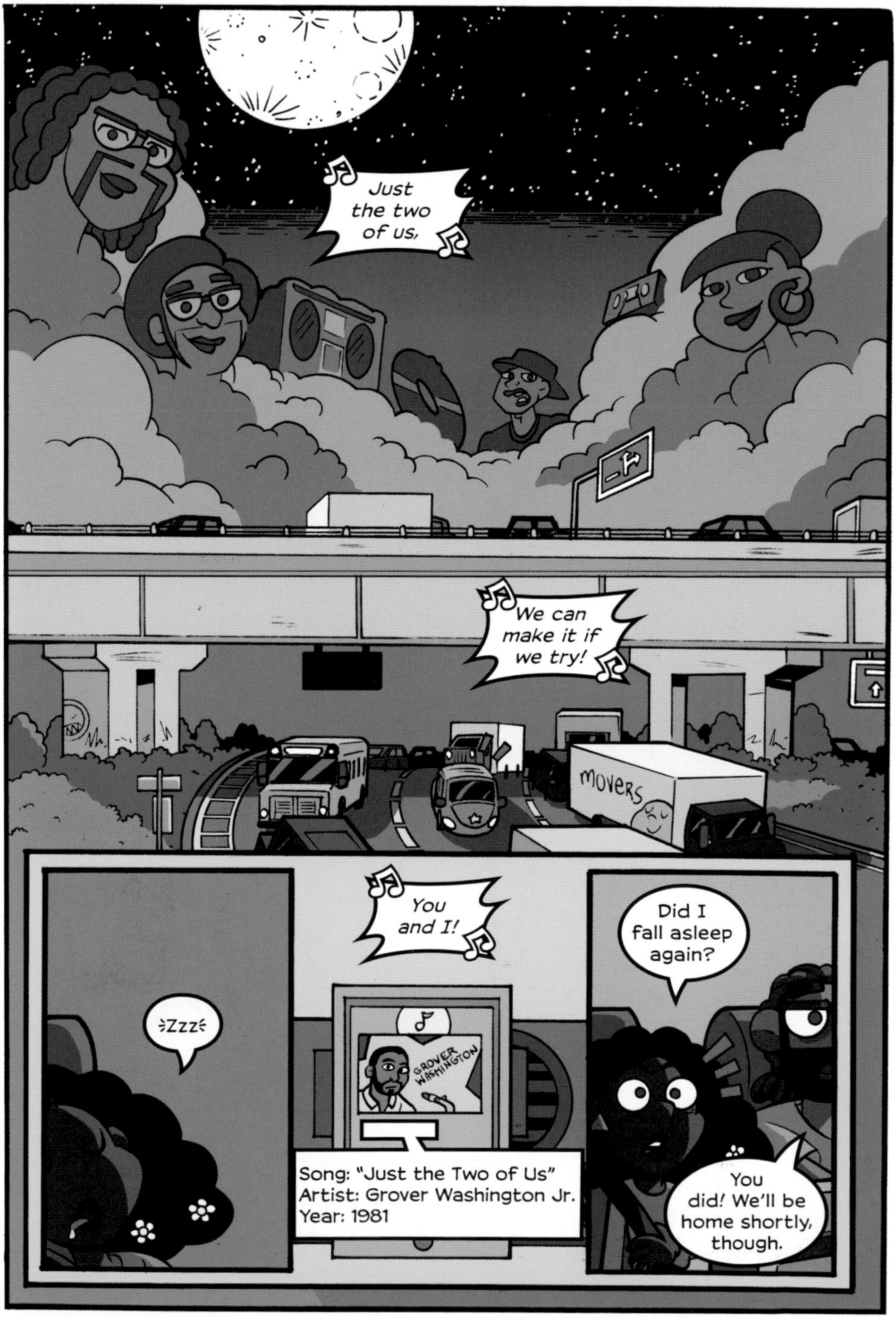
Just the two of us,
We can make it if we try!
You and I!
Zzz
GROVER WASHINGTON
Song: "Just the Two of Us"
Artist: Grover Washington Jr.
Year: 1981
Did I fall asleep again?
You did! We'll be home shortly, though.
movers

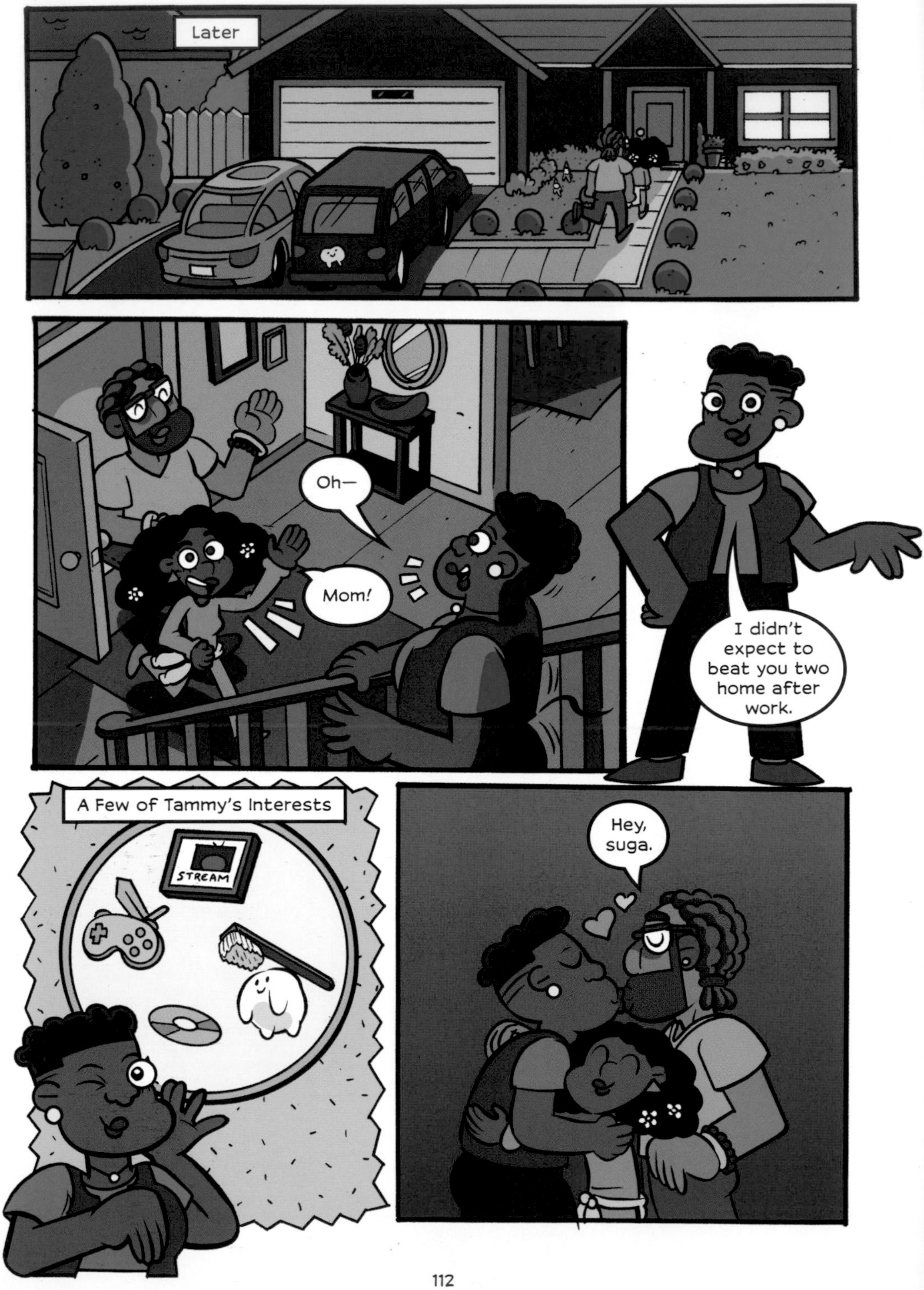
Later
Oh—
Mom!
I didn't expect to beat you two home after work.
A Few of Tammy's Interests
STREAM
Hey, suga.

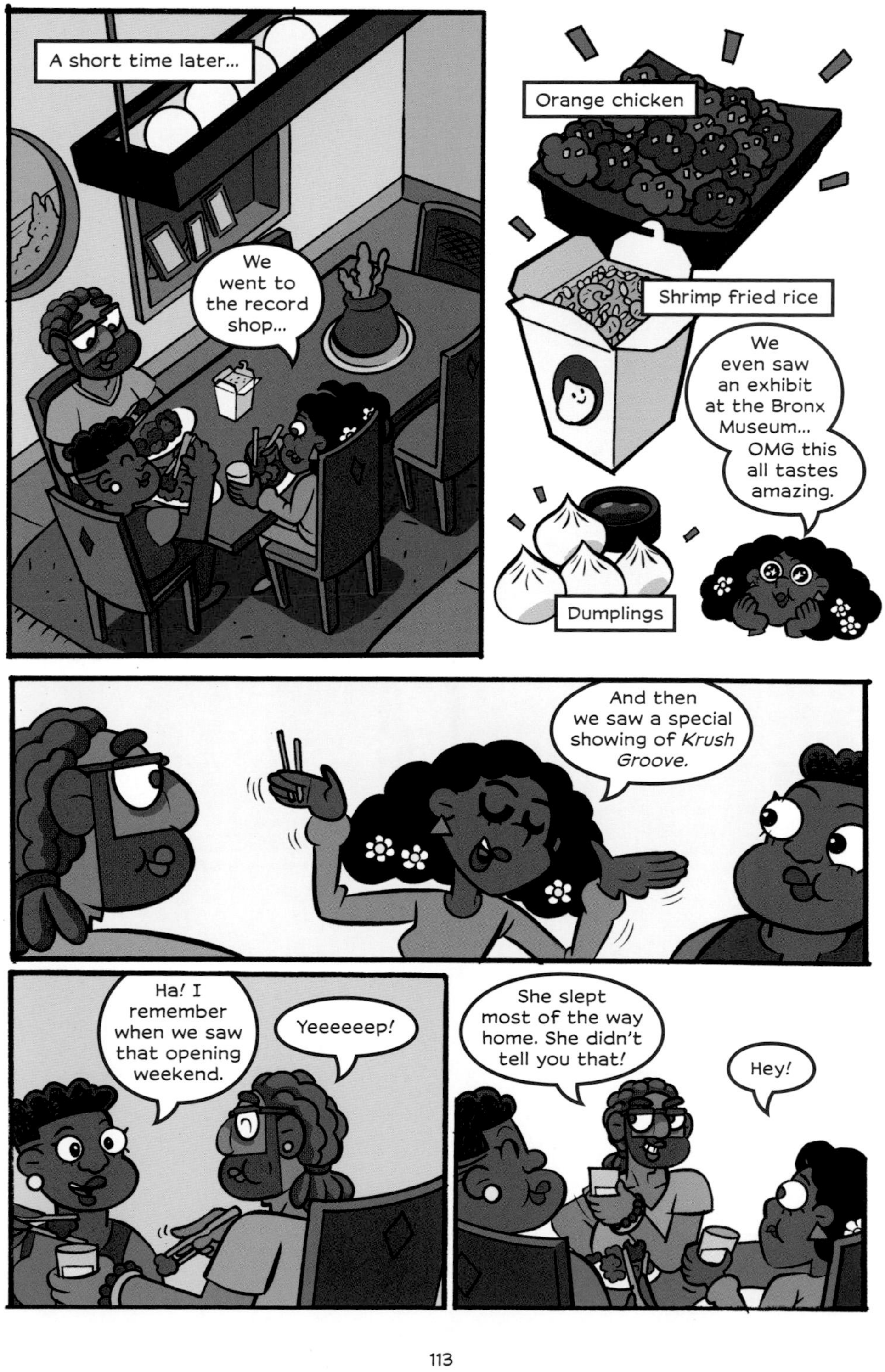
A short time later...
We went to the record shop...
Orange chicken
Shrimp fried rice
Dumplings
We even saw an exhibit at the Bronx Museum...
OMG this all tastes amazing.
And then we saw a special showing of *Krush Groove.*
Ha! I remember when we saw that opening weekend.
Yeeeeeep!
She slept most of the way home. She didn't tell you that!
Hey!

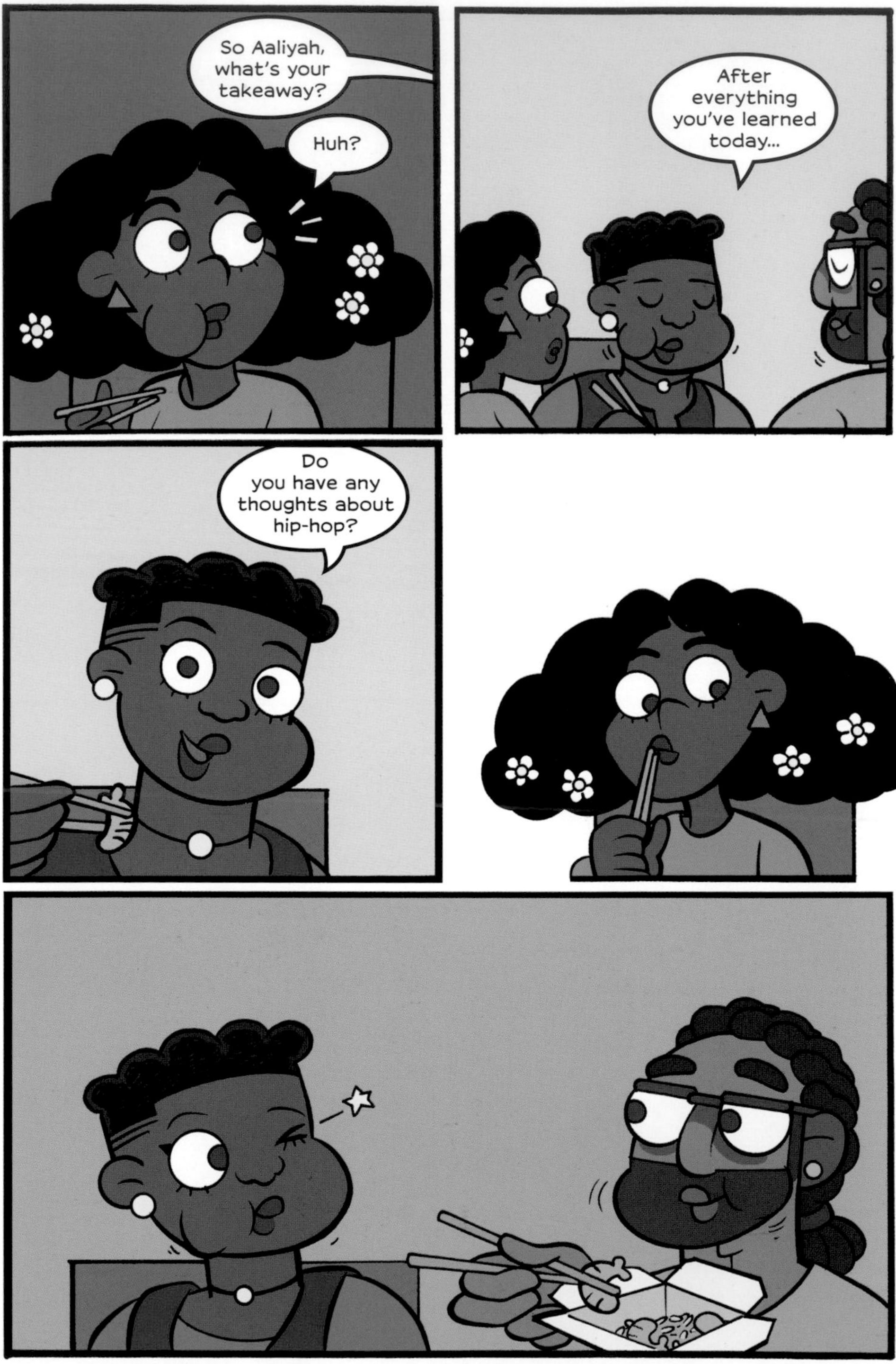

So Aaliyah, what's your takeaway?
Huh?
After everything you've learned today...
Do you have any thoughts about hip-hop?

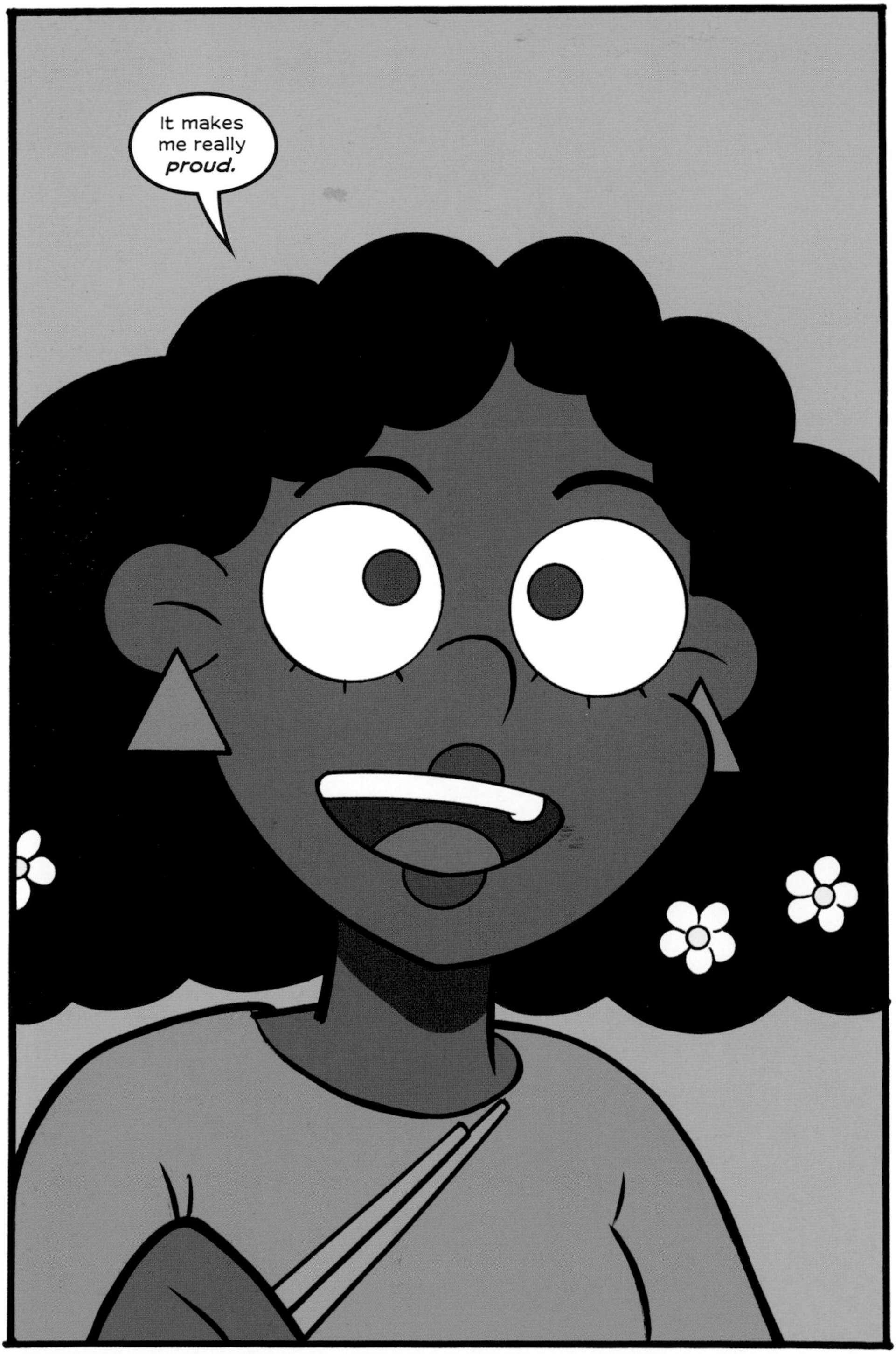
It makes me really ***proud.***

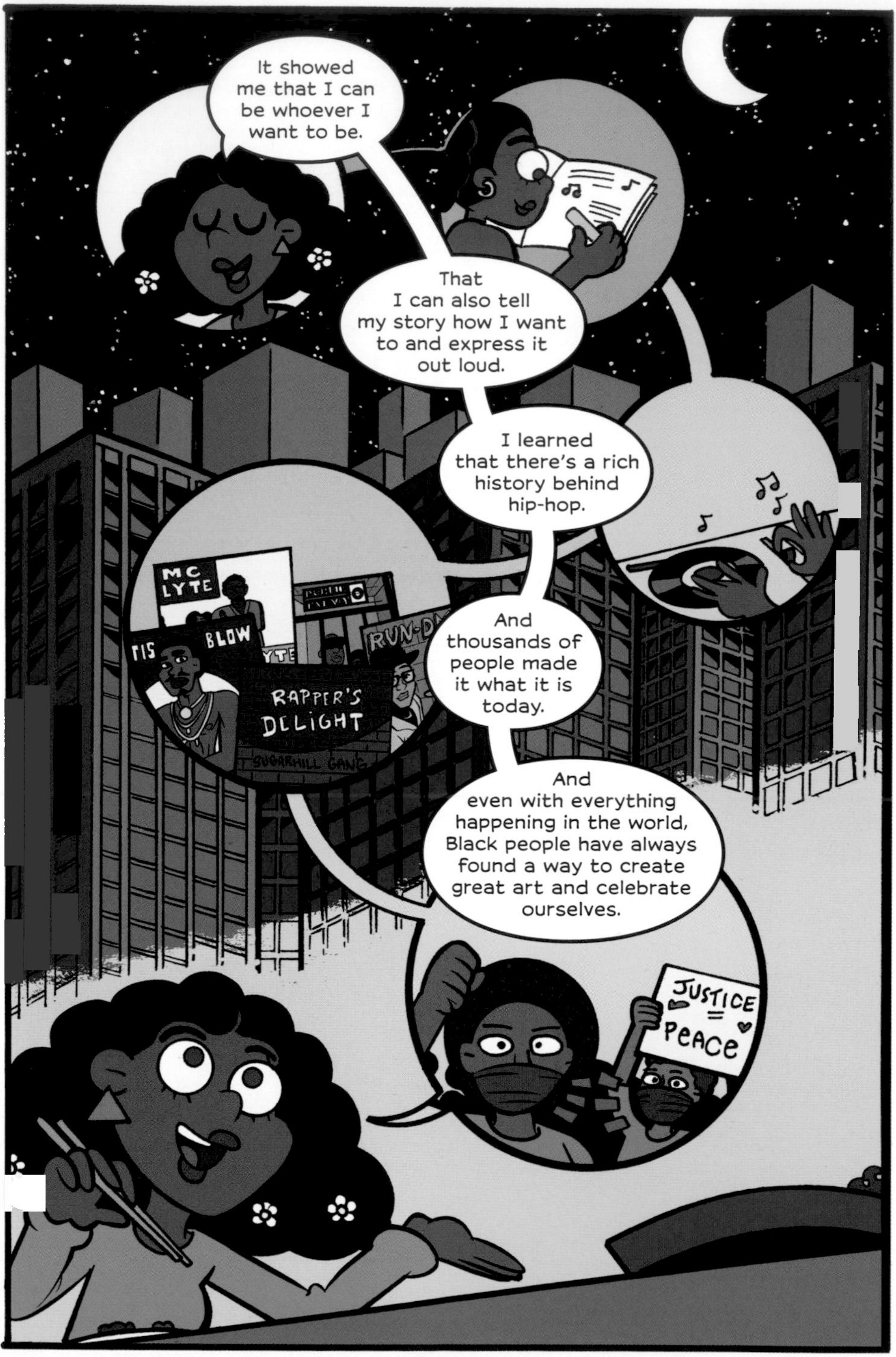
It showed me that I can be whoever I want to be.
That I can also tell my story how I want to and express it out loud.
I learned that there's a rich history behind hip-hop.
MC LYTE
BLOW
RAPPER'S DELIGHT
SUGARHILL GANG
And thousands of people made it what it is today.
And even with everything happening in the world, Black people have always found a way to create great art and celebrate ourselves.
JUSTICE = PEACE

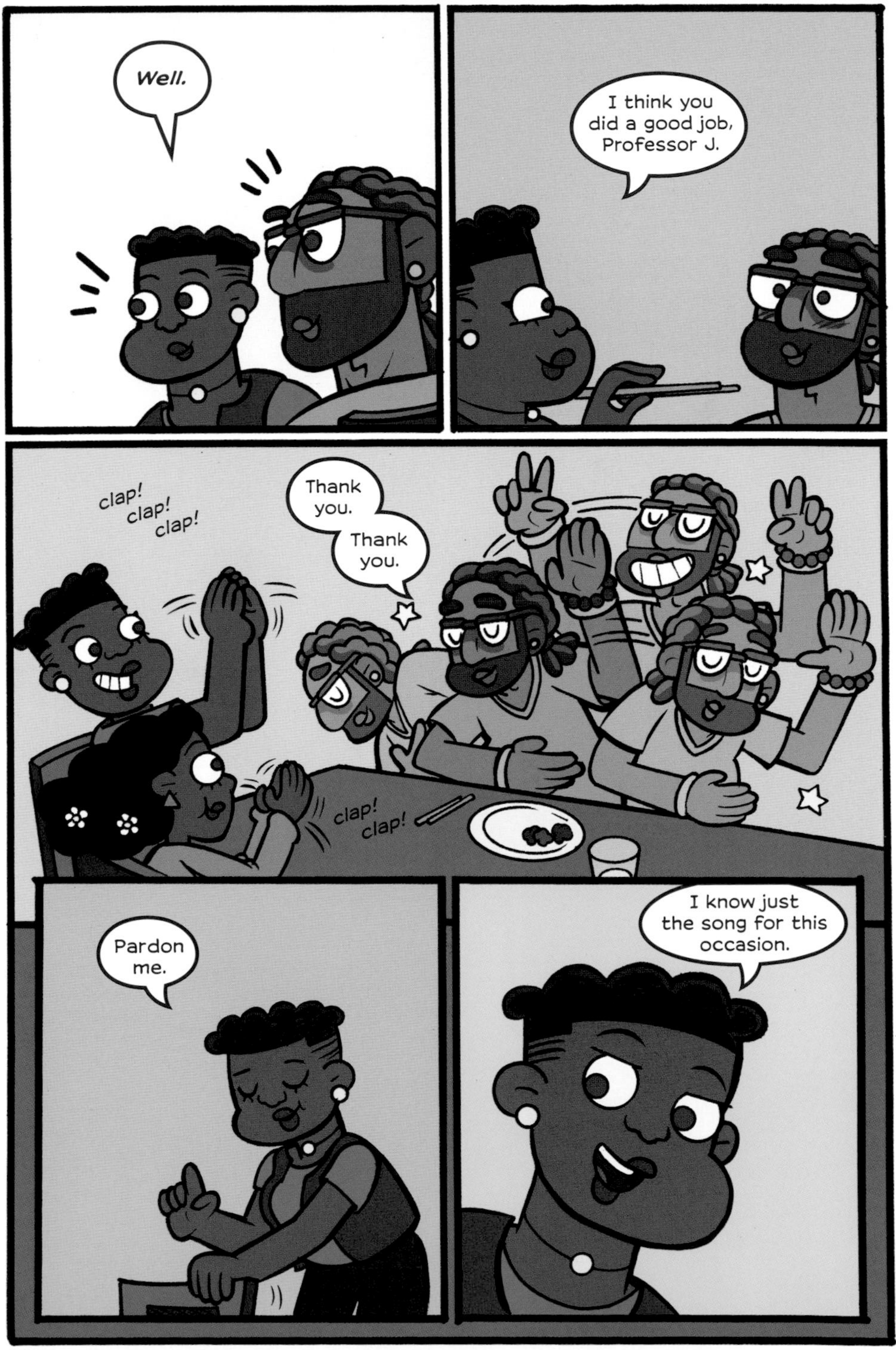
Well.
I think you did a good job, Professor J.
clap! clap! clap!
Thank you.
Thank you.
clap! clap!
Pardon me.
I know just the song for this occasion.

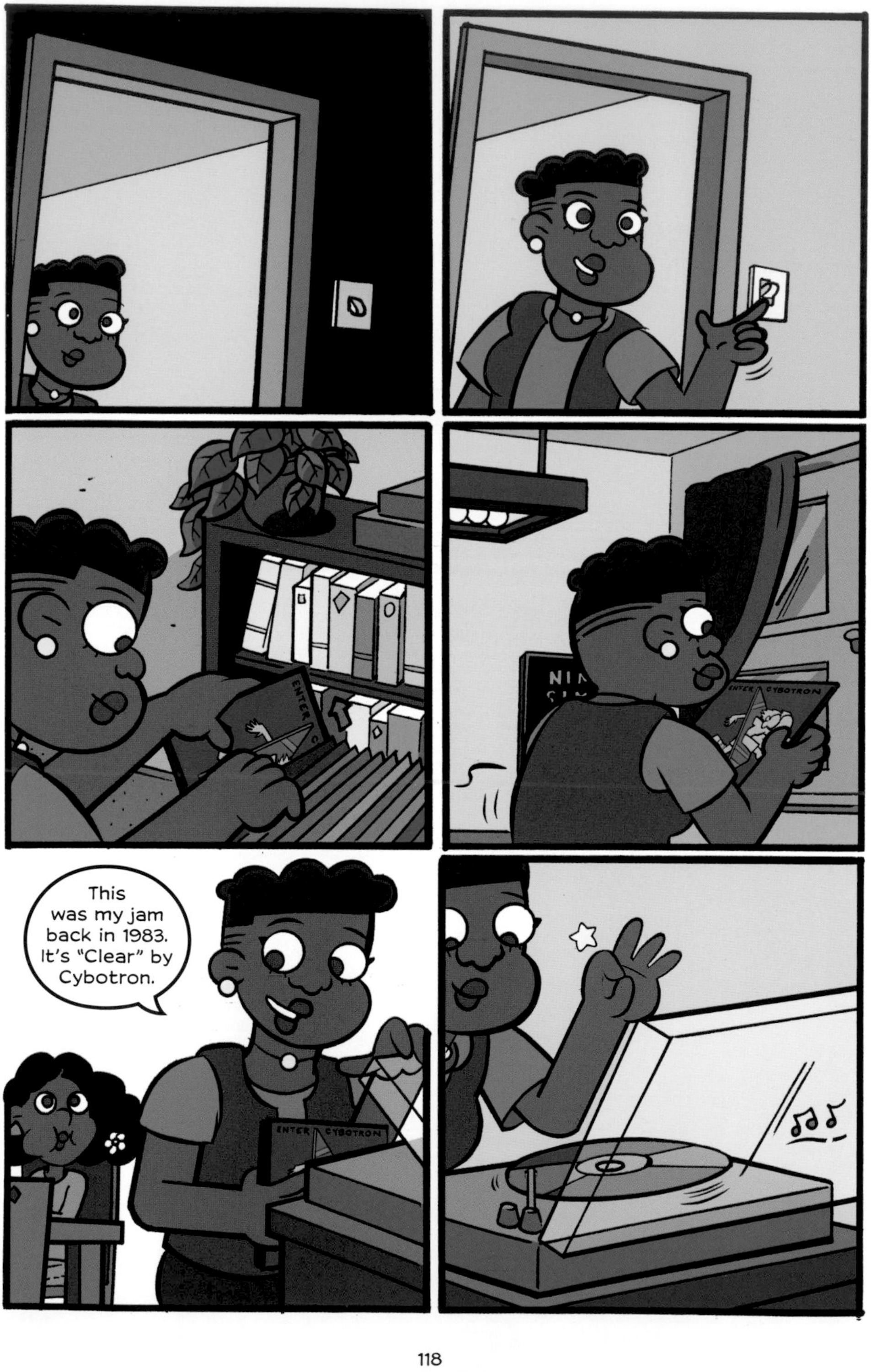
This was my jam back in 1983. It's "Clear" by Cybotron.
ENTER CYBOTRON

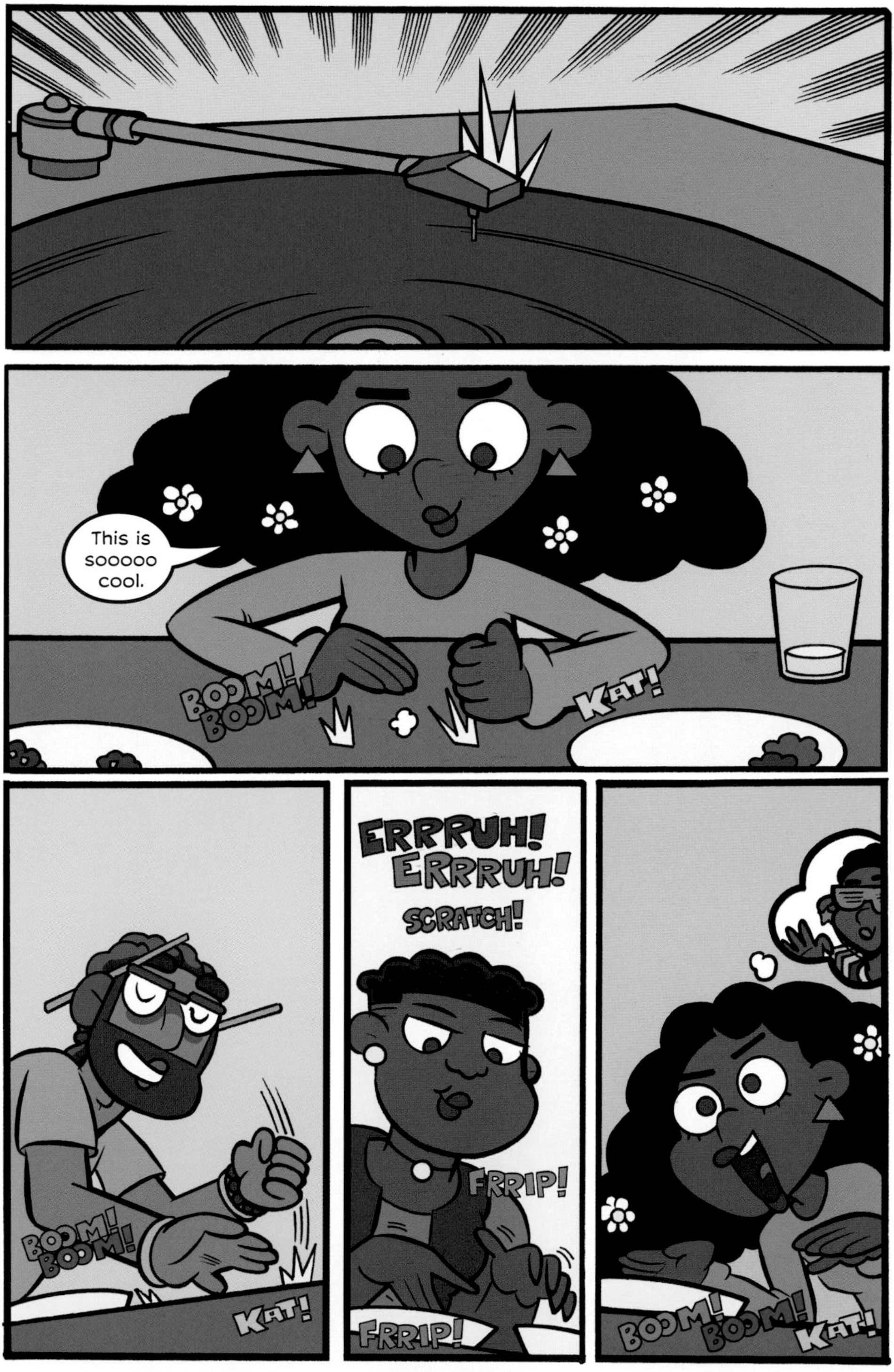
This is sooooo cool.
BOOM! BOOM!
KAT!
BOOM! BOOM!
KAT!
ERRRUH! ERRRUH!
SCRATCH!
FRRIP!
FRRIP!
BOOM! BOOM!
KAT!

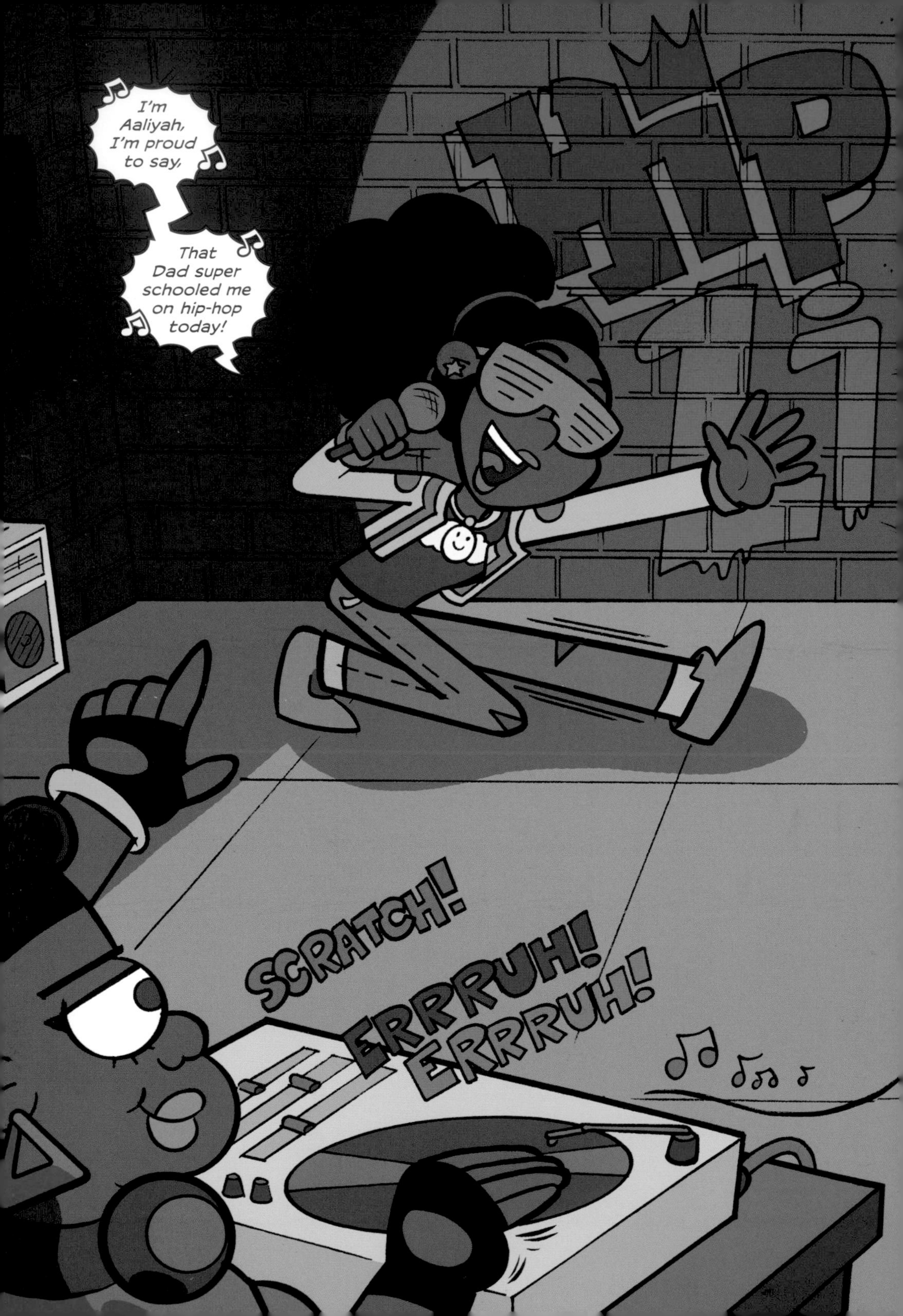
I'm Aaliyah, I'm proud to say,
That Dad super schooled me on hip-hop today!
SCRATCH!
ERRRUH!
ERRRUH!

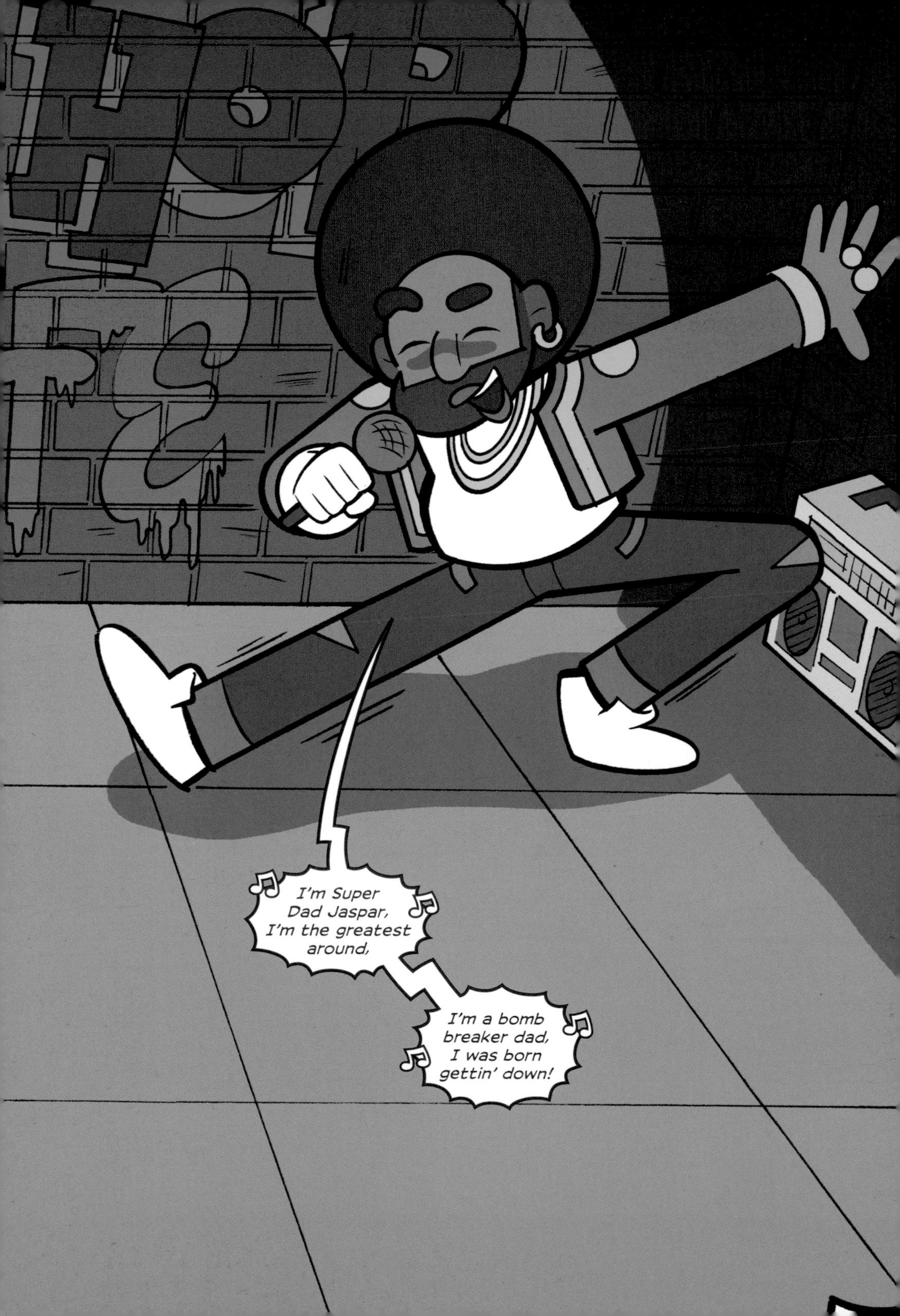
I'm Super Dad Jaspar, I'm the greatest around,
I'm a bomb breaker dad, I was born gettin' down!

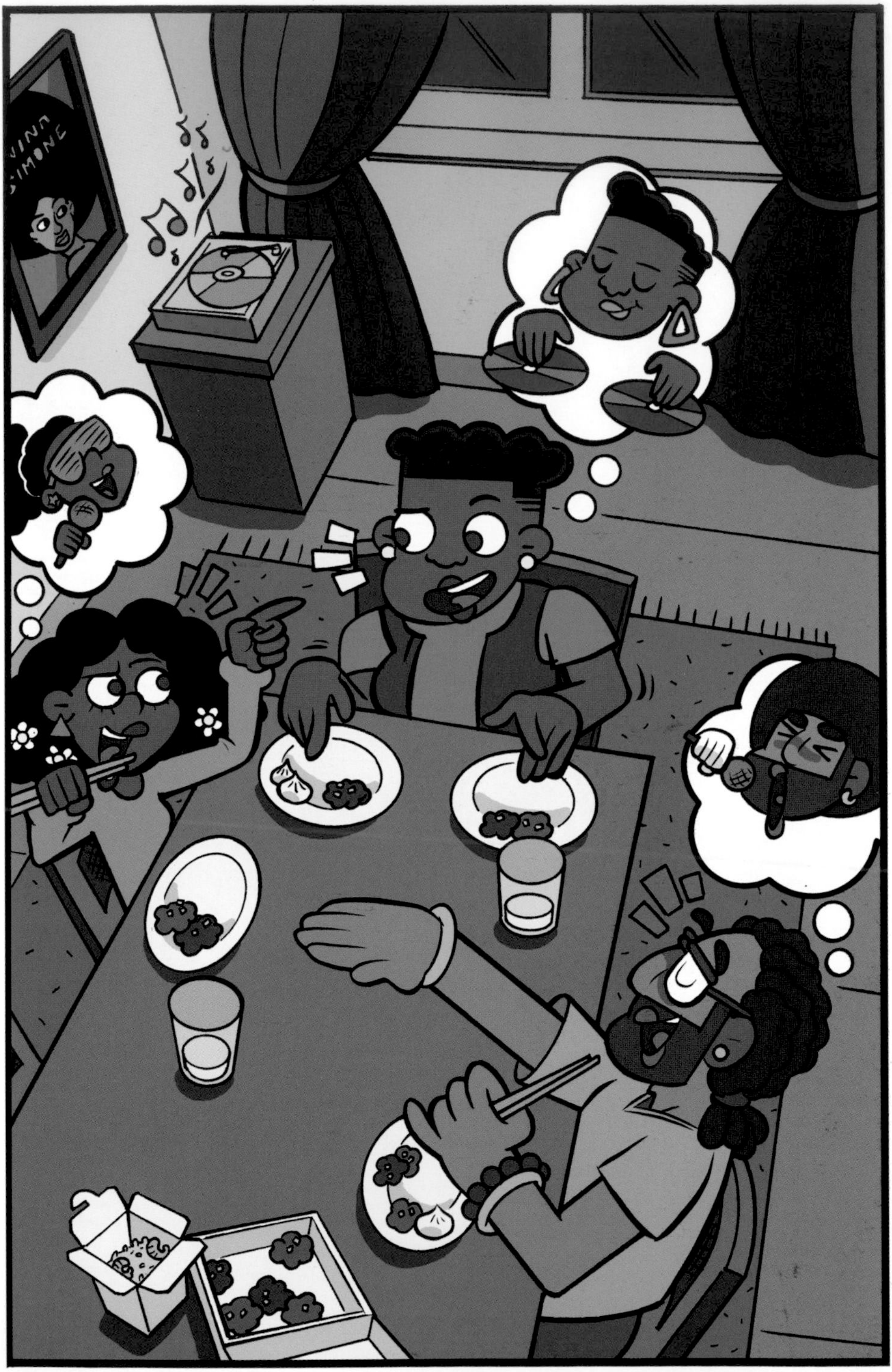
NINA SIMONE

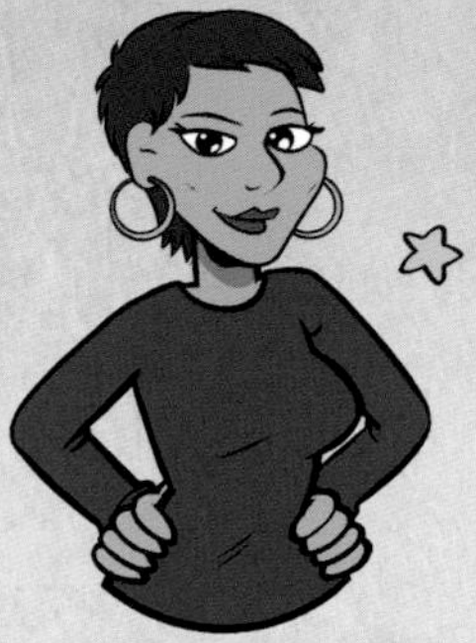

BEHIND THE BEATS

An interview with
Martha Diaz,
cofounder of the Hip-Hop Education Center

What was your first exposure to the sounds and culture of hip-hop?

I discovered hip-hop in the schoolyard when I was about ten or eleven years old. I was invited by a friend to go see "a battle." I thought it was a fight, but it was a dance competition! I remember there was a big boombox blaring music, and I saw the most amazing dancers spinning on their heads and moving like robots and snakes. There were also visual artists drawing in black sketchbooks. It was a community of artists making art and having fun.

What do you think it was about hip-hop that connected so deeply with you?

As a first-generation Colombian American, I grew up without family members. I didn't have cousins, uncles, aunties, and so these new friends became my family. The music, art, and dance were electrifying. We bonded and created a safe space for kids to listen to music, experiment with the arts, learn, and play.

Kids these days discover dance moves using technology that didn't exist in the golden age of hip-hop. Can you talk a bit about how hip-hop culture still managed to go viral and spread through communities?

We didn't have YouTube or TikTok in the 1980s. We had to attend live events. Through flyers, zines, and word of mouth, we often traveled to different cities on buses, trains, and cars to see our friends perform. We became a tight community cheering at dance competitions and mural art projects. It was also a way for us to represent our communities. In the 1990s, the media started to cover some of the events, but it wasn't until we created our own magazines and television shows that we were able to tell our own stories.

In the 1990s, you worked on the TV show _Yo! MTV Raps_, which helped to expose hip-hop music to a global audience. Are there specific memories (whether fun or inspiring) that really stick out as a defining moment from those days?

Cable television was a new technology in the 1980s. We didn't have it in Paterson, New Jersey, where I grew up, until the 1990s. I used to watch _Video Music Box_, _Soul Train_, and _Friday Night Videos_. When I started working at _Yo! MTV Raps_, I was amazed by the cameras and lights—it was a real television set. As an intern, I had to walk the artists to the greenroom, and afterward I helped edit the shows. Meeting so many of my favorite artists was the best part of working at _Yo! MTV Raps_. I loved getting to know performers and seeing how they interacted with their fans. Fab 5 Freddy would interview artists in the community, and local people would gather around and be part of the show. It was the beginning of a new era for hip-hop. We had record-breaking music sales and hip-hop artists representing cities all over the US. New hip-hop scenes were emerging from France, Senegal, Germany, Japan, Brazil, and Canada. Movies like _Who's the Man?_, _Juice_, and _Boyz n_ *the Hood* changed hip-hop cinema. Hip-hop fashion could be seen in fashion runway shows in Paris and Milan. The graffiti artists were in art shows presented by luxurious galleries and museums, and they sold their paintings for thousands of dollars. B-boys and B-girls now traveled around the world to compete against Koreans, Russians, Germans, and Filipinos. Hip-hop's popularity and global presence was undeniable.

Since then you've worn many hats, from filmmaker to curator to activist and more. What are the things that inspire and motivate you the most?

I've always been a problem solver, and hip-hop culture provided me with the skills and tools to change my community. I wasn't very good at the artistic elements of hip-hop, but I was able to bring people together and use my knowledge to teach and to create platforms to talk about issues affecting our community. I also showcased the best movies to inspire and educate by creating the first hip-hop film festival. I was able to share how to use the same tools given to me to make music, movies, and art. I saw how hip-hop empowered youth to be creative, active citizens and entrepreneurial. Hip-hop gave us the opportunity for upward mobility so we didn't have to stay stuck in poverty. I wanted to document and curate this movement so we could see our accomplishments and evolution.

Who are some of the pioneering women in hip-hop who you think deserve more of a spotlight?

Women have been part of hip-hop culture since the beginning. Some of the pioneers include Cindy Campbell, DJ Kool Herc's sister, who was the one throwing the party on August 11, 1973, where the elements of the culture came together. Dancin' Doll was one of the first B-girls. Pebblee-Poo started out as a B-girl in the 1970s and was DJ Kool Herc's first female MC soloist. Then you have Baby Love, who was in the Rock Steady Crew and was the lead singer for the hit song "(Hey You) The Rock Steady Crew." The "Mother of the Mic" aka MC Sha-Rock from the Funky 4 + 1 was the first female rapper in a group to record a song. Most people don't know that Lisa Lee was a member of the Soulsonic Force and the all-female group Us Girls, with Debbie D and MC Sha-Rock. DJ Jazzy Joyce is the first female DJ to compete in an all-male DJ competition. B-girl Bubbles from England did the same by competing in an all-male dance competition and swept them away. Lady Pink helped launch the graffiti arts movement, and Rocky 184 cofounded the Writers Corner 188 as New York's first graffiti crew. There are so many women who have shaped and contributed to the evolution of hip-hop. They are on the mic or turntables, dancing on stage, behind the camera, designing fashion, painting murals, writing about hip-hop, producing events, and signing and managing artists.

You cofounded the Hip-Hop Education Center and many other educational initiatives integrating hip-hop culture. What have you found to be some of the benefits of including hip-hop as an educational tool?

Hip-hop music is the most popular genre on this planet, and it makes sense for educators to use it in the classroom. The hip-hop education movement is a student-centered holistic approach using hip-hop history, culture, and music as a hook, bridge, and/ or discipline to learning and teaching. Hip-hop educators value what students bring into the classroom, such as the different languages they speak, music they listen to, or ethnic and cultural backgrounds. The goal is to learn from student experiences in order to draw out their strengths and help them deal with challenges so they can achieve their goals. For example, young people can learn through different intelligences, such as music, dance (bodily/kinesthetic), graffiti/writing (spatial/visual), and MCing/spoken word (verbal/linguistic). Hip-hop education is culturally relevant to young people, and when using it in lesson plans, we meet students where they are. Furthermore, hip-hop teaches critical thinking, STEM (science, technology, engineering, and mathematics), media literacy, collaboration, time-management, and financial literacy skills, to name a few. In addition to rappers, DJs, and dancers, hip-hop culture offers alternative career pathways and has produced music producers, community leaders, educators, entrepreneurs, politicians, fashion designers, choreographers, writers, curators, and archivists.

You are working now with the Universal Hip Hop Museum alongside legends like Paradise Gray (X-Clan) and Prime Minister Pete Nice (3rd Bass). Can you talk about how that got started and how it will be different from your typical museum?

Three years ago, after serving for many years as an adviser for the Universal Hip Hop Museum, I decided to work with Paradise Gray, their chief curator, and Prime Minister Pete Nice, their cocurator, on their first exhibition. I knew that through working with these legends I would gain a wealth of historical information and could do a deeper dive through the archives and artifacts. The Universal Hip Hop Museum is different because we have access to the people who were there in the beginning of the culture, which is unbelievable and sometimes challenging because everyone has their own point of view. Some of the things in our collection include flyers and posters from as early as the 1970s, Grandmaster Flash's turntable, Biz Markie's rope chain, DJ Kay Slay's record collection, and a throne that belonged to Slick Rick. We have curated three exhibits in the Bronx and two in Malmo, Sweden. The museum is developing a virtual museum, and our new building will open in 2024. It will be a place where you can learn and create, right in the birthplace of hip-hop.

What do you think is the importance of preserving hip-hop history?

It is important to preserve objects that help tell the story of hip-hop culture. When I worked with Tupac's estate, I read Tupac's notebooks, and they gave me insight into his songwriting process and how he viewed the world around him. When I worked on Beyoncé's collection, I saw her talent and hard work ethic as a child through her home videos. Artifacts and archives become evidence that we were there and show how we as a community evolved over time. It is important that we are able to tell our own stories, and we can do this through the preservation and development of collections that can then be shared with museums, libraries, and schools.

If you had to choose your top hip-hop jams to go into your playlist, what would be in the mix?

1. "Every Ghetto, Every City" by Lauryn Hill
2. "I Can" by Nas
3. "My Philosophy" by Boogie Down Productions
4. "Ladies First" by Queen Latifah (ft Monie Love)
5. "Changes" by 2Pac
6. "Afeni" by Rapsody (ft PJ Morton)
7. "Next Year" by Macklemore (ft Windser)
8. "I Am" by Maya Jupiter
9. "Journey of the Lamb" by Will On the Soul (ft J. Cole, Kendrick Lamar, André 3000)
10. "North Star" by Mumu Fresh (ft D Smoke)

EARLY DAYS OF HIP-HOP CULTURE TIMELINE

Written in collaboration with the Hip Hop Education Center and the Universal Hip Hop Museum

Clayton
Fillyau

1962
On James Brown's album *Live at the Apollo*, Clayton Fillyau introduces audiences to the break beat—an interlude in a song when the other instruments drop out to showcase the drummer's rapid-fire rhythms.

1965
Artists, writers, and musicians form the Black Arts Movement as a way of expressing the realities of inner-city living and continuing the fight for civil rights. Poets like Amiri Baraka and Sonia Sanchez often performed their writings accompanied by jazz or blues music and invited participants to respond to their words in the call-and-response format of Black churches.

1966
Disc jockey Hank Spann, aka the Server, builds an iconic radio persona on New York City's WWRL station. His signature baritone and on-air rhymes (with his daily sign-off of "Two steps to the rear, and I'm outta here") inspired a generation of club MCs.

1967
In Philadelphia, Pennsylvania, "tags" (graffiti signatures) of artists like Cornbread, Cool Earl, Kool Klepto Kid, and Topcat 126 begin appearing around the city.

1969
Brooklyn DJ Jonathan Flowers, aka Grandmaster Flowers, opens for James Brown at a concert at Yankee Stadium in New York. Born in the Caribbean Islands, he was influenced by Jamaican sound systems—

mobile speaker setups that blasted R&B at street parties. Flowers was the first DJ to use the term "Grandmaster" to describe his skill at the turntables.

1972

Aretha Franklin releases the album *Young, Gifted and Black* featuring the song "Rock Steady," a term later adopted by the B-boy dance movement.

While working the New York City club circuit, Anthony Holloway, aka DJ Hollywood, incorporates syncopated singing and musical call-and-response segments into his shows. While he was not the first to use this style, his skill at forming extended lyrical rhymes that flowed along with the music gave birth to what would become "hip-hop style" rapping.

Aretha Franklin

1973

Coke La Rock begins improvising rhymes at Bronx dance parties at the request of Clive Campbell, aka DJ Kool Herc. With DJ Clark Kent, Kool Herc and Coke La Rock formed Kool Herc and the Herculords, bringing the DJ (Kool Herc), the MC (Coke La Rock), and the B-boys (Trixie, Wallace Dee, Dancin' Doug, Sau Sau, and Tricksy) together into one cohesive act.

DJ Kool Herc creates the "Merry-Go-Round," a technique that involves spinning the same record on two turntables and repeating a segment of the song—usually a drum or horn solo—so it plays in a continuous loop.

Kool Herc   Coke La Rock

B-boys (and eventually B-girls!) put the Hevalo club on the map with
  weekend competitions in which they challenged each other to do more
  and more complicated dance moves in a big circle called a cypher.

Bruce Lee's *Enter the Dragon*, a staple of the kung-fu action genre that had
  a tremendous impact on Black audiences, releases in the US. Samples,
  dialogue, and other elements of the film would appear in hip-hop
  songs and culture for decades, illustrating how these films spoke to the
  experiences of the inner-city youths who loved them.

The Nuyorican Poets Cafe humbly begins in the Lower East Side, New
  York City, apartment of the writer and professor Miguel Algarín (along
  with his friends/cofounders Lucky Cienfuegos, Miguel Piñero, and
  Bimbo Rivas). It eventually expanded into its own building on East
  3rd Street, where it became a sacred ground in the emerging rhythmic
  poetry/hip-hop music scene.

1974

Joseph Saddler, aka Grandmaster Flash, pioneers hip-hop hardware by
  modifying his DJ setup to include a custom cue monitor he calls the
  "Peek-A-Boo system." The device allowed him to hear a cued-up record
  through his headphones while another record plays through the main
  speakers. Using this system and his impressive hand-eye coordination,
  Flash was able to jump between the same track spinning on two
  turntables, extending the beat as long as he wanted.

The term "hip-hop" starts to catch on and is often credited to Keef
  Cowboy, Lovebug Starski, and DJ Hollywood, all of whom scatted
  variations of the two words in creative ways like, "I said-a hip-hop, a
  hibbit, hibby-dibby, hip-hip-hop and you don't stop."

1976

The Funky 4 + 1 hits the scene featuring Sharon Green, aka MC Sha-Rock, who is considered by many to be the first female MC. In 1981, they would go on to be the first hip-hop group to appear on a national television show when they performed on *Saturday Night Live*, hosted by Blondie's Deborah Harry.

1977

A crew from Fresno, California, known as the Electric Boogaloos help create a dance craze known as "popping" and "electric boogaloo."

Bronx-based Rock Steady Crew is formed by Jojo and Jimmy D, and they recruit new members by way of dance battles to see who was the best of the best. The crew performed at Lincoln Center and would appear in several films. They eventually expanded their membership to separate branches across the globe.

Performing at the Sparkle Club in New York City, Theodore Livingston, aka Grand Wizzard Theodore, brings new innovations to turntablism with his "scratching" and "needle drop" techniques.

1978

Lemoin Thompson, aka Buddy Esquire, brings his self-taught art skills to the New York City dance party scene. He promoted events with quality flyers that stood out from the rest. Esquire's signature style, featuring collages made from publicity photos of the evening's featured performers, would appear on hundreds of flyers over the next several years.

The Electric
Boogaloos

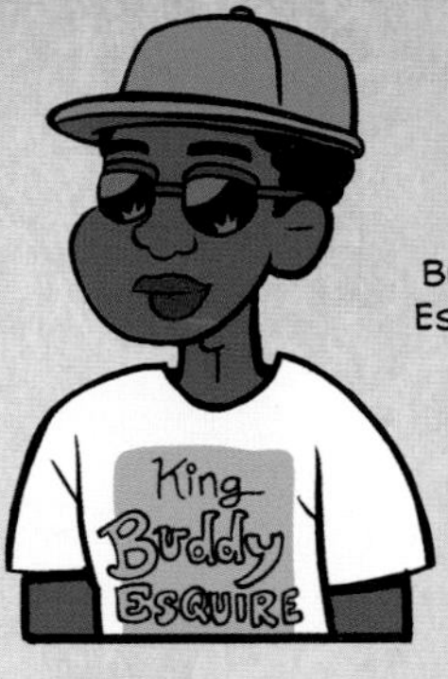
King
Buddy
ESQUIRE
Buddy Esquire

Based in Auburn Hills, Michigan, designer Marc Buchanan leaves his mark on hip-hop fashion with his Pelle Pelle street gear line. Buchanan created colorful embellished leather jackets that would become a mainstay of hip-hop culture. He also made use of windbreakers and baggy clothing to give performers more freedom of movement during shows.

1979

Funk and disco group the Fatback Band drops "King Tim III (Personality Jock)," which many consider to be the first commercially released hip-hop single.

John "Mr. Magic" Rivas pays for time on New York public-access radio station WHBI (now WNWK), creating the first-ever rap radio show.

Wendy Clark, aka Lady B, one of the earliest female rap artists, releases "To the Beat Y'All."

"Rapper's Delight" by Sugarhill Gang reaches the US Top 40, propelling hip-hop onto a global stage. For many people outside of New York City, this was the first rap song they ever heard on mainstream radio.

All-female rap trio the Sequence hits the hip-hop scene with "Funk You Up," released by Sugar Hill Records—its second single after "Rapper's Delight." The Columbia, South Carolina, group was formed by school friends Angie Brown "Angie B" Stone, Cheryl "the Pearl" Cook, and Gwendolyn "Blondy" Chisolm.

All-in-one portable music players known as "boomboxes" or "ghetto blasters" that incorporate a radio, tape player, audio amplifier, and hi-fi speakers become prevalent in Black and Hispanic communities.

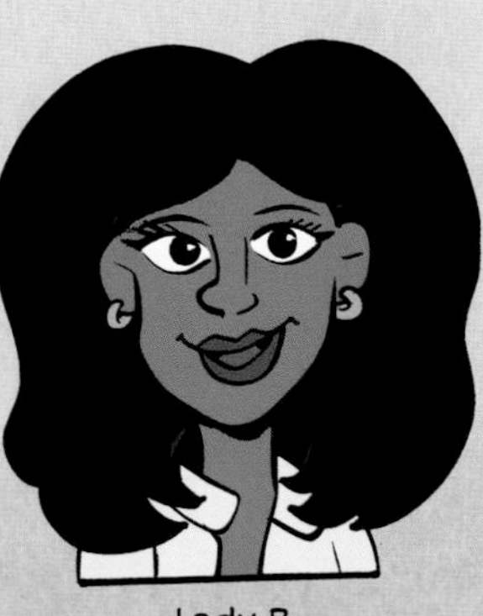
Lady B

1980

Kurtis Blow's "The Breaks" spends six weeks on the *Billboard* charts and is the first rap single to sell 500,000 copies, designating it Gold status. It was also the second certified Gold 12-inch song/single in the history of music and the first rap song to have a chorus.

1981

The ABC network airs a segment of their news show *20/20* dedicated to hip-hop. This was the first national news story about rap music, and it predicted that hip-hop would become a cultural force because "it lets ordinary people express ideas they care about, in a language they can relate to, and put to music they can dance to."

Captain Rapp and Disco Daddy put West Coast hip-hop on the map with the release of their catchy hit, "Gigolo Rapp."

1982

Grandmaster Flash and the Furious Five release "The Message," with vocals by Melle Mel. The song held a mirror up to the social inequality and struggles of Black youth and showed a new side of rap beyond its house-party origins.

The New York City Rap Tour heads to France for the first international showcase of hip-hop culture. The lineup included Afrika Bambaataa and Soulsonic Force; Fab 5 Freddy; Grandmixer D.ST and the Infinity Rappers; Futura 2000; Dondi; Rammellzee; the break-dancing Rock Steady Crew; and the world champion Fantastic Four Double Dutch girls.

Dapper Dan's Boutique opens in Harlem, New York. Owner/designer Daniel Day's elevated street wear would create the iconic looks of countless artists like LL Cool J, Eric B. & Rakim, KRS-One, Salt-N-Pepa, and the Fat Boys.

1983

Wild Style, the first hip-hop movie, is released. It tells the story of a young graffiti artist, played by real-life artist Lee Quiñones, and featured Grandmaster Flash, Fab 5 Freddy, Busy Bee, and more.

Ice-T adds to the growing West Coast rap scene with the electro sounds of "The Coldest Rap" with Jimmy Jam and Terry Lewis, who would go on to be Grammy-winning producers of some of the biggest R&B and pop songs of the decade.

Kurtis Blow becomes the first rap star to be featured on a magazine cover with *Right On!* The issue dedicated to rap music also included a profile on Grandmaster Flash and break dancing.

1984

The Fat Boys release their first album, which many consider to be the first to prominently feature the vocal percussion skill known as beatboxing.

Rick Rubin and Russell Simmons form Def Jam Recordings, a record label started out of Rubin's college dorm that would release albums by some of hip-hop's biggest stars, like LL Cool J, Beastie Boys, and Public Enemy.

Run-DMC sells 500,000 copies of their debut album, making it the first hip-hop record to be certified Gold on the *Billboard* charts. Run-DMC would break records again with their follow-up album *King of Rock*, released in 1985, which would be the first rap record designated Platinum with one million copies sold in its first year in stores.

The movie *Breakin'* hits theaters and captures the attention of youths across the country. Followed by a sequel in the same year, both films star dancers Adolfo "Shabba Doo" Quiñones and Michael "Boogaloo Shrimp" Chambers and feature rapper Ice-T. Chambers and Ice-T also

appeared in the 1983 documentary *Breakin'
'N' Enterin'* that inspired the Breakin'
franchise.

The hip-hop movie trend continues with *Beat
Street*, which focuses on Bronx-based music
and graffiti scenes. Filmed at the legendary
club the Roxy, it includes performances by
pioneers Doug E. Fresh, Grandmaster Melle
Mel & the Furious Five, Jazzy Jay, DJ Kool
Herc, Rock Steady Crew, Soulsonic Force,
and Lawanda McFarland, aka Wanda Dee,
one of hip-hop's first female DJs.

Wanda Dee

1986

Salt-N-Pepa's debut album, *Hot, Cool & Vicious*,
sells more than one million copies in the
US, making them the most successful female
rap group of the time.

Beastie Boys release *Licensed to Ill*, which mixed
hip-hop and punk rock aesthetics. It was the
first rap album to hit number one on the
Billboard 200 chart and the best-selling rap
album of the 1980s.

The first hip-hop comic book, *Rappin' Max Robot*
by Bronx artist Eric Orr, is published. Orr
was a designer of logos and artwork for hip-
hop artists before deciding to create his own
character for the hip-hop community.

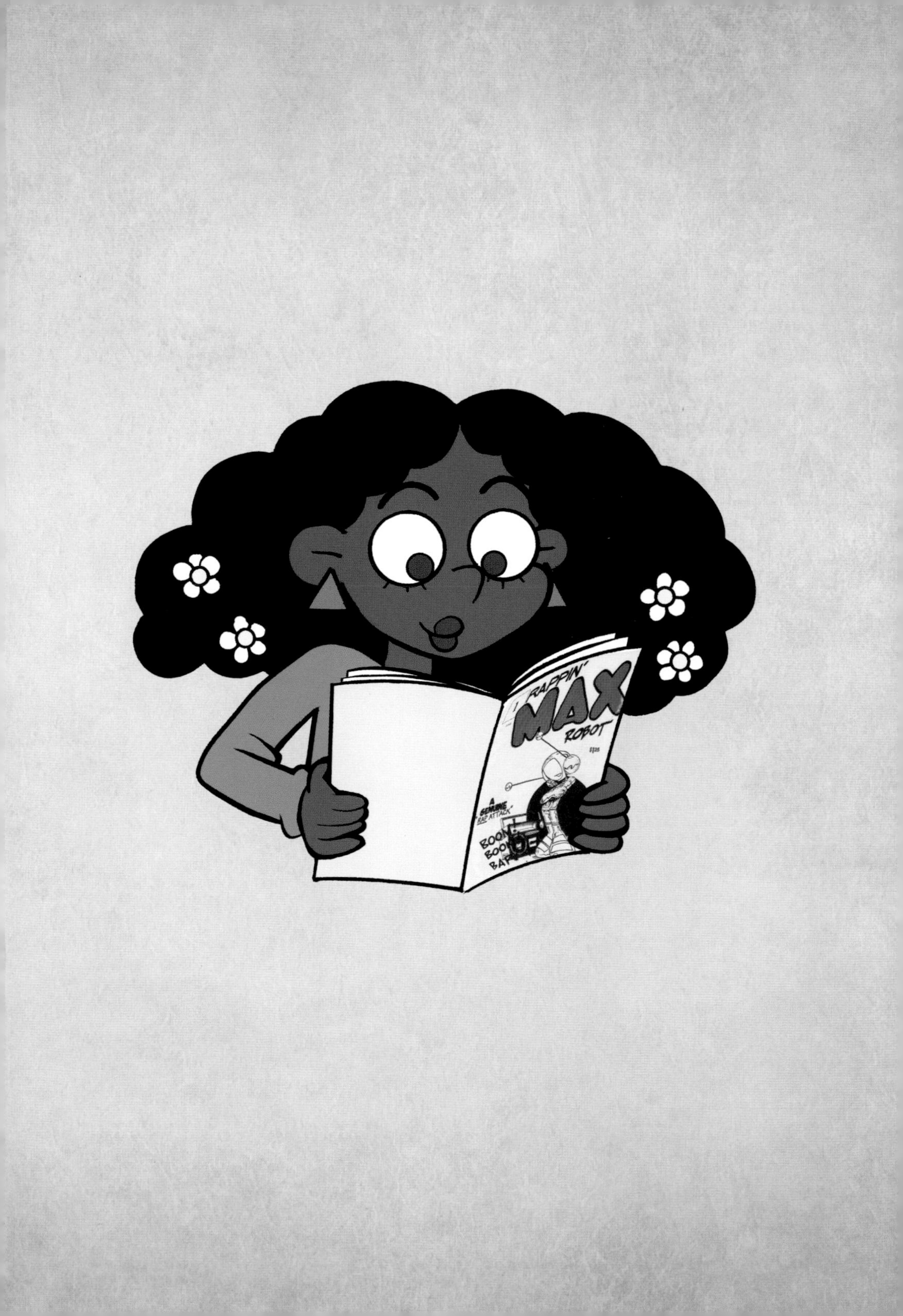
RAPPIN'
MAX
ROBOT
A GENUINE RAP ATTACK